PREACHING: THE ART AND THE CRAFT

also by Walter J. Burghardt, S.J.
published by Paulist Press

TELL THE NEXT GENERATION
SIR, WE WOULD LIKE TO SEE JESUS
SEASONS THAT LAUGH OR WEEP
STILL PROCLAIMING YOUR WONDERS
GRACE ON CRUTCHES

PREACHING:
THE ART AND THE CRAFT

WALTER J. BURGHARDT, S.J.
Theologian in Residence
Georgetown University

PAULIST PRESS
New York/Mahwah

in grateful memory of
John Courtney Murray, S.J. (1904–1967)
–incomparable mentor
–cherished colleague
–dearest of friends

Excerpts from THE LITTLE PRINCE by Antoine de Saint-Exupéry, copyright 1943, 1971 by Harcourt Brace Jovanovich, Inc. Reprinted by permission of the publisher.

Copyright © 1987 by
Walter J. Burghardt, S.J.

Library of Congress Cataloging-in-Publication Data

Burghardt, Walter J.
    Preaching: the art and the craft.

    Bibliography: p.
    Includes index.
    1. Preaching. I. Title.
BV4211.2.B84   1987   251   87-14653
ISBN 0-8091-2906-X

Published by Paulist Press
997 Macarthur Boulevard
Mahwah, New Jersey 07430

Printed and bound in the
United States of America

TABLE OF CONTENTS

PRELUDE

Another book on preaching? I'm afraid so. Forty-five years of priestly experience persuade me that the pressure for more effective preaching must be kept up. The startling assertion of biblical scholar J. Murphy-O'Connor back in 1963 deserves to be repeated today:

> Just as the Reformation four centuries ago, the progressive de-christianization of society today is attributed to a failure of preaching. The factor that more than any other made the Reformation possible was the theological confusion that marked the preaching and teaching of the Faith in the early sixteenth century. Today preaching is admittedly orthodox, but it is often vapid and lacking in vitality. It no longer seems to make converts or to lead to sanctity those who already have the Faith.[1]

But what can yet another volume contribute? Surely nothing substantially new, nothing that has not been said time and again in one way or another. Then why a book by Burghardt? For one thing, fresh emphases in a complex, confusing, changing culture. For another, new ways of looking at timeworn realities: the awesome power of words, the unique force of God's word, the primacy of imagination, models like prophets long dead and preachers still alive, the movement from study to proclamation, the view from the pew, the preacher as pray-er. . . . Pervading all this, an effort to destroy apathy, conquer discouragement, generate excitement, enthusiasm, electricity.

1

Of potential value, too, is the fact that this book has been writ-ten in the twilight of my earthbound existence, after almost a half century of preaching. It is the product not simply of serious re-search but, even more richly, of broad experience, of trial and er-ror, of intense listening. During those years I have grown, have changed—as person, as priest, as preacher. My movement as preacher will be strikingly apparent to anyone who compares my first collection of sermons, *All Lost in Wonder* (Westminster, Md.: Newman, 1960), with my latest set of homilies, *Grace on Crutches* (New York/Mahwah: Paulist, ©1986). From the close of the Second Vatican Council in 1965, but especially since the mid-70s, my preaching has increasingly reflected (1) a return to the Bible, Old Testament and New, for homiletic inspiration and content; (2) a deepened awareness of the link between liturgy, Scripture, and the homily; (3) a priority to imagination over Cartesian clarity; and (4) an anguished concern that faith find expression in the struggle for social justice.

A pilgrim in a pilgrim Church, I am acutely aware that even *my* homilies, in fact my very ideas about the preached word, are on pil-grimage. They are fallible expressions of the inexpressible Word who chose our human language to reveal "the mystery hidden for ages in God" (Eph 3:9). Before this mystery the most fluent of preachers can only stutter and stammer. Like Jeremiah, "I do not know how to speak" (Jer 1:6). I can only trust that, as with Jeremiah, the Lord has at certain gracious moments put His words in my mouth. Please God, the effort in this volume to recapture the char-ism that is preaching will stimulate other preachers to wrestle with words and the Word, to enflesh the word the Word spoke, to fling it out to our world with conviction and courage, with imagination and passion. If not we, then who?

Walter J. Burghardt, S.J.

1

THE WORD MADE FLESH TODAY
Does Language Make a Difference?

I begin this book by speaking of . . . words. Understandably, for a word is the ordinary medium for a preacher's message. Like it or not, I have no choice but to put a subject and a verb together, shape phrases and clauses and sentences and paragraphs, make sense and persuade and inspire through conventional symbols of speech.

Webster's Second Edition Unabridged defines a word as "an articulate sound or series of sounds which, through conventional association with some fixed meaning, symbolizes and communicates an idea. . . . " It all sounds dull as dishwater. Till you escape from sheer definitions and let your mind, memory, and imagination take wing. Let go. . . .

Three stages capture the movement of my thought: the word . . . made flesh . . . today. (1) What is "word"? (2) What kind of word is enfleshed in the liturgical homily? (3) How can the homiletic word be enfleshed today, be incarnated for this believing people?

I

I come to you a weaver of words. Ever since I can remember, I have been seduced by syllables. In grade school my brother and I began the great American novel; to no one's surprise, it aborted. In high school I delighted in debate—either side of any question. But it was the Jesuit juniorate that genuinely focused my verbal future; for there I reveled in the rhythms of the Greeks and Romans, waltzed to English word masters.

I wept to the prophetic plaints of Aeschylus' Cassandra, laughed to the mocking irony of Aristophanes, even croaked to the music of his frogs: "Brekekekex, ko-ax, ko-ax." I agonized with gentle Sophocles over the incest of Oedipus, joined the closing chorus: "Wait to see life's ending ere thou count one mortal blest."[1] I thrilled to Demosthenes assailing Athenian peace-at-any-price, was turned on by his classic description of panic in Athens that begins *Hespera men gar ēn* ("Evening had already fallen").[2] In imagination I invaded Plato's cave and its prisoners, stared transfixed at the fire and the shadows of reality on the wall.[3] Time and again I wept at Socrates' parting words: "I go to die, and you to live; but which of us goes to the better lot, is known to none but God."[4] For all his verbiage, Cicero's command of the idiom could still excite me— whether castigating the conspirator Catiline or analyzing old age. I memorized vast sections of Homer, particularly organ sounds like *polyphloisboio thalassēs,* the shore of "the loud-resounding sea";[5] found a foreshadowing of the Christ-event in Vergil's *Fourth Eclogue:* "magnus ab integro saeclorum nascitur ordo;/ iam redit et Virgo. . . . "[6] I wrote Latin odes in imitation of Horace's "integer vitae,"[7] his "carpe diem" (live today!),[8] his "nunc est bibendum" (it's cocktail time).[9] And many a night I fell asleep, chastely, in the Lesbian arms of Sappho.

On the English scene, Shakespeare's artistry was ceaseless delight. Henry V roaming the camp at night, musing on the burdens of kings: "What infinite heart's ease/ Must kings neglect, that private men enjoy!"[10] Romeo forsaking his very name for Juliet: "Call me but love, and I'll be new baptiz'd."[11] Hamlet's "native hue of resolution . . . sicklied o'er with the pale cast of thought."[12] Shylock's ageless cry of the Jew: "If you prick us, do we not bleed?"[13]

There was more than Avon's bard, of course. With Francis Thompson, I fled the Hound of Heaven's "majestic speed, deliberate instancy." I resonated to Gerard Manley Hopkins comparing the Blessed Virgin to the air we breathe:

> If I have understood,
> She holds high motherhood
> Towards all our ghostly good
> And plays in grace her part
> About man's beating heart,
> Laying, like air's fine flood,
> The deathdance in his blood;
> Yet no part but what will
> Be Christ our Saviour still.[14]

With Cyrano in his last hour, I watched the Venetian-red leaves fall to the ground:

> Yes—they know how to die. A little way
> From the branch to the earth, a little fear
> Of mingling with the common dust—and yet
> They go down gracefully—a fall that seems
> Like flying.[15]

With Carl Sandburg, I experienced Chicago as the "hog butcher of the world"; went "down to the seas again" with John Masefield; sang an ode to Shelley's west wind, "thou breath of Autumn's being"; looked with Keats into Chapman's Homer; blew bugles with Tennyson to "set the wild echoes flying"; heard the revolutionary rustling of Whitman's *Leaves of Grass.*

Newman's periodic sentences entranced me, and sermons such as "The Second Spring" revealed how fact and reason could be infused with imagination and intuition. The paradoxes of Chesterton, that huge man with sombrero, swordstick, and cape, captured my fancy—from the incredible insights into Aquinas to the tantalizing, perhaps debatable "There is a Catholic way of teaching everything, even the alphabet, if only to teach it in such a way as at the same time to teach that those who learn it must not look down on those who don't."

There was all this, and much more. But it was in theology at rural Woodstock in Maryland that words took flesh, that what might have been dilettante seduction became Christian life and death. For in theology the word took on unexpected meaning. In the Old Testament, I discovered, the word is wondrously alive. As John L. McKenzie was to phrase it years later, the spoken word for the Israelites was

> a distinct reality charged with power. It has power because it emerges from a source of power which, in releasing it, must in a way release itself. The basic concept of the word is the word-thing. The power of the word . . . posits the reality which it signifies. But in so doing it also posits the reality which speaks the word. No one can speak without revealing himself; and the reality which he posits is identified with himself. Thus the word is dianoetic as well as dynamic. It confers intelligibility upon the thing, and it discloses the character of the person who utters the word.[16]

That is why *God's* word is particularly powerful.

In the New Testament, I discovered, the word as a distinct reality charged with power is fulfilled to perfection. God not only expresses Himself in human syllables; He expresses Himself in a Word that is itself a person. The same personal Word God utters from eternity, He uttered on a midnight clear—to us. "In Jesus Christ is fulfilled the word as a distinct being; as a dynamic creative entity; as that which gives form and intelligibility to the reality which it signifies; as the self-revelation of God; as a point of personal encounter between God and man."[17]

The word, I learned from St. James, is a perilous thing. "We use it to bless the Lord and Father, but we also use it to curse men and women who are made in God's image" (Jas 3:9). And still, in St. Paul's eyes, the word is an indispensable thing. "How are men and women to call upon him in whom they have not believed? And how are they to believe in him of whom they have never heard? And how are they to hear without a preacher?" (Rom 10:14).

Words, I learned from experience, can be weapons, and words can be healing. Words can unite in friendship or sever in enmity. Words can unlock who I am or mask me from others. Two words, "Sieg Heil," bloodied the face of Europe; three words, "Here I stand," divided the body of Christendom. Words have made slaves and freed slaves, have declared war and imposed peace. Words sentence to death ("You shall be hanged by the neck") and words restore to life ("Your sins are forgiven you"). Words declare a marriage dead, and words covenant a life together in love. Words charm and repel, amuse and anger, reveal and conceal, chill and warm. Words clarify and words obscure. A word from Washington rained down atomic hell on Hiroshima; words from an altar change bread and wine into the body and blood of Christ.

With all this, I feel no guilt in being a weaver of words. A word is real; a word is sacred; a word is powerful; a word is . . . I.

II

This leads to the second level of my argument; for our "word" here is not just any word, it is a liturgical word. If your experience goes back to mid-century, you remember how little the "liturgy of the word" once mattered. A brief but pungent proof: You could miss the whole liturgy of the word without having to confess it. Gloria and Credo, Epistle and Gospel and homily—you could come in out of the cold after all these were said and done, and still "hear Mass," still fulfil your obligation. No manual of morality did more than rap your knuckles lightly.

Why? Because the sole stress was on the sacrifice. One word alone was all-important: the consecratory word. Here was *the* Real Presence; here was the efficacious word, objectively infallible, utterly trustworthy, limpidly clear. No worry about the person, about reader or preacher, songstress or danseuse. No need for lips to be touched by live coals; enough that they whispered distinctly "This is my body." The back of the priest was more symbolic than his face; for the true priest was the hidden priest, the Christ of the sacrifice.

Today's liturgical attitude is refreshingly different, more balanced. In Vatican II's wake, there is fresh stress on the whole word as a locus where God transpires, comes to light. Music, readings, homily, dance—God is there (or can be there), a real presence.[18] My focus is on one of those four liturgical "words," the word that is homily.[19]

What is the liturgical homily, the homiletic word? If you prefer chaste Roman rhetoric, you have an official definition from the Congregation of Rites in 1964: "an unfolding either of some facet of the readings of Sacred Scripture or of some other text taken from the Ordinary or from the Proper of the Mass of the day, taking into consideration either the mystery being celebrated or the special needs of the listeners."[20] From this text, two concerns ought to dominate the homily and its preparation: liturgy and people—this liturgy and this people. This liturgy, because in the Lectionary and the Missal we find the substance of what is to be preached: in the words of Vatican II, "the proclamation of God's wonderful works in the history of salvation"—a proclamation that "should draw its content mainly from scriptural and liturgical sources."[21] This people, because in the liturgy "God's wonderful works" are not just read, not just remembered; they are re-presented, made effectively present. In the words of the Council fathers, "the mystery of Christ . . . is made present and active within us."[22]

The first concern, this liturgical event, the mystery, is the background for the second concern, this people, "the mystery made present." Because it is the indispensable background for the proclamation, for the word made flesh today, I devote to it this second main point. And I suggest that here four critical demands have fashioned four problems which prevent today's homily from being any better than yesterday's sermon: fear of Sacred Scripture, ignorance of contemporary theology, unawareness of liturgical prayer, and lack of proper preparation. A word on each.

First, fear of Scripture. For all too many priests, the Bible is a no-no; they dare not touch it. "The exegetes have taken away my Lord, and I know not where they have laid him." What Jesus himself said, the words the Word proclaimed, the exegetes have hidden like Easter eggs, and the faithful in their paschal finery run around in circles trying to find them. And what do we come up with? What the *early Church* thought Jesus said or meant, or would have said if. . . . Miracles are out, the Magi barely in. Was Jesus virginally conceived, or is virginal conception a physical way of expressing a spiritual reality? Did Jesus "physically" rise from the rock, or doesn't the question make any sense any more? And—more bad news—stop looking for some specifically Christian content to morality that leaps out of the Bible; that, some moralists say, is highly dubious.

And the Old Testament? Forget it! Oust it from the rectory! It no longer announces Christ. Mary is not in Genesis 3:15, Jesus not in Isaiah 7:14; the priest is no longer prefigured in Melchizedek, the Mass in Malachi. The Song of Songs is secular eroticism and would be banned in Boston; the prophets preached social justice.

Scripture is indeed a mystery, if only because it is God's plan hidden in God from eternity. But it is a mystery revealed. The word of God that is Scripture is a unique, incomparable way in which God speaks to us, reveals Himself, challenges us, graces us. Here we come to know Christ as nowhere else. That is why St. Jerome could say that ignorance of Scripture is ignorance of Christ. Difficult as it is, Scripture is still the single most important source for any Christian preacher. Not even dogma supplants Scripture in dignity or content. As Vatican II confessed, the magisterium "is not above the word of God, but serves it. . . . "[23]

Let me be blunt. I have no special competence in Scripture that gives me a head start over the parish priest. We have the same sources: meditation on the word and recourse to the commentaries. Prayer and sweat. When I preached at Catholic University for the golden jubilee of patristic scholar John Quasten's ordination, the liturgical readings emphasized wisdom. They forced me back on biblical dictionaries, on Kittel and Léon-Dufour. It was there I discovered who the wise man is, and what he does that is so wise, and how he comes to be wise. When I preached to the Catholic University community on Holy Thursday, I was faced with the frustrating foot-washing Gospel. As so often, I turned to Raymond Brown's commentary on John. From mild sweat came bright light:

two interpretations of the foot-washing in Johannine circles—and both exciting. Indeed Brown destroyed some old seminary simplicities; but, like most genuine scholars, he uprooted only to plant more richly.[24]

A second obstacle is ignorance of theology. Theology is indispensable for the word because it is the Church's ceaseless effort to understand the word. Once again, an obvious problem: Where do you look? Mid-century theology may have been boring, but you could trust seminary professors to do what Pius XII expected of theologians: "show how the doctrines taught by the living magisterium are found explicitly or implicitly in Scripture and in divine tradition."[25] For that you look in vain: The manuals have vanished, and each theologian has his or her theology—from Baum to Tracy, from Ruether to Rahner, from Curran to McCormick. Theologians question everything, from the first sin to the Second Coming, from abortion to bestiality. Is there any help for the homilist?

Frankly, I see nothing but band-aid remedies until we fill a neuralgic priestly need: continuing education of the clergy. The Church's search for understanding did not grind to a halt when I took my last theology exam; nor is the meaning of God's word preserved immobile in a Vatican capsule. Our basic Christian words, the words we preach, must be constantly recaptured, rethought: God, Christ, and Spirit; sin and redemption; church and sacraments; justice and love; death and resurrection. Books like Dulles' *Models of the Church,* periodic reports like the annual "Moral Notes" in *Theological Studies*—these can help. But until the clergy can read theology with understanding and a critical eye, liturgical homiletics will continue to be impoverished.

A third obstacle: unawareness of prayer—liturgical prayer. John Gallen's thesis is well known: "What the contemporary reform of the Church's liturgy needs most in this moment of its history is the discovery of liturgy as prayer."[26] Liturgical prayer, like all prayer, is a response. The God of mystery touches me, touches the worshiping community, with His presence. The initiative comes from God—not present coldly, abstractly, distantly, but laying hold of me, laying hold of the believing community, at the very core of our being. Prayer is our response to this kind of presence, to the thrilling action of God within us.

But what manner of prayer is the liturgical response? On your answer depends in large measure the kind of homily you construct. For me, prayer is fundamentally and ultimately "sacrifice of praise." Not that I downgrade conversion, petition, thanksgiving. I claim that all three are subsumed ritually in a glorious doxology: Glory to God. . . . In the liturgy I celebrate God. Oh, I do not minimize man or woman. I simply claim that liturgy will be a humanizing experience to the extent that, in playing before God, the human person becomes increasingly image of God. To become human is to praise God.[27]

The point is, the homily is liturgy. In Jungmann's strong sentence, the homily "should emanate from the consciousness that although it is freely created by the liturgist, it is liturgy itself."[28] And the liturgy is prayer. Conclusion? The homily is prayer. The logic is impeccable; only the meaning is debatable. When you proclaim "God's wonderful works," when you help re-present the mystery that is Christ, when with human words you touch the Christ-event to this particular people, what manner of prayer is this? Is it prayer at all?

An examination of conscience, then, to humble the homilist: What is your theology of prayer? Of liturgical prayer? Of homiletic prayer? Do you have one?

The fourth obstacle is the kind of devil that cannot be overcome even by prayer and fasting. To me, the unprepared homilist is a menace. I do not minimize divine inspiration; I simply suggest it is rarely allotted to the lazy. Here I resonate to a story told me some years ago at Belmont Abbey by the famed Baptist biblicist and preacher Dale Moody. A student in his Spirit course at the Louisville seminary wasn't meeting the professor's expectations. So Dr. Moody called him in and (in a delightful drawl I cannot reproduce) said: "Son, you're not doin' all that well in my course on the Holy Spirit. You been studyin'?" "Dr. Moody," the young man replied, "I don't have to *study* about the Spirit; I'm *led* by the Spirit." "Son," Moody asked, "that Spirit ever lead you to the library? If He doesn't soon, you're in deep trouble."

The homilist is in deep trouble if the Spirit does not lead him—lead him to the chapel indeed, but lead him to the library as well.

Implicit in these four obstacles is the major thrust of this second point: The mystery must be preached—God's wonderful works in the story of salvation. From the Spirit of God moving over the waters and a loving God toiling over clay, through the first sin and the first death, through covenant after covenant to the final covenant in God's blood, down to today's "signs of the times," the word must take flesh. Despite the difficulties, God's wonderful works must be preached, especially as they surge up from Scripture and the liturgy. If they are poorly proclaimed, the liturgy will be less effective in making God's works effectively present.

III

This leads to the third level of my argument. I have spoken of the word, and of the word made flesh in the liturgical homily. Now the crucial issue: How can the word be made flesh today? So far, the power of the word and the need for the word. Now, how do you incarnate the word for this people? How can the mystery be made present, not for the Jews of 27 or the Gentiles of 57, but for this congregation in 1987?

Here two realities come together in striking fashion: the insight of the theologian and the hunger of the people. In a typically perceptive article, Yves Congar has addressed the problem of liturgical preaching.[29] He locates three links between word and worship. First, Christian worship is an anamnesis: it is an actualizing memory, an active re-presentation, "of the acts by which God intervened to make a covenant with us and to save us," so that these acts "keep their operative value for the believers of all ages, who make them actual again in the Spirit when they celebrate these acts in faith and thanksgiving."[30] But the liturgy's insights "are more or less veiled"; liturgical texts and forms tend to be immobilized, with rare exceptions are the same for all, whatever their condition; the connection between the Church's sacraments and Christ's pasch is not instantly recognizable. What the homily does is extend the immemorial symbols to a particular time and place, a particular people.[31] The old is expressed anew; it must be, to come alive, to keep alive, to make alive.

Second, worship is a witness to faith—faith being "my response to God's action communicated to me through his Word."[32] The sacraments, Aquinas insisted, are sacraments of faith. In what sense? Because, Vatican II explains, the sacraments "not only presuppose faith, but by words and objects they also nourish, strengthen, and express it."[33] But the peril of liturgy is that it can be impersonal. The homily personalizes what the rite expresses in a common and general way. It should rouse the faith of this people more personally than is possible for liturgical symbols and ritual actions.[34]

Third, Christian worship is a spiritual sacrifice: It consists basically in accepting gratefully God's Eucharistic gift and in uniting to it the spiritual offering of our concrete existence, our total life. The specific function of the homily is not only to explain the liturgical mystery, but to bring the faithful into the mystery "by throwing light on their life so that they can unite it to this mystery."[35] Says Congar in a startling sentence: "I could quote a whole series of ancient texts, all saying more or less that if in one country Mass was celebrated for thirty years without preaching and in another there was preaching for thirty years without the Mass, people would be more Christian in the country where there was preaching."[36]

Theological insight is reinforced by people hunger. Our people are hurting. Not merely the millions consciously squirming in the pews, but the uncounted Christians who are hungry and do not know why. To deepen their Christian living, at times to make it endurable, the homily should throw light on their life in such a way that they can link human living to the paschal mystery. It is not primarily a matter of facts, biblical and theological information. They hurt because, on the one hand, the ritual does not express their faith experience, the symbols do not symbolize, God's wonderful works are just too wonder-full, and, on the other hand, the homilist who should bring liturgy and life together apparently does not know how. He does not speak to their hungers.

What to do? My pressing plea will force you back to my first point; my recommendation revolves around words. That first point was not a tour de force, not narcissistic autobiography. We homilists will not link worship to life unless we become translators. What that involves staggered me in 1978 when I read a remarkable article on justice as a culture problem by that fine Fordham sociologist Joseph Fitzpatrick. In part he wrote:

> . . . I don't know whether you've read Father André Dupeyrat's wonderful little book, *Savage Papua*. Among the Papuans the pig is a sacred animal. The women may nurse the pigs at their breast if there is no sow around to nurse them. In our Scriptures the sacred animal is the lamb. "Behold the lamb of God." This meant absolutely nothing to the Papuans. In order to communicate to the Papuans what "Lamb of God" meant among the Hebrews, Dupeyrat would have to say "Christ is the pig of God." Jesus a pig! In New York? Imagine my going into the pulpit in New York and saying "Glory to God and praise, and to the Lord Jesus who is the pig of God." Yet if I want to communicate to the Papuans the meaning that is communicated to us and to the Hebrews and to the religious tradition of the West, I have to learn what their meanings are.
>
> This is not easy to take. There is no intrinsic relation between the Lamb and the Savior. He was born among the people for whom the lamb was the source of good and the source of clothing, the great economic basis of their life and their society. And the pig was a scavenger. In the parable of the Prodigal, the son is de-

scribed as reaching a hopeless state of degradation—he was feeding pigs. The most wonderful thing a Papuan can do is to feed
pigs. Note how these basic economic realities become symbols.
Religious meanings become projected in them and they become
the context in which our psychological and emotional response to
them as religious symbols eventually gets put in place. Then if
you take the symbol away and put another in its place, our religious experience starts to turn upside down.[37]

The Papuan pig is not only instructive for missionaries; it is a
paradigm for every preacher. In preaching, I must translate.[38]
God's definitive revelation was indeed given through the divine
Word, but it "uses human words that were already current and
loaded with overtones from the surrounding world."[39] When that
revelation is translated into dogma or interpreted by theology, it is
not yet the preacher's word; it is jargon-infested and culture-con-
ditioned. I do not mean it is not true, is not instinct with profound
meaning. I am simply saying that neither the sounds of ancient Sa-
maria nor the rhetoric of Rome or Rahner can pour forth from today's pulpit unchanged, unaltered, unconverted. Not if we intend
to be heard.

My constant question must be: What do these words say to this
congregation? Karl Rahner put it concisely: "The preacher should
be able to hear his own sermon with the ears of his actual audience."[40] John Courtney Murray expressed the same idea more cap-
tivatingly: "I do not know what I have said until I understand what
you have heard." What does this audience hear when I say
"church"? Institution? Community? Sacrament? Herald? Servant?
Disciple? Does their experience of "church" conjure up the qualities
of love and tenderness I associate with my physical mother? And
"holy" has taken on triumphalistic overtones for Christians who see
themselves, their community, and especially Rome as more sinful
than saintly.

Take a more likely example, the monosyllable that makes the
world go round: love. Here, if anywhere, the committed Christian
confronts confusion. On the one hand, the whole Christian "thing"
is love, or it is hoax. On this, God's own word rings loud and clear:
God *is* Love; whatever exists, man or mountain, blue marlin or
robin redbreast, stems from love divine; out of love God gave His
only Son to earth and cross; on the twin command of love rest the
law and the prophets; love towers above faith and hope; unless I
love my brothers and sisters, I cannot claim to love God.

On the other hand, the word "love" is frightfully mangled, manipulated. Dr. James Shannon put it vividly to a Christian Family Movement seminar: We use love to describe "the motive for the voluntary death of Jesus Christ on Calvary, the subject matter of hard pornographic movies, the bond of affection between Flower Children at Woodstock, the intimate union of a husband and a wife, and the unbuttoned promiscuity of Fire Island on a weekend."[41] And so he suggested a moratorium on the word "love"; during the moratorium, experiment with other words, words that say precisely what we mean. I would add: Let not the liturgist sell short those who just sing about love—where the naked syllables ("When you say love, you've said it all") are admittedly inadequate, but the beat, the rhythm, the music makes for meaning.

Admit it: The homiletic movement from Scripture through theology and prayer to the present liturgical moment is a frightening function, a dismaying task. It is not simply a matter of escaping the malapropism—not imitating the acting mayor of New York City who assured a Harlem audience: "My face may be white, but my heart is as black as yours." What is time-consuming and soul-searing in each homily's preparation is that I must (1) grasp the genuine meaning of a word as it emerged from the mouth of Jeremiah or the pen of Paul or the contemplation of a Johannine community, (2) touch it to the paschal mystery celebrated by the Church, and (3) transform it so that the word takes on the personal and cultural clothes of this moment, of these believers. Here is the agony of preparation, here its occasional ecstasy.

I am not boasting when I confess that I consume four hours in preparation for every minute in the pulpit. Some of it goes into research, sheer information. In preaching on the Bread of Life, for example, it was important for me to discover that Jesus' discourse in John 6 is colored by two themes; scholars call them the sapiential and the sacramental. Jesus feeds us with his word and he feeds us with his flesh; the "bread from heaven" which "gives life to the world" (Jn 6:33) is God's revelation and Christ's flesh. Some of those hours are spent in mulling, over days at times—what this scriptural data might have to say to a community living the paschal mystery today—until a promising central idea bursts forth. Ah yes: In today's context of human hungers, talk about the Bread of Life will sound awfully empty, suspiciously hollow, unless we who feed on the Eucharistic Christ are ourselves eucharists for the life of the world. It is a question of real presence. If I am to be a eucharist for the life of the world, my feeding on the flesh of Christ must take me from church to world. I must begin to be present to others, present where they are, present in ways that respond to their needs, to their hungers. *I* must be present—not merely my money or my mind—somewhat hidden at times but always totally committed, because as a Christian, as a Christ, my life is love and only love can bring life.

From that point my hours are given over to . . . words. Precisely here is a preacher's crucifixion. A word is not an entry in Webster; it is colored by living experience. The Eucharist is indeed a bread that gives life; but when *you* hear the word "life," you hear something quite different from the 200,000 skin-and-bones starving who "live" in the streets of Calcutta, build tiny fires to cook scraps of food, defecate at curbstones, curl up against a wall to sleep—perhaps to die. Yes, a word is real, is sacred, is powerful, but inevitably a word is . . . I. This makes a double demand on a preacher: I must sense what my people hear, and I must say what I mean.

But clarity is not enough. A homily is not a catechism or a manual of dogma or a textbook in theology. The word flings forth a challenge; it is a summons to decision; God wants a reply. In Semmelroth's words, "in the word of preaching the flood of historical redemptive events is grasped and brought before man for his decision. Again and again men are addressed in preaching and moved to fashion their lives in accordance with what is said."[42] But really, are they so moved? God's grace is indeed all-powerful, but it dashes against two powerful Catholic adversaries: a homilist dead below the larynx, and a minimal vocabulary dominated by abstract nouns ending in -tion. If I am to persuade, my whole person should be aflame with what I proclaim. If I am to move, the words I utter must be chosen with care and love, with sweat and fire. That is why, before I set pen to paper, I listen to Beethoven or Tchaikovsky, Vivaldi or Mary Lou Williams, Edith Piaf or the theme from "Doctor Zhivago"; I read poetry aloud, Shakespeare or Hopkins, T. S. Eliot or e. e. cummings—something to turn me on, so that the end result will not sound like a Roman rescript or a laundry list. To challenge, the word must come alive.

Ultimately, *I* am the word, the word that is heard. And—I say it fearfully—it is not a clever rhetorician the people need, but a holy homilist. Holy in what sense? Because aware that I am only *a* word, not *the* word: If God does not speak through me, I am "a noisy gong, a clanging cymbal" (1 Cor 13:1). Because my homily is a prayer: In preparation and pulpit, I stand before God in praise of Him, not of my own rhetorical perfection. Because aware of my own weakness: I too need the word I preach, I too need forgiveness, I too am vulnerable, I am a *wounded* healer. Because, like my hearers, I too ceaselessly murmur "I believe, Lord, help my unbelief." Because I am in love: with the things of God, with the people of God, with God Himself. Because the hungers of God's family are my hungers: When they bleed, I weep. Unless some of this breaks through, the word may indeed be proclaimed, but it will hardly be heard. The word is . . . I.

Dear preachers actual and to be: The word can be made flesh today. But only on condition that we take the word seriously, handle it sacredly. Every word: the scriptural word, the sacramental word, the secular word, the homiletic word. For all our pulpit problems, I am not disheartened. I take heart from two disparate sources: the Christian faithful and four lines of verse. In 46 years of priestly preaching, not once have I encountered an unresponsive congregation, not once a believing community that could not be stirred. And on those occasions when I have been most acutely aware of a chasm, of a gulf that yawns between the audience and myself, between their experience and mine, I draw Christian hope from Rod McKuen:

> I make words for people I've not met,
> those who will not turn to follow after me.
> It is for me a kind of loving.
> A kind of loving, for me.[43]

2
SIR, WE WOULD LIKE TO SEE JESUS
Preaching As Imagining

Do you remember Saint-Exupéry's *The Little Prince?* I'm thinking specifically of the opening pages:

> Once when I was six years old I saw a magnificent picture in a book, called *True Stories from Nature,* about the primeval forest. It was a picture of a boa constrictor in the act of swallowing an animal. Here is a copy of the drawing.

> In the book it said: "Boa constrictors swallow their prey whole, without chewing it. After that they are not able to move, and they sleep through the six months that they need for digestion."
> I pondered deeply, then, over the adventures of the jungle. And after some work with a colored pencil I succeeded in making my first drawing. My Drawing Number One. It looked like this:

I showed my masterpiece to the grown-ups, and asked them whether the drawing frightened them.

But they answered: "Frighten? Why should any one be frightened by a hat?"

My drawing was not a picture of a hat. It was a picture of a boa constrictor digesting an elephant. But since the grown-ups were not able to understand it, I made another drawing: I drew the inside of the boa constrictor, so that the grown-ups could see it clearly. They always need to have things explained. My Drawing Number Two looked like this:

The grown-ups' response, this time, was to advise me to lay aside my drawings of boa constrictors, whether from the inside or the outside, and devote myself instead to geography, history, arithmetic and grammar. That is why, at the age of six, I gave up what might have been a magnificent career as a painter. I had been disheartened by the failure of my Drawing Number One and my Drawing Number Two. Grown-ups never understand anything by themselves, and it is tiresome for children to be always and forever explaining things to them.

So then I chose another profession, and learned to pilot airplanes. I have flown a little over all parts of the world; and it is true that geography has been very useful to me. At a glance I can distinguish China from Arizona. If one gets lost in the night, such knowledge is valuable.

In the course of this life I have had a great many encounters with a great many people who have been concerned with matters of consequence. I have lived a great deal among grown-ups. I have seen them intimately, close at hand. And that hasn't much improved my opinion of them.

Whenever I met one of them who seemed to me at all clear-

sighted, I tried the experiment of showing him my Drawing
Number One, which I have always kept. I would try to find out,
so, if this was a person of true understanding. But, whoever it
was, he, or she, would always say:

"That is a hat."

Then I would never talk to that person about boa constrictors, or primeval forests, or stars. I would bring myself down to
his level. I would talk to him about bridge, and golf, and politics,
and neckties. And the grown-up would be greatly pleased to have
met such a sensible man.[1]

In recent years I have argued that four problems prevent today's homily from being any better than yesterday's sermon: fear of
Sacred Scripture, ignorance of contemporary theology, unawareness of liturgical prayer, and lack of proper preparation.[2] The list
has a lamentable lacuna. I have left out the most serious lack of all:
imagination. Without imagination the preacher limps along on one
leg. You may have memorized Mark and ransacked Rahner, you
may be an expert in things liturgical and put onerous hours into
your homily; but if your homily is only a masterpiece of Cartesian
clarity, you are in deep trouble. If you are for ever explaining things
to grownups, drawing recognizable Christian hats, you are hardly a
homilist.

To make this outrageous thesis palatable, let me develop it in
three stages. First, what are we talking about when we speak of
imagination? Second, what has imagination to do with preaching?
Third, if imagination is so awfully important, what ought we homilists to do about it?

I

First then, what is this creature we call imagination?[3] To begin
with, what is imagination *not*? It is not the same thing as fantasy.
Fantasy has come to mean the grotesque, the bizarre. That is fantastic which is unreal, irrational, wild, unrestrained. We speak of
"pure fantasy": It has no connection with reality. It is imagination
run wild, on the loose, unbridled, uncontained.[4]

What is it, then? Imagination is the capacity we have "to make
the material an image of the immaterial or spiritual."[5] It is a creative
power. You find it in Rembrandt's self-portraits, in Beethoven's
Fifth Symphony, in the odor of a new rose or the flavor of an old wine.
You find it in storytellers like C. S. Lewis and John Shea, in dram-

atists like Aeschylus and Eugene O'Neill, in poets from Sappho to
e. e. cummings.

Now, when I say "capacity," I do not mean a "faculty" like intellect or will. I mean rather a posture of our whole person towards
our experience.[6] It is a way of seeing. It is, as with Castaneda, looking for the holes in the world or listening to the space between
sounds. It is a breaking through the obvious, the surface, the superficial, to the reality beneath and beyond. It is the world of wonder and intuition, of amazement and delight, of festivity and play.

Is all this too imaginative to be clear? Then let me sketch, in
clear and distinct ideas, some of the ways in which imagination—
specifically, religious imagination—comes to expression.

1) A vision. I mean "the emergence either in dream, trance, or
ecstasy, of a pattern of images, words, or dreamlike dramas which
are experienced then, and upon later reflection, as having revelatory significance."[7] Examples? Isaiah's vision of the Lord in the temple (Isa 6); Ezekiel's "four living creatures" (Ezek 1); Moses and
Elijah appearing to Jesus and the disciples on the Mount of Transfiguration (Mt 17:1–9); Joan of Arc's "voices"; Teresa of Avila's visions of Christ; St. Margaret Mary's vision of the Sacred Heart.

2) Ritual. The form of ritual is action—action that is public, dramatic, patterned. A group enacts the presence of the sacred and
participates in that presence, usually through some combination of
dance, chant, sacrifice, or sacrament.[8]

3) Story. I mean a narrative—that is, a constellation of images—
that recounts incidents or events. As Sallie TeSelle puts it, "We all
love a good story because of the basic narrative quality of human
experience: in a sense *any* story is about ourselves, and a *good* story
is good precisely because somehow it rings true to human life. . . .
We recognize our pilgrimage from here to there in a good story."[9]
For the religious imagination, three types of stories are particularly
important: parable, allegory, and myth.

The parable is a developed simile, usually quite short, in which
the narrative is at once fictitious and true to life; from it a moral or
spiritual truth is extracted. In a specially forceful way we recognize
our pilgrimage in the parables of Jesus: "The kingdom of heaven is
like treasure hidden in a field" (Mt 13:34). "There was a man who
had two sons" (Lk 15:11). "There was a rich man clothed in purple
. . . [and] a poor man . . . full of sores" (Lk 16:19–20).

Allegories are developed metaphors prolonged into continu-
ous narratives, in which a series of actions is symbolic of other actions, while the characters often are types or personifications. You

remember Bunyan's *Pilgrim's Progress,* the dream allegory that tells of the journey of Christian and Christiana through "the wilderness of this world" to Sion; Spenser's *Faerie Queene,* that richly imaginative work of moral allegory; Lewis' *Chronicles of Narnia,* a milestone in theological allegory, high festivity in the kingdom of the imagination, the Christian quest in terms a child can understand. Add to these Herman Melville's *Moby Dick,* James Joyce's *Finnegans Wake,* William Golding's *Lord of the Flies,* and John Barth's *Giles Goat-Boy.*

The myth is basically verbal. "It is a narration which conveys the meaning of human existence in relation to its destiny or origin, or the destiny or origin of the social group, nature, or cosmos of which it is a part, as these are grounded and penetrated by the sacred."[10] And so we can speak legitimately of the Creation myth or the Christian myth. For myth is not opposed to fact or to fancy. Its raw material may be fact or it may be fancy, "but its purpose is not to add yet another facet to our squirrels' nest of facts stored against some winter of the mind, nor to create an entertaining fantasy to titillate aesthetic delight." It intends "to narrate the fundamental structure of human being in the world. By the concreteness of its imagery, the universality of its intention, its narrative or story form, the myth evokes the identification and participation of those for whom it functions as revelatory."[11]

4) Symbol. What symbol means is not easy to say; for even within theology it does not have a univocal sense. Let me define it, with Dulles, as "an externally perceived sign that works mysteriously on the human consciousness so as to suggest more than it can clearly describe or define."[12] Not every sign is a symbol. A mere indicator ("This Way to Washington") or a conventional sign (a word) is not a symbol. "The symbol is a sign pregnant with a depth of meaning which is evoked rather than explicitly stated."[13] It might be an artifact: a totem, a crucifix, the brazen serpent. It might be a person or an event: Moses leading the Israelites out of Egypt, Jesus Christ crucified and risen. It might be sacred writings: the Bhagavad Gita, the Old and New Testaments. It might be a story: parable, allegory, myth.

5) The fine arts. I mean painting and poetry, sculpture and architecture, music, dancing, and dramatic art. I mean da Vinci and John Donne, the Pietà and Chartres, Beethoven's *Missa Solemnis,* David whirling and skipping before the Ark of the Covenant, the mystery dramas of the Middle Ages. I mean film, the movies.

From all this two significant conclusions emerge. First, imagination is not at odds with knowledge; imagination is a form of cognition. In Whitehead's words, "Imagination is not to be divorced from the facts: it is a way of illuminating the facts."[14] True, it is not a process of reasoning; it is not abstract thought, conceptual analysis, rational demonstration, syllogistic proof. Notre Dame of Paris is not a thesis in theology; Lewis' famous trilogy does not demonstrate the origin of evil; Hopkins is not analyzing God's image in us when he sings that "Christ plays in ten thousand places,/ Lovely in limbs, and lovely in eyes not his/ [plays] To the Father through the features of men's faces."[15] And still, imaging and imagining is a work of our intellectual nature; through it our spirit reaches the true, the beautiful, and the good.

Second, the imagination does not so much teach as evoke; it calls something forth from me. And so it is often ambiguous; the image can be understood in different ways. Do you remember the reporters who asked Martha Graham, "What does your dance mean?" She replied: "Darlings, if I could tell you, I would not have danced it!" Something is lost when we move from imagining to thinking, from art to conceptual clarity. Not that imagination is arbitrary, that *Swan Lake* or the Infancy Narrative or *Hamlet* or the Transfiguration is whatever anyone wants to make of it, my gut feeling. Hostile to a valid imagination is "the cult of imagination for itself alone; vision, phantasy, ecstasy for their own sakes; creativity, spontaneity on their own, without roots, without tradition, without discipline."[16] Wilder is right: "Inebriation is no substitute for paideia."[17] And still it is true, the image is more open-ended than the concept, less confining, less imprisoning. The image evokes our own imagining.

II

My second question: What has imagination to do with preaching? Not much; just everything. The scholar of mythology Joseph Campbell did not think much of us clergy; he said we have no imagination. Part of the reason is our older education: Imagination was identified with "bad thoughts," and bad thoughts were sexual phantasms, and these we confessed. Moreover, as the Carmelite William McNamara has complained, all through school we were taught to abstract; we were not led to contemplation, to immediate communion with reality, to loving admiration, experiential awareness. We were not taught to simply "see."

To put the problem in vivid relief, let me contrast two theories of preaching. Recently I read the contention of a priest that we should scrap the Vatican II homily and get back to instructional sermons. The critical Catholic problem, he felt, is abysmal Catholic ignorance. Our people, particularly the young, do not know "the faith." A trinitarian God and an incarnate Son, original and actual sin, one true Church and seven real sacraments, created grace and Uncreated Grace, the Mass as sacrifice and the pope as vicar of Christ, mortal sin and the Ten Commandments, the immorality of birth control and abortion—this is what our faithful must be taught. Vatican II? Why, Catholics don't know Baltimore Catechism One! And especially these days, when elementary Catholic education is vanishing, there is only one viable way to teach: via the Sunday sermon. Give them the dogma, the doctrine, and give it with consummate clarity, with unquestioning certitude.

I cannot agree. I grant that many a Catholic is distressingly ignorant of God's revelation, does not know what God took flesh to tell us. Somehow, somewhere they should learn this. But not *ex professo* in a homily. The homily, like the liturgy of which it is part and parcel, should proclaim, re-present, make effectively present "God's wonderful works in the history of salvation"; "the mystery of Christ" should be "made present and active within us."[18] But this is not done by a laundry list of dogmas to be believed, doctrines to be accepted. It is done by imagination.

Why? Because indoctrination plays upon one faculty of the human person: the intellect's ability to grasp ideas, concepts, propositions. It pays little heed to an old scholastic axiom, "Nothing is present in the intellect that was not previously present in the senses." Our ideas are triggered by sense experience. On the whole, then, the more powerful the sense experience, the more powerfully an idea will take hold. If I want to sell you on Spaghetti Bolognese or Beef Burgundy, I don't hand you a recipe; I let you smell it, taste it, savor it. If I want you to "see" the Holocaust, I won't just say "six million were exterminated"; I'll let you see the gas ovens, the mountains of human bones. It is not enough to show you the score of Handel's *Messiah;* you must drink it in with your ears. It is one thing to hear "I love you," quite another to experience love's touch.

My thesis? The homily is a fascinating wedding of all those ways in which imagination comes to expression: vision and ritual, symbol and story (parable, allegory, and myth), the fine arts. This is the homily at its best, the homily that makes God's wonderful works come alive, immerses in the mystery, evokes a religious response.

A response—there's the magic word! The homily might be dif-

ferent if the task of the liturgy were simply to *recall* God's saving
works, simply to *remember* the mystery that is Christ. Then I might
merely explain lucidly what it all means. But there is more. If the
liturgy must make the mystery "present and active within us," a
homily should be evocative. I mean, it should help the believer to
open up to God speaking now. Not a cold assent to a proposition;
rather, "What do you want from me, O Lord?" And the most effective approach to this is not ratiocination, not demonstration; it is
imagination.

The evidence for imagination's incomparable power surrounds
us. We keep saying "A picture is worth a thousand words." Americans spend billions each year on movies, theatre, concerts. Students
study to stereo, skip lectures readily when Bruce Springsteen comes
to town. Jesuits too read the comics before the front page, go wild
over sports—poetry in motion. Our children's supreme educator,
for good or ill, is TV. Even the commercials, that sell products from
head to foot essential for human existence, sell us with the greatest
array of imaginative talent since the creation story in Genesis 1 and
John's vision on Patmos.

And we homilists (so our patient people complain) mount the
pulpit or approach the podium with the imagination of a dead fish.
"Today, my dear brethren, Holy Mother Church in her age-old wisdom urges us once again to fix our eyes on eternal verities, to scorn
passing fancies and the temptations of this world, to recognize in
this valley of tears that we have no lasting habitation, that our hearts
have been made for God and will be restless until they rest in Him."
It recalls what a reviewer once said of Msgr. Ronald Knox, English
convert, satirist, master of style: "one can look in vain in his *Sermons*
for such unctuous phrases as 'Holy Mother the Church,' which
some preachers use as carelessly and frequently as sailors use ob-
scenities to conceal their inability for sustained communication."[19]
The same Knox was once twitted by a bishop for reading his sermons from a prepared text—twitted a bit too long. At last Knox
said: "Ah yes, Your Grace, I recognize the validity of your observations. I sensed it one day when I was about to mount the pulpit
with my manuscript in my hand and I heard a gentleman in the first
pew whisper to his wife, 'My God, another bloody pastoral!' "

The homily is an instrument; God uses it to speak to the soul.
God speaks. The external word is indeed mine; but if God is to
speak, my word has to open the way, not close off all avenues save
mine. Not, therefore, "When you go back to your kitchen, this is
what you must do." Rather, so artistic a presentation of a message

that different people hear from God what they need to hear. Like a great piece of music—Bach's church cantatas, full of symbolism, allusion, and word painting in the context of the Lutheran service—the homily will have different meanings for different listeners, will touch them not where I live but where they live, where God wants them to live.

Here imagination is indispensable. The image is more open-ended than the concept; the image evokes imagining. This is not indifferentism: From my homily you should not emerge with a Unitarian God, an Arian Christ, abortion on demand. No; I presume, or insinuate, or proclaim the tradition. Remember Wilder: "Inebriation is no substitute for paideia." And still I am not so much exposing as evoking, not so much imposing on the ignorant a revealed truth with specific applications as drawing the already faithful into the mystery of Christ in such a way that *they* can apply it, can say yes to a living God speaking now. The priest, Urban Holmes insists, is "one who incites people to imagine."[20]

III

My third question: If imagination is so awfully important, what ought we homilists to do about it? When I first approached this point, I fumbled long and wearily with specifics; I wanted, you see, to give you concrete applications! Read storytelling theologian John Shea; tune in on the apocalyptic vision of the TV preachers; immerse yourself in Lewis and Tolkien; shift your language from the abstract to the concrete; remember that the verb carries the action; listen to the flowers.

I do not retract all that; those suggestions could be of help. But suddenly I realized that we have a more basic need. What Catholic homilists require is a conversion; we need fresh insight into our priesthood. I can best illustrate this from my own life. Here I wed three elements: the "I," the revelation, the people.

First, I who communicate. For the first half of my priestly life, I was the most objective of human beings. Objectivity had been rooted in me—by scholastic philosophy, by a theology that lived off magisterial affirmations, by spiritual masters who stressed reason and will, suspected emotion and experience. The subjective had illegitimate parents: Protestantism and Modernism. At the altar, then, and behind the confessional screen, in teaching and preaching, in lecturing and counseling, the "I" was submerged, that Christ alone might appear. I rarely said "I," that only the truth might transpire. Until one day in the early 60s, when I had given a remarkably lucid response to a young lady's religious question. She looked at me a moment, then said: "And what do *you* think?" It was a harrowing moment. I am not an ecclesiastical computer, spewing forth the data fed me. I too am a symbol, a sign that says more than my words can express. In the pulpit *I* may well be the most powerful image of all.

Second, the revelation we communicate. How was it initially communicated? In my more callow days we had no problem: Divine revelation consists of truths set forth in the Bible and in authoritative Church pronouncements. God has embodied His revelation in propositional language so that it can claim our unswerving assent. Now I do not deny that revelation can be mediated through true propositions. I simply point out that a fresh vision permeates our century, permeates me: Revelation is symbolic disclosure.[21] Revelation is always mediated through an experience in the world—specifically, through symbol. I have no room to argue this here; let me illustrate it by one example, a key theme in the New Testament: the kingdom of God.

> As Norman Perrin points out, the "kingdom of God" in the preaching of Jesus is not a clear concept or idea with a single, univocal significance. Rather, it is a symbol that "can represent or evoke a whole range or series of conceptions or ideas" and thus bring the hearer into the very reality borne by the preaching of Jesus. Perrin profusely illustrates the symbolic nature of this language as found in the proverbial sayings of Jesus, in the Lord's Prayer, and especially in the Gospel parables. The constant factor in these diverse materials, he maintains, is the symbol of the kingdom of God, which had for Jewish audiences the power to evoke the faith-experience of God's dramatic action on behalf of His people and to elicit an appropriate response. To seek to pin down some one definite meaning of the term "kingdom of God," according to Perrin, would be to overlook the polysemic character of symbolic communication.[22]

This does not mean that revelation cannot be translated into objective doctrinal statements. It means that our biblical symbols, from the theophanies of Sinai through the cross of Christ to the descent of the Spirit, are too rich to be imprisoned in any single conception. Moreover, the knowledge that symbols give is not cold, abstract information; it is "participatory knowledge." A symbol is an environment I inhabit, live in, the way I live in my body; I recognize myself within the universe of meaning and value it opens up to me.[23] And because revelation is this sort of truth, it can transform us, initiate us into a saving relationship with God; it can radically influence our commitments and our behavior; and it can give us insight into mysteries reason cannot fathom.

Third, the people with whom we communicate. Early on, I took for granted that they came to the liturgy to learn, that the sheep needed to be led. The assumption is clear in an address I gave two decades ago to the Catholic Homiletic Society on preaching dogma.[24] I do not disown the address, but it was one-sided: How do I preach the truth attractively? I hardly mentioned the people "out there." Their responsibility, as far as I can reconstruct it, was to give ear to my clear message and be seduced by its beauty. Late in life I have begun to grasp why some pulpits confront the preacher graphically with the request of the Greeks to Philip: "Sir, we would like to see Jesus" (Jn 12:21). How simple a request . . . and how stunning! Here is our burden and our joy: to help believing Christians to see Jesus—not with our eyes but with their own.

Given fresh insight, a kind of conversion, on these three levels—a homilist more open and free, a revelation charged with symbols, a people wanting to see Jesus—you will inevitably preach imaginatively, prepare imaginatively. First, you will find yourself inescapably part and parcel of your homily. What you preach will strike sparks because *you* are aflame with it. The word you speak will say so much more than the dictionary definition because that word has taken flesh in you. You have been captured by a dream, enraptured by a vision; you have your own "voices"; the world of the senses excites you; like Teresa of Avila, you can be ravished by a rose. You will feel ceaselessly reborn, thank God each dawn with e. e. cummings "for most this amazing day . . . for everything which is natural which is infinite which is yes."[25]

Second, God's word will never again seem "stale, flat, and unprofitable." For you will have discovered, with the Benedictine liturgiologist Nathan Mitchell, that "every symbol deals with a new discovery and every symbol is an open-ended action, not a closed-off object. By engaging in symbols, by inhabiting their environment, [you will] discover new horizons for life, new values and motivation."[26] The biblical symbols will overwhelm you with their many-splendored possibilities, their refusal to be imprisoned in a formula, their openness to fresh imaginings. You may even start saying, not "The kingdom of heaven is . . . ," but "The kingdom of heaven is like. . . ."

Third, once you realize that your people want not catechesis or theology but only to see Jesus, you are forced to find ways to satisfy their thirst. Rome and Rahner are only a foundation. For all their objective importance, neither John Paul's encyclical *Redemptor hominis* nor the "supernatural existential" are calculated to turn the faithful on. And so, like it or not, you will learn to dream dreams and see visions, retell the parables of Jesus in a modern idiom. You will create your own world of Christian imaging, learn not only to pray but to play, look for the holes in the world, listen to the space between sounds.

The alternative is terrifying. Without imagination we homilists are no more than pied pipers, and just as dangerous as the original. Like the Piper of Hamelin, we dress in a suit of many colors, pipe our strange melody, and many of the children follow us. But where do they end up? Where the children of Hamelin ended up. Look again at Saint-Exupéry's Drawing Number One:

Doesn't it frighten you? You may answer: "Frighten? Why should anyone be frightened by a hat?" But my drawing is not the picture of a hat. It is a cave, a cave packed with children, a closed-up cave, a cave with no air, no exit, no freedom. Doesn't *that* frighten you?[27]

3
SHUDDER, YOU COMPLACENT ONES
Ancient Prophet and Modern Preacher

The subtitle of this chapter implies two things. First, there is such a person as an ancient prophet. Second, there is a resemblance between the ancient prophet and the modern preacher. In this context let me do three things. First, I shall search out what qualities, what features, what approaches characterized certain ancient prophets—I mean, the Hebrew prophets. Second, I shall suggest that certain of those qualities, features, approaches ought to mark the modern prophet—in our case, today's preacher and homilist. Third, I shall grapple with some facets of biblical prophecy, some traits of the Hebrew prophets, that seem to clash with our understanding of a homilist's task.

I

First then, the ancient prophets. What were the biblical prophets like? What manner of men were they? How did they act? How did they address the people?[1]

To begin with, the Hebrew prophet is extraordinarily sensitive to evil, to injustice—so much so that at times he seems to pay excessive attention to trivialities, to what *we* might deplore but have learned to live with. "To us a single act of injustice—cheating in business, exploitation of the poor—is slight; to the prophets, a disaster. To us injustice is injurious to the welfare of the people; to the prophets it is a deathblow to existence: to us, an episode; to them, a catastrophe, a threat to the world. . . . To the prophets even a minor injustice assumes cosmic proportions."[2]

Second, and in consequence, this "man who feels fiercely,"[3] who is stunned by human greed, whose prophecy is the voice God has lent to the silent agony of the plundered poor, this man in whose voice God rages, this man rarely sings, he castigates; his images do not shine, they burn; his words do not aim to edify, they are meant to shock. Listen to Isaiah (32:11):

> Tremble, you women who are at ease,
>   shudder, you complacent ones;
> strip, and make yourselves bare,
>   and gird sackcloth upon your loins.

To the ancient society that prized three possessions above all else—wisdom, power, and wealth—Jeremiah thundered: "Thus says the Lord: 'Let not the wise man glory in his wisdom, let not the mighty man glory in his might, let not the rich man glory in his riches; but let him who glories glory in this, that he understands and knows me, that I am the Lord who practice steadfast love, justice, and righteousness in the earth; for in these things I delight, says the Lord' " (Jer 9:23-24).

Third, the Hebrew prophets make little concession to human weakness, no effort to mitigate the sinner's guilt. Here are no ethicists carefully calculating culpability, touched by ignorance and infirmity, excusing this omission or palliating that rape, making fine distinctions. No. With their sweeping allegations, their ceaseless generalizations, their unbelievable exaggerations, the prophets were unfair to Israel.[4] Listen to Hosea: "There is no faithfulness or kindness, and no knowledge of God in the land; there is swearing, lying, killing, stealing, and committing adultery; they break all bounds and murder follows murder" (4:1–2). Measure the prophets by statistics and they fail every test. They were concerned not with sheer facts but with the meaning of facts, of human acts. This, the genuine image of human existence, sheer statistics could never express. And so Heschel does not find exaggeration when the rabbis assert: "Whoever destroys a single soul should be considered the same as one who has destroyed a whole world. And whoever saves one single soul is to be considered the same as one who has saved a whole world."[5] The prophet's truth is not our truth; it is a transcendent truth. He sees life, human action, from God's high vantage, from the conviction of Job that before a God who finds angels imperfect no mortal can be righteous or pure (cf. Job 4:17–19; 15:14–16).

What lies behind this? An agonizing realization that this is not just another people. Here is a land, a people, that was chosen by God to transform the world. And this people, the beloved of the Lord, "kept sacrificing to the Baals, and burning incense to idols" (Hos 11:2). In Jerusalem "God's kingship and man's hope were at stake."[6] And so, to the prophets, if few are guilty, all are responsible.

Fourth, the Hebrew prophet is an iconoclast. He challenges sacred institutions, sacred beliefs, sacred persons. To those who keep mouthing "This is the temple of the Lord, the temple of the Lord, the temple of the Lord" Jeremiah responds: "Do not trust in these deceptive words" (Jer 7:4). The temple will not save them, will not assure God's protection. For this, they must amend their ways, execute justice (v. 5). Otherwise the house of God becomes a den of robbers (v. 11). And this house of God, desecrated by idolatry, will be destroyed (v. 14). And as long as faithfulness is far from the people, as long as they reject God's law,

> To what purpose does frankincense come to me from Sheba,
> or sweet cane from a distant land?
> Your burnt offerings are not acceptable,
> nor your sacrifices pleasing to me.
>
> (Jer 6:20)

And to the kings who were anointed to shepherd Israel Ezekiel cries out: "The weak you have not strengthened, the sick you have not healed, the crippled you have not bound up, the strayed you have not brought back, the lost you have not sought, and with force and harshness you have ruled them. So they were scattered, because there was no shepherd; and they became food for all the wild beasts" (Ezek 34:4–5). Even the enemy of Israel—whether Assyria (cf. Isa 10:5–6) or Nebuchadnezzar (cf. Jer 25:9)—may be God's instrument in history. In the name of God the prophet dares to castigate what is most sacred to Israel, what is awesome and holy.

Fifth, the Hebrew prophet is a man embarrassed, lonely, frustrated. He is embarrassed because, while others are predicting peace and prosperity, he threatens disaster and destruction. If the hearts of the people do not change, they will die. He is lonely because he alienates simply everyone: not only the wicked but the pious, not only cynics but believers, not only princes but priests, not only false prophets but judges. Little wonder that Jeremiah laments (Jer 20:14, 17–18):

> Cursed be the day
>   on which I was born!
> The day when my mother bore me,
>   let it not be blessed!. . . .
> because He did not kill me in the womb;
>   so my mother would have been my grave. . . .
> Why did I come forth from the womb
>   to see toil and sorrow,
>   and spend my days in shame?

There is indeed some delight: "thy words became to me a joy and the delight of my heart" (Jer 15:16). And still the prophet is frustrated. Jeremiah can declare to the people: "For twenty-three years . . . I have spoken persistently to you, but you have not listened" (Jer 25:3). What is surprising is not that the people turned a deaf ear to the prophets; what is surprising is that the people tolerated them. For "To the patriots, they seemed pernicious; to the pious multitude, blasphemous; to the men in authority, seditious."[7]

Sixth, the Hebrew prophet is not merely a messenger of God. He is that indeed; for he repeats over and over again "Thus says the Lord." In a genuine sense, he is God's mouthpiece. But he claims to be more than a messenger. He stands in the presence of God, stands "in the council of the Lord" (Jer 23:18), "is a participant, as it were, in the council of God, not a bearer of dispatches whose function is limited to being sent on errands. He is a counselor as well as a messenger."[8] He is not a hireling; he is God's associate. At times he challenges the Lord's intention:

> O Lord God, forgive, I beseech thee!
>   How can Jacob stand?
>   He is so small!
>
>   (Amos 7:2)

And "the Lord repented . . . : 'It shall not be . . . ' " (v. 3). The prophet's response to God is not always "Thy will be done"; at times he prays "Thy will be changed." "In the presence of God he takes the part of the people. In the presence of the people he takes the part of God."[9]

The point is, the prophet is a person transformed. Remember what Samuel said to Saul when he anointed him prince over Israel: "Then the spirit of the Lord will come mightily upon you, and you shall prophesy with them [a band of prophets coming down from the high place] and be turned into another man" (1 Sam 10:6; cf. v.

5). As a messenger, he delivers the word; as a witness, he bears testimony that the word is divine. He reveals God, makes an invisible God audible. Not by proving or arguing. His words are charged with divine power.

Seventh, the prophet's words are charged with divine power because he has experienced God's own pathos.[10] He is not particularly interested in God's essence; his God is not the Wholly Other. He has experienced the God of the covenant, a God involved in history, a God who has a stake in the human situation, is intimately affected by events. He has experienced God "as living care."[11] He has seen sin not only as human failure but as divine frustration; man's predicament is God's predicament. And so the prophet has experienced not only a loving and compassionate God, but a God who is disappointed, indignant, angry.

> Never in history has man been taken as seriously as in prophetic thinking. Man is not only an image of God; he is a perpetual concern of God. The idea of pathos adds a new dimension to human existence. Whatever man does affects not only his own life, but also the life of God insofar as it is directed to man. The import of man raises him beyond the level of mere creature. He is a consort, a partner, a factor in the life of God.[12]

Little wonder that Heschel sees as the special characteristic of the prophet "not foreknowledge of the future, but insight into the present pathos of God."[13] His fundamental experience is "a fellowship with the feelings of God, *a sympathy with the divine pathos*. . . . "[14] He not only hears God's voice; he feels God's heart. How, then, can he ever speak dispassionately, serene and unruffled? How can his words be ever other than aflame, afire with a God whose living is caring?

II

A man extraordinarily sensitive to evil and injustice, who feels fiercely and shocks rudely, who concedes little to human weakness and exaggerates mightily, who challenges sacred institutions and beliefs and persons, who is embarrassed and lonely and frustrated, who is God's counselor as well as His messenger, whose words are charged with divine power because he has experienced God's pathos—these seven facets of prophetic preaching raise an agonizing issue. Is the Hebrew prophet a model for the modern prophet, for today's preacher and homilist?

Let me respond speedily that in several ways the prophets from Isaiah to Malachi can be, must be, a pattern for our own prophetic speech. First, many of us have lost, or have never had, the neuralgic sensitivity to evil and injustice that should mark every prophet. Some surely share that sensitivity; but it is usually those who have experienced firsthand the sorry existence of the poor and the imprisoned, the hungry and the downtrodden. More of us simply deplore injustice; we are against sin; we take up collections for the homeless Lebanese.

In this connection, I remember vividly a remarkable sermon I heard several years ago at the annual Ohio Pastors Convocation. A black pastor from Texas preached to us on the Good Samaritan. Commenting on the priest and Levite who passed by the half-dead victim of robbers, he noted that these two gentlemen were perfectly at home in Jerusalem. They could handle anything that had to do with the temple: circumcision and the Torah, the altar of incense and the table for the showbread, the animals to be sacrificed and the ark of the covenant. What they could not handle was "the évent on the Jericho road." The phrase still haunts me: "the évent on the Jericho road." How often have I "passed by on the other side" (Lk 10:31, 32)? And how has it affected my prophetic word, my preaching?

Moreover, there is so much evil and injustice over the globe that we grow used to it. We were shocked when TV first brought war into our living rooms; now we can wolf our pizzas and slurp our Schlitz to the roar of rockets and the flow of blood. It's commonplace; we see too much of it; it's part of the human tragedy. It no longer grabs our guts—no more than broken bodies in the Orange Bowl.

When that happens, our preaching will not reflect a second significant facet of Hebrew prophecy: We will not "feel fiercely." And we must. When I began to preach four decades ago, the Catholic stress was on the clear and distinct idea. Our seminary education, in philosophy and theology, emphasized objectivity. We were dispassionate searchers for truth, cool critics of error and heresy—beetle-browed, lynx-eyed, hard-nosed, square-jawed. Imagination was for poets. We did not show our emotions. Emotions were for women, and women could not be ordained. For, to credit a 1959 doctoral dissertation at the Catholic University of America,

Man tends to be more realistic, woman, idealistic. . . . The logical mind of the man is far more dependable in time of crisis than would be the female intuition. Emotional stability must be found in a priest, and in this the man excels the woman. To look at a problem objectively is most necessary to the priest. Man is objective, woman, subjective. A man is slower in passing judgment; he considers a problem fully before attempting a solution, a quality which is absolutely necessary for the priest.[15]

I am not arguing here for the ordination of women. I am insisting that for effective preaching the analytic mind is not enough by half. I do not mean that we should rant and rave in the pulpit. I do mean that our people should sense from our words and our faces, from our gestures and our whole posture, that we love this sinning, struggling community with a crucifying passion; that we agonize over our own sinfulness, our failure to be holier than we are; that we weep with the refugees whose tears water the ways of Lebanon; that we too are awfully vulnerable, prey to the loneliness that ravages the human heart; that we too must at times cry out "I believe, Lord, help my unbelief"; that the heavy-burdened can look to us not so much for answers as for empathy; that our celibacy has not made us crotchety old bachelors but opens us warmly to all who need the touch of our hand; in a word, that we too share the dread-full human condition. And, not least, they should sense that we joy in our priesting, would not exchange it, literally, for "the world."

To come through to our people in that way, we have to "feel fiercely." It cannot be forced or faked; it cannot be imported from without. It comes from prayer and sweat, from a willingness to let go of an imprisoning self, from a sharing in "the joys and the hopes, the griefs and the anxieties of the people of this age, especially those who are poor or in any way afflicted."[16]

Third, I submit that the Christian preacher, like the Hebrew prophet, must prove a ceaseless challenge to the community. It may sound strange to you, exaggerated, unseemly, that I speak of us preachers as iconoclasts. I mean that our task, in part, is to shatter false images, to destroy idols. That these parade in the cloak of the sacred—institutions, beliefs, persons—only makes our task more sensitive, more delicate; it does not remove our responsibility.

I am not suggesting that the pulpit is for Savonarola, that we preach to castigate, to condemn, to flay the people before us. But must we not insist to them, with Jeremiah, that the temple of stone in which they worship does not save; that though the Church is a community of salvation, only Jesus saves; that the more important temple is this flesh of ours which is the living temple of the Spirit? Must we not constantly preach that the faith which is a firm acceptance of revealed propositions is sterile without the faith which is a total self-giving to the revealing God? Should it not leap forth from what we say and how we say it that the shepherds, whether pope or pastor, are servants; that we see ourselves in our shepherding as all too "unprofitable servants"; that it is not only the laity but ourselves who are ceaselessly summoned to conversion; that our homilies are directed in the first instance at our own lives?

But the sacred institutions that call for challenge are not only those that have been solemnly blessed in a religious rite. They include those attitudes, life styles, and ways of acting that mark our culture as less than Christian. Some years ago, at the annual convention of the Catholic Theological Society of America, a prominent University of California sociologist, Robert Bellah, reported a frightening phenomenon re-emerging in North American society, taking it over: the rugged individualist of the late nineteenth century, responsible to no one except one's self. More than that, Bellah has concluded that the one institution which ought to be a counterforce to rugged individualism, because it claims to be a social body whose members are dependent one on another for life in the Spirit, is largely ineffectual; for the Catholic Church has not so much influenced American society as been influenced by it. We too are becoming rugged individualists; for too many of us commitments are contracts to be broken when the going gets rough or a brighter offer beckons. Is it impertinent for the modern prophet to apprise his people of this peril, this Baal, in their midst, even to challenge them on their fidelity to the Pauline doctrine of a single body in which no one can say to another "I have no need of you" (1 Cor 12:21), their commitment to Vatican II's vision of an interpersonal, interpenetrating community united to the Father and to one another through Christ in the Spirit?

Fourth, it is the rare preacher who is rarely lonely and frustrated. I doubt that we echo Jeremiah's plaint "Cursed be the day on which I was born!" But the loneliness that is built into our priesthood presses upon our preaching. For all the TLC in our lives, for all the affectionate people who cross our paths, we walk very much alone. Few of us share their lives, save at a respectful distance. And we talk alone. Not Trappist solitude; my homily has to be born of people and their needs. I mean rather that preaching is prayer, a homily is liturgical prayer, a paean of praise for God's wonderful works among His people, an inspired word that helps others to see Jesus with their own eyes, hear him with their own ears.

But this demands, above all, that I listen. The experience of the prophet must be my own experience. Like him, I have to hear what God says to me: in the word I read on the sacred page, in the word that is the Church's reflection on God's revelation down the ages, in the word God speaks to the depths of my heart, in the voices of the world around me. But to hear is not enough. I must struggle with that word, at times wrestle with God. For with me too the word can fall "on rocky ground" with "no depth of soil," can fall "upon thorns" that grow up and choke it (Mt 13:5, 7). I must make that word my own, lay hold of it not only with cold intellect but with my rebellious emotions. Most taxing task of all, I must live the word I preach. What I hear should shape and reshape who I am and what I do.

That, my friends, is a lonely toil. Not indeed without joy, not without satisfaction, not without moments of ecstasy. But if you have not experienced how lonely, almost unbearably lonely, the modern prophet's task can be, then either you are uncommonly graced by God or . . . you're not really working at it!

Hand in hand with loneliness runs the prophet's frustration. It takes different forms. Some preachers may resonate to Jeremiah's "For twenty-three years . . . I have spoken persistently to you, but you have not listened." More frequently, I suggest, we are discouraged by the gulf that yawns between the high holiness we preach and the low level of so much of "Christian" existence (including our own); and all too rarely do we actually see the increase God alone can give to the seed we sow. "Nice sermon, Father" or "Great message, Reverend" is well meant but is hardly revelatory of the human heart. I am reminded of a cartoon in the *New Yorker*. A pompous gentleman and his equally pompous wife are descending the steps of an imposing Gothic church, and she is saying to him: "I thought the rector gave a particularly fine sermon this morning. You know, it's so easy to offend people like us."

As for myself, my frustration often reflects the feeling St. Augustine confessed in that remarkably perceptive work of educational psychology sometimes translated *The First Catechetical Instruction*:

For my part, I am nearly always dissatisfied with my discourse. For I am desirous of something better, which I often inwardly enjoy before I begin to unfold my thought in spoken words; but when I find that my powers of expression come short of my knowledge of the subject, I am sorely disappointed that my tongue has not been able to answer the demands of my mind. For I desire my hearer to understand all that I understand; and I feel that I am not speaking in such a manner as to effect that.[17]

For the consolation of catechists and preachers who feel that way, Augustine has a three-pronged answer. (1) It is never quite as bad as you think. (2) Endure for love's sweet sake. "For then only is a work truly good, when the purpose of the doer is winged with love, and as if returning to its own place, rests again in love."[18] (3) As best we can, let God speak through us.

Fifth, our words, like the words of the prophets, should be charged with divine power, not primarily because we have been ordained to preach, but because we have experienced God. Not a God who dwells only in light inaccessible, outside time and space. No, a God who is intimately involved in history—in our history. A God who shows Himself, not only in a burning bush millennia ago, but in today's passionate cry for freedom and today's quest for "roots." A God whose pulsing image is every one of us. A God who *became* one of us.

Here our scholasticism can get in the way. It is difficult to experience "as living care" a God whom we conceive as Immovable Mover, a kind of Christian Buddha staring unblinkingly into space. Now this is not the place to deny divine immutability. But this I do say. We shall be effective preachers, preachers in the prophetic mold, to the extent that we experience and preach a living God, a loving God. Loving not only because He gave us His only Son 20 centuries in the past, but because right now what happens to me somehow happens to Him. Whatever intellectual contortions I must suffer to reconcile this with a God who is a single, eternal Pure Act, I still must experience and preach a God who "not only rules the world in the majesty of His might and wisdom, but reacts intimately to the events of history . . . does not stand outside the range of human suffering and sorrow [but] . . . is personally involved in, even stirred by, the conduct and fate of man."[19]

III

So then, five of the seven facets of prophetic utterance can and should echo in our own preaching. We too should be keenly sensitive to evil and injustice; we too should feel fiercely; we too should challenge the idols in our community and our culture; we too can expect to find loneliness our lot, frustration inescapable; we too have to experience God "as living care." In this third point, let me grapple with the two remaining traits of the Hebrew prophets, traits that seem to clash with our understanding of a homilist's task.

First, the Hebrew prophets conceded little to human weakness and exaggerated mightily. Is there place for this in the pulpit? You might argue that Jesus himself, a fair enough model for preachers, flayed the scribes and Pharisees pitilessly: "Woe to you, scribes and Pharisees, hypocrites!" (Mt 23:13). Jesus himself used hyperbole to get a point across: "If anyone comes to me and does not hate his own father and mother and wife and children, yes, and even his own life, he cannot be my disciple" (Lk 14:26). Even so, I am convinced that in our time and culture such rhetoric would be not only ineffective but counterproductive.

The people who sit so patiently before us are indeed a motley lot—Christians of varying hues, different stripes. By the law of averages, some live an intense religious life, most fulfil the basic commandments, a few may be candidates for the Mafia. But they listen to us because they believe; otherwise they would leave after our opening paragraph and make for the nearest bar. We are addressing believers, the faith-full. They are here because they want to worship God, to live a Christlike existence. Unless I have a clear mandate such as inspired Jeremiah and Jesus, I shall refuse to flail them for weakness and hypocrisy. What they need is to be brought into contact with Christ, who alone can make them strong, heal their hypocrisies. They are pleading with us as the Greeks pleaded with Philip: "Sir, we would like to see Jesus" (Jn 12:21).

How can I help them to see Jesus? I have developed this already.[20] Very briefly, it calls for imagination; and the homiletic imagination makes three demands. (1) It calls for a preacher who is aflame with the message he carries, who has himself been captured by the Christian story, enraptured by the Catholic vision. (2) It calls for an imaginative presentation of God's word that reveals the many-splendored possibilities of the biblical symbols, their open-endedness, their refusal to be imprisoned in a single formula, their ability to initiate us into a saving relationship with God. (3) It calls for a loving awareness of people—people thirsting to see meaning in their lives, Christ in their lives, and hoping against hope that we can speak to their needs.

Do this and you need rarely reprove; for we reprove best when we share vision, raise sights, open horizons. Nor do I see much point today in prophetic exaggeration—except perhaps to suggest that much which to us seems an exaggeration is simply raw reality from the side of God. Not too long ago we pretty much agreed that not for all the world might one directly, intentionally destroy an innocent life. Today we blithely destroy 50 million little innocents a year, and we are talking seriously of annihilating entire cities if push comes to nuclear shove. We just might need the judgment of our friends the rabbis: "Whoever destroys a single soul should be considered the same as one who has destroyed a whole world."

A second problem for our wrestling: Hebrew prophets were God's messengers. Now, in some genuine sense, the preacher of today is a messenger of God. If I am preaching God's word, I may legitimately say with Isaiah "Thus says the Lord." I am God's mouthpiece; I speak for Him and at times I repeat His very words. But this raises two neuralgic questions—one academic, the other quite practical.

The academic question need not delay us long. It is a question that was raised long before modern biblical criticism came into being. Very much an issue in ancient rabbinic discussion was the question, how much was actually spoken by God and how much was phrased by Moses. In *Exodus Rabbah* 28.3 on Exodus 19:8 ("And all the people answered together and said, 'All that the Lord has spoken we will do.' And Moses reported the words of the people to the Lord."), God is portrayed as thinking, "When I say to them, 'I am the Lord your God,' they will ask, 'Who is speaking? God or Moses?' " My point here is, only human beings use words. Not only my word, therefore, but the biblical word as well is a human word, time-conditioned, subject to our human limitations. I may indeed say "Thus says the Lord," but I must recognize that when I say this I am giving expression to what God says to me with no words—or at best in the human words of Scripture. The problem need not induce homiletic indigestion, but since it is not impertinent to your preaching, I recommend that you read Raymond Brown's penetrating article " 'And the Lord Said'? Biblical Reflections on Scripture As the Word of God."[21]

A more practical problem is what I do with God's word. Here it is not a simple matter to be God's messenger, to carry His mind and will to others. It is not just a question of avoiding two extremes: the fundamentalism of TV preachers and the facile "This is the way I feel about it." I can avoid both extremes and still have to struggle with God's word. It was easier for Ezekiel and Zechariah. They seemed to know exactly what God wanted them to say: "The word of the Lord came to me" (cf. Ezek 1:3; Zech 1:1). Once I get beyond the sheer text of the Old Testament and the New, the word of the Lord comes to me slowly, at times indistinctly; I am not sure what He wants me to say; often I agonize whether it is His word I am uttering or only mine. I must wrestle with Scripture and its multifarious exegetes, come to grips with the Church's tradition and its parti-colored interpreters, uncover the needs of a complex people in a changing world, help make the mystery of Christ present and active in their concrete existence. Not as dangerous to my health as the commission of the prophets, but far more complicated. The word of the Lord came to *them*; you and I must come to the Lord—best on our knees.[22]

It has been an exciting experience these several months, "kibbutzing" with the Hebrew prophets. As I close this glowing report, two thoughts pertinent for our own preaching refuse to ebb away: the prophets' incredible intimacy with their Lord and their passionate concern for a chosen people. Both are crucial to our kerygmatic commission. To listen to the word, to hear it, we must love the Lord who speaks it—love Him with all our mind and heart, all our strength and spirit. And to speak that word ourselves, to inflame the hearts of the faithful, we must love this paradoxical people, this struggling, sinning, saintly people of God's special selecting—love them with a crucifying passion. Only if we love dare we address to them the word that sears as it heals. Only if we love dare we proclaim "Hear, O new Israel! The word of the Lord has come unto me."

4
THE LORD OPENED THE MOUTH OF
THE ASS
The View from the Pew

This chapter may strike preachers as a digression, since I am moving for the moment from the pulpit to the pew. If it is indeed a digression, it is not an impertinent one; for I am simply asking preachers to take a closer look at their audience before they enflesh God's word for today, before they immerse people imaginatively in the paschal mystery, before they dare to clone the ancient prophets. The homily is not a Platonic "idea" suspended in midair. It presupposes (1) a vision of parish, (2) an awareness of a specific congregation within the parish, and (3) only then a preacher addressing himself to that congregation.

I

First, a vision of parish. The word "vision" is dreadfully vague. Certain dictionary definitions do not concern us here. We are not talking about "an imaginary, supernatural, or prophetic sight beheld in sleep or ecstasy." We are not interested in the mystics' "direct awareness of the supernatural." I mean, quite simply, "a way of seeing" something. If, for example, you think of Jesuits as a crafty, insidious, well-disciplined, tightly-knit, 007 type of male creaturehood creeping stealthily into the power structures of church, state, and society, you have a "vision" of the Jesuits. The vision may not be totally accurate, but you have in fact a way of looking at that curious amalgam of men whom a retired soldier organized almost four and a half centuries ago. Green Berets of the Spirit?

Here we are talking about a vision of parish: How should we see, how should we envision, a parish? Technically, the vision is simple enough. A parish is a segment of a diocese under the direction of a priest known as the pastor or parish priest, who is charged with the care of the people in that area who have been officially entrusted to him. This is clear, canonical; and it will help you if you are taking a parish census or an envelope collection. But we are concerned with far more than a definition. What is a parish, a congregation, all about? Why does it exist? What is supposed to happen there?

You can speak of it, as Matthew Fox does so eloquently, as a journey, "becoming a people." You can speak of it as a ceaseless process of conversion. You can speak of it as a continuing development in faith. These are different aspects of a single reality, ways of focusing on a reality too rich and complex to be imprisoned in a definition. I suggest that it is all of these. Putting them together in a bit of a synthesis, I conclude: A [Catholic] parish is a group of Catholic Christians who are in process of becoming a people by deepening and expanding their faith through a ceaseless process of conversion.

The group is in process of becoming a people, a community. They are, therefore, at once a community and not a community. They are indeed a community; for all acknowledge Christ as Lord and Savior, all profess the same basic beliefs, are sanctified by the same sacramental system, are bound by the same code of laws—and all this in obedience to the bishop of Rome and the bishop at home. And still they are not the community they should be. A parish is fashioned initially out of individuals who love God but normally do not particularly love one another. They do not hate one another; they simply do not know one another. And many parishes stay that way. Isolated individuals, or at best isolated family units, congregate in the one place once a week, do their solitary thing, and go back home pretty much as they were when they came. Nourished indeed individually, but to all appearances no more a community than before.[1]

Tragic, for a parish is the Church in miniature; it is the single Body of Christ localized. And so it must be fashioned into a oneness where, as St. Paul puts it, "The eye cannot say to the hand, 'I have no need of you,' nor again the head to the feet, 'I have no need of you'" (1 Cor 12:21), where "If one member suffers, all suffer together; if one member is honored, all rejoice together" (v. 26). The problem is, we rarely have the social structure for this in a city parish, a Saturday-evening and Sunday-morning affair where the hearts that go up to heaven hardly go out across the pews.

Still, this is part of the parish pilgrimage. The parishioners of St. Martin-on-the-Rocks are not journeying to a better life with blinders. They are part and parcel of a process: they have to become a people, a little church, where grace is not a narrow pipeline from heaven to each parishioner but flows through all to each, where every man, woman, and child strives consciously to be a channel of grace for the whole, where, as Karl Rahner put it, all of us are mediators for one another.

How do they become a people? By deepening and expanding their faith. Catholic faith, you see, is not primarily a matter of propositions: "I believe in one God the Father almighty; I believe in His Son, who became man, died for our sins, and rose from the dead; I believe in the Holy Spirit, the Lord, the Giver of life; I believe in the Catholic Church, the forgiveness of sins, the resurrection of the body, and life everlasting." It includes all that, of course; but faith is more than the acceptance of propositions. Remember the New Testament Letter of James: "You believe that God is one; you do well. Even the demons believe—and shudder" (Jas 2:19).

Catholic faith surrenders to God and His Christ not only the mind: "I accept as true whatever you say." No, I surrender my whole self. And I do so within a community that is the Body of Christ. In saying a total yes to the risen Christ, I am saying yes to the total Christ, head and members, vine and branches. True faith, therefore, is a loving faith. And the love, to be faith-full, must go out to every limb that forms part of the whole Christ. That is how faith builds community: Our love goes not only up but out. It sounds the death knell for the me-and-Jesus spirituality.

How is such faith deepened and expanded? Through a ceaseless process of conversion. I mean a constant turning to Christ . . . through Christ. It is relatively rare, I believe, that a Christian has turned totally from Christ, is alienated from God, is in rebellion against Him. My experience of Christians is very much my experience of myself: turned radically to Christ in mind and will, but dreadfully weak in living the logic of that primal conversion. You cannot call me sinner, because my face is set towards Christ. But you can call me sinful, because so many of the actions that should express who I am, a committed lover of Christ, give the lie to that person. So much of my life is superficial. I mean, so many of my human acts are not fully human, do not commit me as a total person. They

THE LORD OPENED THE MOUTH OF THE ASS

are neither sin in the radical sense nor conversion. They do not en-slave me to Satan, they do not commit me to Christ. The danger in such semi-Christian living was strongly stated in the last book of the Bible: "I know your works: You are neither hot nor cold. Would that you were cold or hot! So, because you are lukewarm, and nei-ther cold nor hot, I will spew you out of my mouth" (Rev 3:15–16).

Christian parish living is a continual movement towards the risen Christ. Not simply as individuals—as a single body that reso-nates to the indwelling Christ it is trying to image, resonates to St. Paul's cry to the Christians of Galatia: "There is neither Jew nor Greek, there is neither slave nor free, there is no male-and-female; for you are all one in Christ Jesus" (Gal 3:28).

II

Which brings me to the second stage in my development: We move from the parish to the congregation, from the people as an amorphous group in "low cost" and condo to the highly visible au-dience resting restlessly on its haunches as I begin to homilize. They are indeed what I have described: a group of Catholic Christians who are in process of becoming a people by deepening and ex-panding their faith through a ceaseless process of conversion. My homily should promote that process. But to do that effectively, I must recognize that, at this specific moment in the history of hom-iletics, I rarely face an audience drooling in anticipation of my mes-sage. Even *God's* word on my lips has trouble making it out of the sanctuary.

What keeps God's word from getting through to a congrega-tion or to an individual believer? Obstacle number 1: You are here because you have to be, because Sunday Mass is a serious obligation, because otherwise there's a chance you may blister in hell. Little or no openness here, either to the preacher or to God. With this cast of mind, you don't expect God to speak to you; you want the homily to be short; you are easily distracted; you simply put up with the whole bloody thing; you'd rather be somewhere else, anywhere else. Little wonder Jesuit William O'Malley's sixth commandment for preachers reads: *"Presume disinterest. . . .* [W]hile you are poring over the readings for next Sunday's homily, presume a cold audi-ence. Presume that they would rather feed their children to croc-odiles than listen to you."[2]

Obstacle number 2: You approach the liturgy with a prejudice.

Prejudice *a*: You don't like the liturgy. The vernacular Mass is for the birds; "To Jesus' Heart All Burning" has been supplanted by "I Wanna Hold Your Hand"; and oh, that kiss of peace! Prejudice *b*: You don't care for sermons. From sheer temperament or Sundays of sickening experience, sermons turn you off. Prejudice *c*: You can't take that priest. He mumbles, rambles, stumbles; or he sports a scraggly beard straight out of the late 60s; or he's a young whippersnapper still wet behind the ears; or he's old enough to know better. Prejudice *d*: You've had it "up to here" with a Church in politics: bishops sounding off on nuclear arms or withholding taxes in protest, Marxist priests toting Russian rifles in Nicaragua, sisters disbursing tax monies for abortions, ceaseless collections for shiftless minorities.

Obstacle number 3: You come here to be alone with your God. You used to be able to, for you came into a house of God hushed in reverence. Now everything is noise, activity, hustle and bustle, "everybody sing!" You can't even kneel—there aren't any kneelers, no Communion rails, no vigil lights. And the statue of our Lady is straight out of *Glamour*.

Obstacle number 4: You're not going to learn anything. After all, you've had eight to 16 years of Catholic education, and there's nothing new sounding from that pulpit; it's all like a TV repeat. Recently I heard a young priest say to several relatives at dinner: "What did you get out of the bishop's letter at Mass this morning?" "Oh," one replied, "I didn't really listen. It was on abortion, and we know all about that."

Imagine what would happen if you went to *Swan Lake* or to the *Return of the Jedi* in some such frame of mind. Someone made you come; you can't stand Tchaikovsky or George Lucas; you really want to be alone with your psyche; or you know everything there is to know about ballet or outer space. You have to use the ticket, but let no one ask you to like it. Oh, you might accidentally be caught and ravished by the performance; but not likely. You'd be distracted, bored; you'd yawn, pick your nose, sneak looks at your Timex, doze off. You would hardly leave the theatre a different person, uplifted, carried out of your small self. You might even be irritated, resentful, angry.

So with the liturgy, so with the homily. If you come with a grudge or a bias, irritated or indifferent, then I, the homilist, am your enemy. I'm part of the conspiracy: canon law, bishop, pastor, celebrant, preacher. Get the homily over with; get to the Consecration. I'm interrupting your Sunday—sleep or golf, TV or crab feast, whatever. If you were one of the old-timers, you'd sneak out the back for a smoke during the sermon. How can God possibly speak to your heart?

So much for the negative. But almost anyone can analyze what is awry in an attitude; the positive poses the greater problem. What should characterize a Christian congregation if it is to profit from a homily, if it is to hear and respond to the word of God from the lips of a man?

Basic to it all is a living faith. By faith I do not mean simply that you "believe all that the holy Catholic Church teaches," or even simply that you have committed yourself totally to our Lord and Savior. I mean a special something that should flow from this belief, from this commitment. I mean, first, that you come to the Eucharistic celebration because you are convinced that you are about to celebrate the most important social act in Christian history: The Christian community is about to worship its God in the primary way the Lord commanded. Here is the center of divine life, of grace, of forgiveness and conversion, of thanksgiving and praise. Here is where God meets His people as nowhere else. Here is where the new covenant is confirmed, where we memorialize, as no place else, the death of the Lord until he comes. Here is what Vatican II called "the outstanding means by which the faithful can express in their lives, and manifest to others, the mystery of Christ and the real nature of the true Church."[3] Nothing you do this day, or any day, outstrips in its potential for grace the act you will place in common with your fellow worshipers on that holy spot. Such should be your frame of mind, your mindset.

Within that facet of your faith, within the conviction that in the Eucharistic action God meets His people not exclusively but in privileged fashion, what worshipful attitude is best calculated to let you hear what the Lord is saying, what your Lord wants from you? I suggest . . . openness. The obstacles I have outlined are all features of a closed mind, a closed heart. What is needed is the boy Samuel's response when the Lord called "Samuel! Samuel!" He answered: "Speak, Lord, for your servant is listening" (1 Sam 3:9–10). Not, as ethicist Paul Ramsey once mused, "Speak, Lord, and your servant will think it over."

The trouble is, such a response is not automatic, is not triggered by some psychological open-sesame. It calls for a faith at once profound and practical. I mean a conviction that, somewhat as God's sacraments work their power in you through the instrumentality of a weak human being, God's word speaks to you through the mouth of even a bungling homilist. I am not contending that everything he says to you, every word he utters however inept or foolish, becomes God's word. I *am* saying that in this fellow's liturgical preaching, God is trying to tell you something.

This is not magic, but neither is the liturgical homily a William Buckley show, where human learning and rhetorical skill, dramatic flair and ready wit, are the highest factors. Here God must be allowed to work His grace. My own homiletic experience humbles me. Some of the most effective, grace-producing remarks I have emitted are those I was not personally smitten by. "It was so wonderful, Father, when you said 'God loves you.' " Not a particularly original observation. But someone was ready for it, needed it, was open to it.

And remember—at least in my own theory of preaching—you are listening not so much to what *I* have to say as to what *God* has to say through me. Oh yes, you hear me (no way of escaping it); but actually the question is, what is God trying to tell you through my feeble language?

Another way of putting it: You dare not listen to a sermon the way you watch TV, ready to tune out as soon as it gets dull, as soon as *The Edge of Night* loses its soap, or Quincy starts raving and ranting for justice' sake, or Kojak's lollypop gets on your nerves.[4] I am not applauding mediocrity, settling for inferiority. I've been as caustic as the laity in my criticisms, am known to many a reader of religious news for one syndicated sentence: "We homilists mount the pulpit or approach the podium with the imagination of a dead fish." I simply insist that you will miss much of God's own whispering to you if you focus sheerly on the humanity or inhumanity of the preacher.

You may remember the story of Balaam in the Book of Numbers (chap. 22). The Moabites were in deadly fear of the Israelites, newly freed from Egypt, who threatened to overrun them. So Balak, king of Moab, sent for Balaam, a priest-diviner from Mesopotamia, and asked him to lay a curse on the Israelites. Balaam refused to do so, but still went along with the princes of Balak, riding on his ass. Three times the ass refused to go on when an angel with drawn sword would have slain Balaam; three times Balaam struck the ass to make him move ahead. The ass finally spoke to him, rebuked him for his anger and violence. As the popular story saw it, God Himself spoke through Balaam's beast: "The Lord opened the mouth of the ass" (v. 28). Now if God can speak through a harassed ass, He can surely speak through the dullest and most plodding of preachers. Not an ideal, just a fact.

III

All of which leads to my pregnant third point: the preacher. How does a homilist address effectively a congregation composed in large measure of men and women who expect little or nothing from a sermon, or confront him with all sorts of prejudices, or just want to be left alone—Catholic Christians who do not look for their faith to be deepened or expanded, do not anticipate any kind of conversion?

If such you are, I approach you much as I would approach a congregation hanging on my lips, panting in feverish expectation. I approach you as a people of faith, a people drawn here by God— if not quite by Augustine's cords of love. Oh, I know that apathy and bias are obstacles to grace: Teresa of Avila burning with yearning for Christ is richer promise for grace than the three-piece suit wrinkling spastically on the pew, anxious for the whole blessed thing to end. But I do not change an apathetic audience, a prejudiced people, by assailing its apathy, by pummeling its prejudice. I convert by being converted.

What do I mean? Negatively, I mean it is not enough that I preach the gospel by divine or ecclesiastical commission, that I have the right to say to you "Thus says the Lord." This by itself will shake no one's apathy, dispel no one's prejudice, save perhaps the scrupulous or the neurotic. Positively, I mean that, far from occupying a position atop the parish, "far from the madding crowd's ignoble strife" (Thomas Gray), I come through to you as one who shares your struggle—the struggle to become a people, a living community. I am part of the people, part of you. In harmony with my description of a parish, this makes at least three demands on me.

First, it should become clear to you from my preaching that I too am a pilgrim, I too am "on the way." Put another way, when preaching to you I am preaching first to myself. In a sense, this reverses, or at least reinterprets, the ageless homiletic commandment "Know your audience." Of course the people in front of me make a difference. I agree wholeheartedly with Augustine as he speaks of his own catechetical instructions: "It . . . makes a great difference . . . whether there are few present or many; whether learned or unlearned, or a mixed audience made up of both classes; whether they are townsfolk or countryfolk, or both together; or a gathering in which all sorts and conditions of men are represented."[5] Without denying this, I am confessing that I preach most effectively when I am acutely aware of the prophet Nathan's accusation to King David: "You are the man" (2 Sam 12:7).

Let me make this uncommonly concrete. Some years ago I gave the homily during the Holy Thursday liturgy at the Franciscan Renewal Center in Scottsdale, Arizona. The title: "I Have Given You an Example." In the latter half of the homily I asked how we become eucharists for the life of the world. Right where we are, I answered, right where we live. As Jesus did. He did not move past Palestine, did not look to see what he could do for Lebanon. He helped people as they crossed his path, seemed even to choose his special friends as he found them. And so for you and me. The distance, for most of us, is not geographical. People can occupy the same space as we do and still be as far away as the Lebanese or Japanese. We create our own distances. And I went on to say:

The other day, right out of the blue, I indulged in a fantastic fantasy: "A Day in the Life of Jesus." It begins with breakfast. While his mother is preparing his bagels and cream cheese, Jesus is reading the Jerusalem *Post*—comics first, then the sports pages. A few grunts in response to Mary's tries at conversation, then he bolts a bagel, grabs another on the flight from table, a hurried peck on the cheek with his mouth full—and off he goes to meet the Twelve outside the Sheraton Sinai.

All day long they run across people; people are his job. But the "kitchen cabinet," Peter, James, and John, have their instructions. "Keep the scribes and Pharisees away; they're as bad as *Post* reporters, always trying to catch me in a contradiction. Watch out for that woman who hemorrhages; she'll get blood all over my new tunic. Remember, I don't like Samaritans; they don't like us, and they're just not our kind of folk. If you accept an invitation to dinner, make sure it's with a respectable host like Simon; tax collectors and adulterers give me a bad name. And, for the Lord's sake, don't promise any more cures on the Sabbath; I've had enough trouble with the local officials. When that centurion asks about his sick kid, tell him in a nice way that I'm tied up; better say "overcommitted." By all means, get an SRO crowd for my next sermon, but don't let them touch our boat; and make sure they go home by sundown, else we'll have to send Judas with all our money to the nearest Deli. By the way, John and James, if your mother comes around once more asking seats for you on the dais in my kingdom, I'm going to tell her flat-out to "buzz off." And Peter: I know I agreed to eat at your house tonight. But your mother-in-law has this high fever; she'll want me to sit by her all evening, soothe her burning brow with my cool hand, give her

one of those endless blessings. We'll never get to the Manischew-
itz."

Fantasy? Yes—about Christ. No more than a modest satire
about many Christians. I thought it was real funny—till I
changed the title to "A Day in the Life of Walter Burghardt."
Then, as we youngsters used to say in a simpler age, it was as
funny as a rubber crutch.[6]

I am not claiming that, to arouse an audience from apathy or
to abate its bias, I have to identify myself expressly as a culprit
among culprits. I do claim that, to shape a pilgrim people, I must
preach precisely as a pilgrim. Not simply in the secret chambers of
my mind, my intention. The pilgrim in me should be palpable to
you: I do not stand above you, I sit beside you.

A second demand. I have said that a parish is a group of Catholic Christians who are in process of becoming a people by deepening and expanding their faith. And I insisted that faith is more
than the acceptance of propositions. To be genuinely faith-full, you
surrender to God and His Christ not only your mind but your whole
self. Living faith, loving faith, is a total yes to the total Christ, head
and members.

The pertinent point here is this: If liturgical preaching is to
contribute to your growth in faith, it is not enough that my *homily*
be a resounding call to self-surrender, an eloquent challenge to an
unreserved yes. *I* must come through to you as a man of faith. Not
indeed without my infidelities; no more than Paul am I "already
perfect" (Phil 3:12). And still, what you must sense in my sermon is
that these are not disembodied words, syllables floating in space,
eternal verities in a Platonic world of "ideas." For all my reliance on
the word of God, ultimately *I* am the word I preach. Herein lies the
power of the word and its weakness. Its power? The Christ who
speaks through me. Its weakness? The human vessel through whom
Christ has to flow.

Hence the risk, the glorious Christian risk, in any live homily.
A cassette is not quite I, not by half. In the assembly you see *me*—
every gesture or lack thereof, every change of expression. You hear
me—not just a voice from the past. In the seeing and the hearing,
you touch me, you scrape beneath my skin. Oh yes, if I'm a consummate actor, Laurence Olivier or Woody Allen, I might deceive you.
I might spout a message that moves your hearts despite my disbe-
lief, gives life even though I do not live it. But most of us are not
such accomplished Thespians. Most of us are open to the devastat-

ing remark a very young teen-ager made to his mother on leaving a Sunday Mass: "Mother, I don't think that priest believes what he was saying."

More positively, I am not so much concerned about the ability of a perceptive Christian to see my Christian infidelities. More positively, I have to, I must want to, speak in such a way that this congregation can react: "Wow! He really believes this stuff. He really believes that Jesus is alive and well, that to save your life you have to lose it, that to live humanly you ought to love God above all else, love everyone else as much as you love yourself. The words are flowing from his life; he seems to be suffering to live them."

A third demand. I have said that a parish is a group of Catholic Christians who are in process of becoming a people by deepening and expanding their faith through a ceaseless process of conversion. Conversion. Now conversion, a ceaseless turning to Christ, is not a process which a preacher simply recommends to a needy congregation, somewhat as Johnny Carson might recommend the latest in protective shields for women. No. When I repeat John the Baptist's "Repent" (Mt 3:2), I ought, like John, to be "preaching in the wilderness" (v. 1). In my wilderness. Calvin Klein may have replaced "camel's hair," a Lacoste belt John's "leather girdle," beef fondue his "locusts and wild honey" (v. 4). Such details, though not impertinent to conversion, can be incidental. What is indispensable, if preaching is to contribute to congregational conversion, is that my homily be part and parcel of my constant turning to Christ. It should proceed from conversion, express conversion, promote conversion.

Not necessarily radical conversion, casting off the slough of deadly sin to be clothed anew in amazing grace. Not so much Augustine's "Your right hand had regard to the profundity of my death and drew out the abyss of corruption that was in the bottom of my heart."[7] More commonly, the slow, sluggish, day-to-day, up-and-down, frustrating effort to grow into Christ, to get to be in his image. Aware of this, experiencing this, I can speak to the heart of a people—strong at times but never harsh, sweetly reasonable but never saccharine. It is my own story my homily should retell, even when that perilous "I" is not pronounced expressly. And that story is most effective when my turning to Christ reflects the conversion experience of the community, when it reproduces daily the prayer of the publican, the toll collector: "Lord, be merciful to me *the* sinner" (Lk 18:13).

It's a liberating experience, believe me. I no longer have to mount the pulpit as one who dwells with God in light inaccessible, remote from "the perils of Pauline" on earth. But genuinely liberating only if, like St. Paul, I continually carry the marks of Christ's passion in my flesh. Only if I share in some way the poverty of the poor to whom I preach so trippingly the poverty of Christ. Only if the love I would have lavished on wife and children is spent on all the loveless and unlovable who cry out to me. Only if my vow of obedience delivers me from a damnable preoccupation with my own wants, my own good pleasure, my own satisfaction, rather than the will of God and the agonizing needs of God's people.

As I close this chapter on the preacher and the parish, I realize how little I've said about the "nuts and bolts" of homiletics. It's been with malice aforethought. I see no point in eye contact unless "my eye is sound" (Mt 6:22; Lk 11:34). No sense projecting my voice if my sound waves are disembodied. No use constructing a classical sentence if the phrases are not charged with the Christ in me.

The view from the pew may be jaundiced in part, colored by all manner of morbidity. And that's a problem indeed. But what our parishioners see in the pulpit is not quite as important for the parish as what they do *not* see. Too often, I fear, they do not see a pilgrim who walks beside them, a man of faith who loves God and them with a crucifying passion, a constant convert reaching out to touch the hem of Jesus' garment.

To help fashion a parish after the mind of Christ, we have a long way to walk—preacher and parishioner. I have only one exhortation: Let's walk together.

5
LORD, TEACH US HOW TO . . . PREACH
From Study to Proclamation

Long centuries ago, a student in a select school looked longingly at his teacher and begged him: "Teach us how to pray." Because that particular teacher was filled with the Holy Spirit, and perhaps because his human intelligence was uniquely wed to divine Wisdom, he did teach the class how to pray: "When you pray, say . . . " (Lk 11:1–2).

For decades, seminarians beyond counting have looked longingly at their professors and mutely or vocally begged them: "Teach us how to preach." And the masters in theology, though presumably enlightened by the selfsame Spirit, have failed to serve up a satisfying "When you preach, preach like this. . . . " Some have coldly rejected the request as foreign to their function, as the burden of a different discipline, the task of homiletics. Others, charitably or desperately, have tagged practical applications onto theological theses: a paragraph of kitchen Christology, an appendix in ecclesiology on the family as a little church, and so on weakly into the night. The theologian was infrequently a preacher, and the homiletics professor was rarely a theologian. And so the newly oiled priest has departed the seminary for the parish with a theology that often bored him and seemed discouragingly irrelevant, and a course or two in homiletics that stressed technique, skills, know-how. Wired for sound, not fired for proclamation.

In consequence, we continue to reap the plaintive protests of our parishioners: Why have so many priests so little to say? Aren't they "turned on" by this God they've studied so long at our expense?

54

Whatever happened to these young fellows when they "left the world"?

Less passionately phrased, the problem might read: How can we move more effectively from classroom to pulpit, from study to proclamation? There is no instant answer, no infallible injection, no universal lesson. The homily that "sends" worshipers to the vaults of St. Patrick's Cathedral in Manhattan may fall flat on the grass of a rude chapel in Micronesia. No preaching pattern works for the Curé d'Ars *and* Norman Vincent Peale, for the apostle Paul *and* John Paul II, for Bossuet *and* Burghardt. From the very same pulpit, to the selfsame people, different preachers will preach differently. One preacher's "style" is another preacher's poison.

It is not my task, therefore, not my intention, to write other preachers' homilies, to set before them, in living color, "the very model of a modern major" homilist.[1] I shall attempt something far less arrogant and far more basic, something I have come to see with increasing intensity as the years roll on. It is my contention that between study and proclamation there is frequently a missing link. That link is experience: experience of God, experience of God's people, experience of God's wonderful works. That link spells the difference between the journeyman and the master. To make this thesis perceptible and palatable, let me unfold it in three stages, under three rubrics: (1) study, (2) experience, (3) proclamation.

STUDY

First, study. By study I mean a searching for knowledge, a searching that is organized, disciplined, methodical. It might take a solid semester or a single hour. It might be a complete course in Christology or a serious "Saturday Night Live,"[2] with Padre Sarducci feverishly plundering Raymond Brown on Jesus' enigmatic words to Pilate, "*You* say I am a king" (Jn 18:37). In any event, it is a deliberate effort to learn something in student style.

Now my four decades and more of preaching persuade me that very little I have studied is impertinent to preaching. From anthropology to zoology, whatever I learn about God's creation is potential grist for my homiletic mill. Not that I study every subject, or any subject, simply to see how I can apply it to the pulpit. Such study, such "despoiling of the Egyptians,"[3] not only does violence to the autonomy of a science; it risks turning superficial, and it contributes little or nothing to my constant conversion. My point is rather this:

Whatever I study can offer fresh insight into God's awesome activity in the story of salvation.

Here Lutheran theologian Joseph Sittler has been remarkably helpful to me. For Sittler has insisted that it is a mistake to imprison the Christian doctrine of grace within the rubric of redemption, while delineating our day-to-day "natural" experiences (Vatican II's "joys and hopes, griefs and anxieties") under the rubric of creation. Concretely, Sittler insists that our basic ecological error is that we Christians have separated creation and redemption. The reason why we can worship nature in Vermont and at the same time manipulate nature in New York is because, in our view, the redemption wrought by Christ leaves untouched the creation wrought by God. And once we wrench redemption from creation, once we put nature out there and grace in here, as long as we omit from our theology of grace the transaction of man and woman with nature, it is irrelevant to Christians whether we reverence the earth or ravish it.[4]

Our Catholic tradition tended, for all too long, to draw an excessively hard and fast line between nature and grace, between the secular and the sacred. The peril of too sharp a distinction is that nature and the secular can be misprized and despised. No, God's salvific story is everywhere to hear and discern: not only in "the heavens" that "are telling the glory of God" (Ps 19:1) but all over our planet, from the ovum and sperm that join to shape a child to the Atari and the atom. The divine milieu, as Teilhard de Chardin saw, is not only the mystical body of Christ; it is the cosmic body of Christ. The material for a sermon, therefore, its matter, is literally without limit.

But lest this chapter be limitless, I focus on two areas of study particularly pertinent for the preacher. The first is Scripture—Old Testament and New. I shall speak of Scripture more fully in a later chapter; here let me simply suggest its importance for preaching and its challenge. No need to argue Scripture's peerless importance; give ear to Vatican II:

> Like the Christian religion itself, all the preaching of the Church must needs be nourished and governed by Sacred Scripture. In the sacred books, you see, the Father who is in heaven comes to meet His children with extraordinary love and speaks with them. So remarkable is its power and force that the word of God abides as the support and energy of the Church, the strength of faith for the Church's children, the food of the soul, the pure and perennial source of spiritual life.[5]

If that is true, if for those striking reasons all our preaching should find its direction and its sustenance in Scripture, a twin challenge confronts us. One facet of the challenge is general, the other quite specific. On broad lines, my homily should be recognizably biblical. For all my radiant 20th-century rhetoric, I must confess that there is an incomparable power, an unrivaled richness, in the sheer text of Scripture. Why? Raymond Brown has put the reason pithily: "In the Bible God communicates Himself to the extraordinary extent that one can say that there is something 'of God' in the words. All other works, patristic, Thomistic, and ecclesiastic, are words *about* God; only the Bible is the word *of* God."[6] And the scriptural symbols, from the covenant through the kingdom to the cross, are matchless for their capacity to evoke a religious response.

But if I am to mediate the unique power of God's word to others, the Bible cannot remain a mere reference book, a handy volume of quotations for all occasions. Scripture must be the air I breathe. I must develop a love for God's word that reflects the vivid advice of St. Jerome: When your head droops at night, let a page of Scripture pillow it.[7] Only so will *my* words too burn with Isaian fire; only so will the ancient symbols come alive on my lips; only so will the "good news" come across to the faithful as news indeed, and as very, very good.

This is highly important, this immersion in the Bible like an embryo in amniotic fluid. But by itself it is not enough; something more specific must supplement it. After all, God is not simply "talking," making sound waves. He is saying something: "Thus says the Lord." "Amen, amen, I say to you." To recapture what that is calls for disciplined study. What did the Lord actually mean when He proclaimed through Jeremiah: "This is the covenant which I will make with the house of Israel after those days . . . : I will put my law within them, and I will write it upon their hearts; and I will be their God, and they shall be my people" (Jer 31:33)? Not my personal preference for beatitudes; rather, why Matthew and Luke are so different, why Luke has Jesus talking about real poverty, Matthew poverty in spirit. And how do you reconcile the radical Jesus on riches with the moderate Jesus: the Jesus for whom wealth is "totally linked with evil"[8] and the Jesus who counsels a prudent use of possessions; the Jesus who tells some people to give it all away and the Jesus who advises others to share what they have; the Jesus who forces you to choose between money and God, and the Jesus who loves a rich man who keeps both his wealth and God's commandments?

I am not suggesting that to be an effective preacher you must become a professional exegete. I am not identifying what a biblical text meant to its human author *then* with what God might be saying to His people through the text *now*. I am even prepared to grant, with Gadamer and contemporary philosophical hermeneutics, that a so-called "classical" text, be it the Bible or a score of Chopin, "has a fulness of meaning which by its very nature can never be exhausted," that "the meaning mediated by the [classical] text actually exceeds the conscious intention of the author," that the reader's understanding can help constitute the meaning of the text, "as the interpretation of the artist is constitutive of the music."[9] If that is true, then the ordinary Christian, operating within the understanding of the faith community and out of his or her life experience, can grasp what the text is basically saying. "Just as one need not be a professional musician to enjoy a symphony, or a literary critic to enjoy *Moby Dick*, one need not be a professional exegete to understand the Gospel of Luke."[10]

And still the preacher dare not disregard scholarly exegesis. Sandra Schneiders has phrased it tellingly, in the context of philosophical hermeneutics:

> The advantage of the exegete is analogous to that of the professional musician. Obviously, one who can play Chopin can, other things being equal, enjoy Chopin more deeply than the musically uneducated but appreciative listener. Even more importantly, unless *someone* can play Chopin, the ordinary person will never have the chance to appreciate his music. . . . Through the work of exegesis the text becomes more available and more understandable, just as through the playing of the musician the music becomes more available and more enjoyable.[11]

If I am to preach the word of God effectively today, a double don't is in order: (1) Don't bypass the exegete. (2) Don't parrot the exegete. The paradox is startling: I am more likely to grasp what God's word says today if I have mastered what God's word meant yesterday.

The second area of study particularly pertinent for the preacher is theology. Simply because theology is the Church's incessant struggle to grasp God's word and to express it. It is theology's privilege and burden to search out *where* God has spoken, where God speaks: from the burning bush in Midian to the gas ovens in Auschwitz, from the word that was creation to the Word that was made flesh, from the Church gathered in council to the skeletons starving in Calcutta's streets, from the Book that somehow reveals the heart of God to the trace of God on the face of humanity.

It is theology's task to uncover and interpret *what* God has said, what God says now. It is to theologians of the past 1800 years—from Irenaeus and Origen, through Aquinas and Luther, to Tillich and Rahner—that we owe our deeper understanding of so many love-laden mysteries. I mean, who *Christ* is: what it means to be divine and what it means to be human—both in the one unique package. What the *Church* is: not only or primarily pope or bishops, but the whole interpersonal community united to the Father and to one another through Christ in the Spirit. What *grace* means: the vast, deep realm that is the relationship between a triune God and the human person. What it means to say that God has revealed Himself to us in His dying/rising Son, that God channels His life to us in the sacraments, that Christ is really present in the Eucharist, that death is not the close of life but its glorious, Christlike continuance days without end.

True enough, it is not theology I preach; for the pulpit is not a classroom. But without theology I risk preaching platitudes (Remember Mayor Daley's "Chicago must rise to higher and higher platitudes"?). Our homilies are rarely heretical. They fail, fall short, flounder rather because they are stale and flat, vapid and insipid, dreadfully dry and boringly barren. One reason? They are not pregnant with the inexhaustible riches that is Christ; they carry so little substance, so little sap to slake the parched spirit.

EXPERIENCE

Serious study, therefore, is important for the preacher. Exegesis and theology exist because each word God speaks is at once mysterious and open-ended, never totally understood. Exegetes and theologians help the homilist to take that word from wherever it is spoken, wrestle with it, feel its fire, and fling it out to live people with new life, fresh flame.

But sheer study is not enough. To preach effectively, to speak God's word somewhat as Isaiah and Paul did, it is not enough to know *about* God; I must know God. In half a century, I have learned a great deal about God. With Aquinas, I have learned that God is Immovable Mover, Uncaused Cause, Necessary Being, Absolute Perfection, Supreme End. With Paul, I have risen from "the things that have been made" to God's "invisible nature," to "His eternal power and deity" (Rom 1:20). With John, I believe "God so loved the world that He gave His only Son" (Jn 3:16), gave him to a crucifying death that I might have life. I resonate to Joseph Mary Plunkett when he sees Christ's "blood upon the rose,/ And in the stars the glory of his eyes./ His body gleams amid eternal snows,/ His tears fall from the skies."[12] I thrill when I read in Gerard Manley Hopkins that I can find God in man and woman, that "Christ plays in ten thousand places,/ Lovely in limbs, and lovely in eyes not his/ [plays] To the Father through the features of men's faces."[13]

But believe me, this is not enough. From my own checkered past, I urge on all preachers a burning, humbling question: For all you know *about* God, do you really know God? Almost a decade ago Karl Rahner fashioned a moving essay in the form of a letter from Ignatius Loyola to a modern Jesuit. A significant segment of the letter has to do with Ignatius' experience of God. Here simply some excerpts:

> I was convinced that first, tentatively, during my illness in Loyola and then, decisively, during my time as a hermit in Manresa I had a direct encounter with God. This was the experience I longed to communicate to others. . . . I am not going to talk of forms and visions, symbols, voices, tears and such things. All I say is I knew God, nameless and unfathomable, silent and yet near, bestowing himself upon me in his Trinity. I knew God beyond all concrete imaginings. I knew him clearly in such nearness and grace as is impossible to confound or mistake. . . .
>
> God himself: I knew God himself, not simply human words describing him. . . . This experience is grace indeed and basically there is no one to whom it is refused. . . . When I say that it is as possible to encounter God in your age as in mine, I mean God really and truly, the God of incomprehensibility, the ineffable mystery, the darkness which only becomes eternal light for the man who allows himself to be swallowed up by it unconditionally. But it is precisely this God, he and none other, whom I personally experienced as the God who comes down to us, who comes close to us, the God in whose incomprehensible fire we are not, in fact, burnt away but become ourselves and of eternal value. The ineffable God promises himself to us; and in this promise of his ineffability we become, we live, we are loved and we are of eternal value; through him, if we allow ourselves to be taken up by him, we are not destroyed but given to ourselves truly for the first time.[14]

Of each preacher I would ask: Can you say that, like Ignatius, you have truly encountered the living and true God? Can you say that you know God Himself, not simply human words that describe Him? If you cannot, I dare not conclude that you are an unproductive preacher; for the same God who "is able from these stones to raise up children to Abraham" (Mt 3:9) can use the most sere of sermons to move the obdurate heart. But I do say that if you know only a theology of God, not the God of theology, you will not be the preacher our world desperately needs.

To know God, it is not enough to be brilliant and well read. The Father, His Christ, their Spirit—these must come through to you as real persons, real as the most tangible flesh-and-blood man or woman you know. Your personal experience of God, how God speaks to you, this is not mine to define or explore. It may be the thunder of Sinai (Exod 19:19) or the "still small voice" on Horeb (1 Kgs 19:12). It may be the theophany to a rebellious Job, where God transpires not to defend His wisdom but to stress His mystery. It may be Francis of Assisi stigmatized on Alvernia or Augustine and Monica enravished at Ostia. It may be John of the Cross's ascent of Carmel or Ignatius' illumination at the Cardoner.

More likely, your encounter with God will mean that you are increasingly sensitive to four phenomenological aspects of your relationship to God in Christ.[15] (1) You will find yourself absorbed by a *living* presence, a divine activity more real than your physical surroundings. (2) You will be aware of a *holy* presence that fills you with awe and fear, the while it warms and draws you—what Mouroux called "a kind of rhythm between hope and fear, each mutually supporting and generating the other."[16] (3) You will know an inexpressible *loneliness;* for in the presence of Love you will still be far from Love, agonizingly aware that to find yourself you must lose yourself, to grasp God you must risk all. (4) Even within sorrow you will sense a profound *joy,* strong and unshakable, a joy that refuses to be imprisoned, must burst forth to be shared with others.

In the last analysis, as the fourth-century theologian and mystic Gregory of Nyssa saw so perceptively, there is only one way to know God, and that is to be like Him, to get to be in His image. And so

> the knowledge of God to which [Gregory] gives preference in his thinking is that of participation in His virtues, in His holiness— that knowledge which is essentially union. . . . And how participate in that holiness of God? By following Him through faith, eyes closed, wherever He leads; by opening one's heart always to

a further and deeper submissiveness; by divesting oneself of every favor already received through unceasing yearning for what is always beyond; in a word, by the ecstasy which is a going out of oneself. . . . [17]

Our people are hungry for preachers who, like Magdalene, have seen the risen Lord. My darkest moments in homiletics are not when my theology is porous. My darkest moments are when I have ceased to pray—when the familiar phrases fall trippingly from my pen and tongue but it is all rote, prepackaged, with the life-giving juices dried up. My preaching is least effective when I experience nothing—neither God's presence nor His absence.

Not unexpectedly, the same problem surges with respect to God's images on earth. My homiletic experience cries aloud that Christian anthropology is not enough. Important indeed, but insufficient. The preacher our people desperately need not only knows *about* woman and man. Our people need preachers who live what Aquinas put so acutely: "There are two ways of desiring knowledge. One way is to desire it as a perfection of one's self; and that is the way philosophers desire it. The other way is to desire it not [merely] as a perfection of one's self, but because through this knowledge the one we love becomes present to us; and that is the way saints desire it."

This is not to denigrate anthropology. I am simply saying that the most profound knowledge is in peril of staying sterile unless it is charged with love. My knowledge of the human condition is Christian and salvific, my insight into man and woman will find effective expression, if it touches me to the other, to the countless men and women whose days are faithless or hopeless or loveless.

The paradox is, the flow is not one way. Here is reciprocal causality, a two-way street. If knowledge leads to love, love deepens knowledge. It has taken me a lifetime to learn that love lavished on others is not time stolen from theology, from anthropology, from homiletics. Please God, our preachers will increasingly learn, not so much from reading as from loving, how "Christ plays in ten thousand places . . . through the features of men's faces."

Something similar can be said about the rest of God's creation. It is not enough for me to plumb its secrets; I should experience the subhuman as sacred. Everything that exists, from ocean floor to outer space, is precious because it reflects the God whose whole being is summed up in a monosyllable: He *is*. And everything that lives, from the simple amoeba through a field of wheat to the sul-phur-bottom whale, is more precious still, because it images the God who *is* Life. This breath-taking trace of God throughout His universe is not ours simply to know, to recognize, to analyze. To preach persuasively, I had better love it!

Perhaps what I have said so far can be summed up neatly. A solid sermon presupposes serious study, if only because the word I preach is not so much my word as God's word; and God's word is a challenge not to my piety alone but to my intelligence as well. Sheer study, however, is insufficient; for to study is, in large measure, to recapture the ideas and insights, the discoveries and experiences, of others. If I am to do more than parrot the exegete and theologian, if I am to touch God's living word to a living people, I have to hear that word with my own ears, see the risen Christ with my own eyes, experience for myself the Lord God and the loving work of His hands.

Let me point up and conclude this segment on experience with a story I have borrowed from Henri Nouwen.

> One day a young fugitive, trying to hide himself from the enemy, entered a small village. The people were kind to him and offered him a place to stay. But when the soldiers who sought the fugitive asked where he was hiding, everyone became very fearful. The soldiers threatened to burn the village and kill every man in it unless the young man were handed over to them before dawn. The people went to the minister and asked him what to do. The minister, torn between handing over the boy to the enemy or having his people killed, withdrew to his room and read his Bible, hoping to find an answer before dawn. After many hours, in the early morning his eyes fell on these words: "It is better that one man dies than that the whole people be lost."
>
> Then the minister closed the Bible, called the soldiers and told them where the boy was hidden. And after the soldiers led the fugitive away to be killed, there was a feast in the village because the minister had saved the lives of the people. But the minister did not celebrate. Overcome with a deep sadness, he remained in his room. That night an angel came to him and asked, "What have you done?" He said: "I handed over the fugitive to the enemy." Then the angel said: "But don't you know that you have handed over the Messiah?" "How could I know?" the minister replied anxiously. Then the angel said: "If, instead of reading your Bible, you had visited this young man just once and looked into his eyes, you would have known."[18]

PROCLAMATION

Study impregnated with experience—a powerful preparation for preaching. But as yet I do not have an actual sermon or homily; the word I shall personally proclaim has not taken specific shape. How shape it? No single system ensures success for all. Still, for what it is worth, let me develop the *modus operandi* I sketched towards the close of this book's first chapter. Here I recapture a real-life situation: the Second Sunday of Advent 1982, cycle C, a homily I was asked to deliver at the National Shrine of the Immaculate Conception in Washington, D.C.[19]

Stage 1: What shall I talk about? This is the mulling stage, the search for a subject, the general topic. It has to focus on Advent, of course. But what approach to Advent? I could fashion my homily directly from the liturgical readings (Baruch 5:1–9; Philippians 1:4–6, 8–11; Luke 3:1–6), but something else intrigues me more. I recall, from a lecture by Raymond Brown, that three persons dominate the Advent liturgy—three persons who prepare in different ways for the coming of the Savior: Isaiah, John the Baptist, Mary. And the feast of the Immaculate Conception is almost upon us— three days away. I have my topic: Advent with Mary.

Stage 2: How, in point of fact, do Advent and Mary link up? This calls for study in two areas: What is the Advent liturgy all about, and how does the mother of Jesus fit into it? Advent, I find, is a period of expectation; we are waiting. For what? We focus on two events. We put ourselves back into the situation of an expectant people, on tiptoe for the first coming of the Messiah; and we rekindle our expectation of his final coming. Baruch waits for the first coming, Paul for the final.

And what of Mary? As I search the Scriptures and canvass the commentaries, I conclude that Mary and Advent fit together strikingly. Not primarily because we celebrate Mary's birthday on September 8, subtract nine months, and celebrate her conception on December 8. Mary is an Advent figure because she reveals more remarkably than anyone else how the Christian should wait for Christ. First, the way she waited for Christ's *first* coming. Not only like every other Jew waiting for the Promised One. She waited uniquely, as no other in history: He for whom she was waiting was nestling within her, in her flesh. She was waiting only to see his face and to offer him to the world. Second, the way Mary waited for Christ's *second* coming. In a word, she was his disciple—the very model of what discipleship means. "My mother and my brothers, they are the ones who listen to the word of God and act on it" (Lk 8:21). That, at its best, is Mary: she who hears God's word and does it. Such was Mary at the gospel's beginning; such was she throughout her life (check this theme in Luke); such was she beneath the cross; such was she after the ascension of her Son, waiting with the Eleven for the descent of the Spirit.

Stage 3: How organize all this? The material seems to suggest three points, three questions. The first two stem quite naturally from my study: (1) What is the Advent liturgy all about? Expectant waiting for Christ. (2) How does Mary fit into Advent? History's most remarkable model of waiting: She listened to God's word and acted on it. But a third question challenges not my study but my experience: What does Mary say *to us* these Advent weeks? She suggests how we in our time and circumstances are to wait for Christ. Not only for his second coming, "with great power and glory" (Mk 13:26), but for his constant coming each day, in poverty and powerlessness that make his crib look like a castle. Jesus comes to us in the hungry and thirsty, in the stranger and the naked, in the sick and the shackled (cf. Mt 25:35–40). The hungers of the human family cry out to us: hunger for bread, for justice and peace, for understanding and love—hunger for God. Their cry is not only a human cry; God is speaking to us. We are disciples of Jesus, in the image of Mary, only if we listen to that anguished word and act on it, as God gives us to act.

Stage 4: I develop each point in detail, compose in methodical fashion, order my ideas with rigor and vigor. Here clarity, for all its importance, is not enough. A homily is not a catechism, not a theology text, not a curial rescript; it calls for a religious response. And so I struggle with language, wrestle with words; Webster's Unabridged is my second bible. I pause to read Shakespeare aloud, Gerard Manley Hopkins, T. S. Eliot, Tennessee Williams, John Henry Newman. I listen to Beethoven's *Ninth Symphony* or Barber's *Adagio,* a ballet like *Swan Lake* or a dash of country music. For the bare message can be deadeningly dull; it must come alive, take wing. To play on the human heart, my words must leap and dance, quiver and shiver, burn and cool. That is why, when I speak to my Advent people about the hungers of the human family, I move briskly from abstractions to "the living skeletons in Mother Teresa's Calcutta and the downtrodden in D.C., the bombed-out in Lebanon and the MX in Wyoming, the slums in El Salvador and the pimps and prostitutes in Times Square, the schizoid psyches in St. Elizabeth's and the lonely old on your street."

But for my words to come alive, *I* must come alive. This realization drives me back, time and again, not to study but to experience. How do I touch God in love, feel the scars of His people, trace His face in sky and earth?

Stage 5: When I think I have finished, I work through every sentence of the homily with a fine comb. I do not need this much on Isaiah, that extra phrase on John the Baptist. A purple patch here, a bit too subtle there. Needless bloodletting in this provocative sentence. Block that metaphor, excise that banality, lessen the alliteration. Not a single unnecessary word.

I have mapped out one man's movement from study through experience to proclamation. If it strikes the parish priest as onerous and time-consuming, I shall not attempt a rebuttal; it takes me 60 or 70 hours to shape a 15-minute homily. No one who preaches every Sunday (and short homilies on weekdays) can afford such an expenditure of time. A handful of suggestions, therefore, to keep my method from becoming a hothouse plant that has no practical place in parochial ministry.

1) Try the method (mull, study, organize, write, rewrite) but on a much-reduced schedule. Shall we say ten hours a week? Can't spare the time, you reply. Not true. Not if you realize that the Sunday liturgy with its homily, the community's weekly worship, is the most significant ministerial activity that engages the Catholic priesthood.

2) Recognize that the ten hours I recommend need not all be spent at your desk. There is hardly an experience in your day that is not grist for your proclamation. I do not mean that you carry a notebook, jot down every single thing that passes for real. I do mean that everything you see, hear, touch, taste, and smell is part of your human and Christian experience, can therefore shape the word you preach and the way you preach it. *Chariots of Fire* and Woody Allen's *Zelig, The Gods Must Be Crazy* and *Amadeus;* the photo of Mother Teresa cradling a naked retarded child in the rubble of West Beirut; the Op. Ed. page on nuclear warfare or sexual morality, on child abuse or international terrorism; the taste of canneloni and the cool breeze caressing your cheek; thousands of Cambodian refugees ravaged by tuberculosis, dysentery, malaria; an article in *Manhattan, Inc.* by a Manhattan minister thrust into Harvard's Graduate School of Business Administration; Amy Grant singing "Doubly Good to You"; the touch of a hand, the feel of a flower, the look of love in another's eyes; a harrowing walk through hospital wards; the "bag lady" you hurry past on the street; the Christ who each day pillows

himself on your tongue and graces your body. These experiences and a thousand more combine to fashion the person you are; let them shape your homily as well.

3) Believe firmly that whatever price you have to pay, whatever sacrifice of sleep or pleasure, the effects will far outstrip all that. Effects on your people: time and again, fresh insight into the mind of Christ, often a burning yearning to listen to the Lord and say yes, at crucial moments just the courage to be. Effects on you: a continuing education, ever-new experience of the risen Christ, constant conversion. Yes, conversion; for you will soon discover, perhaps to your surprise, that in the first instance you are preaching to yourself. It is then that the people listen more eagerly to the Lord and his preacher—if the preacher has seen the face of the Lord.

4) Look ahead to next Sunday's sermon not as a chore but as a chance, not an obligation but an opportunity. The faithful in front of you do not expect you to reduce the national budget or bring peace to Nicaragua. They ask only that you speak to them of the God who has spoken to you—spoken to you through books and the Book, on your knees and on your streets, in your daily dying/rising that mirrors the paschal mystery. You have much of Christ to offer them, if you will only wed sweat, blood, and tears to a conviction that God has indeed, and deliberately, chosen "what is foolish in the world to shame the wise, what is weak in the world to shame the strong" (1 Cor 1:27).

Do this and, I promise you, your life and your preaching will sing the joyous eucharist of the poet e. e. cummings:

> I thank You God for most this amazing
> day: for the leaping greenly spirits of trees
> and a blue true dream of sky; and for everything
> which is natural which is infinite which is yes
>
> (i who have died am alive again today,
> and this is the sun's birthday; this is the birth
> day of life and of love and wings: and of the gay
> great happening illimitably earth)
>
> how should tasting touching hearing seeing
> breathing any—lifted from the no
> of all nothing—human merely being
> doubt unimaginable You?
>
> (now the ears of my ears awake and
> now the eyes of my eyes are opened)[20]

This, at bottom, is my homily: thanksgiving for most this amazing day, for everything which is natural, for everything which is infinite, for everything which is yes.

EPILOGUE

In its original form this chapter was an address delivered at the First National Ecumenical Scriptural-Theological Symposium on Preaching, convened at Emory University in Atlanta by the Word of God Institute in celebration of its tenth anniversary of apostolic service in the renewal of preaching (December 1982). The prepared response to my address by Elisabeth Schüssler Fiorenza was so insightful, persuasive, and moving that I have asked and received her gracious permission to reproduce it here. I agree with reviewer Willard F. Jabusch that it "should be required reading for all male preachers."[21]

Response
Elisabeth Schüssler Fiorenza[22]

Professor Burghardt has very eloquently outlined how the homilist moves from study to proclamation. He has stressed the necessity for careful study of Scripture and theology. He has emphasized the importance of the preacher's experience of God, "the Father and His Christ," and finally he has outlined the five stages of "one man's movement from study through experience to proclamation." The argument of the paper is insightful, formulated with great care, and well balanced. I envy his skill as "a weaver of words."

We are all in debt to Father Burghardt for his stimulating presentation. It goes without saying that his constructive proposals are both suggestive and provocative and I have no serious disagreement to register. In my response I should therefore like to underline his emphasis on experience and on the study of Holy Scripture by singling out three points or areas where I would want to complement his suggestions and at the same time to offer a somewhat different perspective on the interrelationship between experience, study and proclamation. Such a different perspective comes from my expertise not as a homilist but as a Scripture scholar and a feminist theologian. The three areas I wish to focus on are: (1) the interpretation of present experience not only of the homilist but of all the people of God, (2) the interpretation of past experiences of the people of God in Scripture, and (3) the move from experience to proclamation.

I. Interpretation of Present Experiences of All the People of God

Dr. Burghardt addresses foremost the homilist and his God-experience. His movement from study to experience to proclamation entails three major components: the first is study, the third and last is proclamation. The interlocking link in his proposal is experience. Experience is so to speak the missing link between study and proclamation. How does Father Burghardt understand experience? It is defined as the "experience of God, the experience of God's people and the experience of God's wonderful works." God's people are not the subject of experience but are here conceived of as a part of the object of the homilist's experience. Moreover he maintains that in order to preach the homilist must not just know something *about* God. Experience is specified as the homilist's experience *of* God and it is this almost mystical experience of God that provides the link between study and proclamation. The homilist's experience is paradigmatic for Christian God-experience today.

Yet some of the major insights of recent theology stem from the application of the sociology of knowledge to theology. Raw experience or even common experience does not exist, but what exists are particular and individual experiences. All human experience insofar as it is human experience is bound to particular historical situations, is bound to specific cultural contexts, and is determined or at least influenced by the individual's social status and professional role in society and church. This social conditioning of experience holds true also for the human experience of God. There is not an abstract common experience of God, but human experience of God is a particular experience that reflects and is shaped by its historical conditions in time and space, in culture and gender socialization. It is for this reason that I think it is important to look at experience not just as a link but also as a starting point of the movement from study to proclamation. The conditioning of experience poses the hermeneutical circle: where do we begin; how do we reflect upon our own experiences; how do we become conscious of our own presuppositions; how do we articulate our assumptions; how do we make explicit our institutional commitments?

My own critical starting point is not that of the homilist or the ordained cleric but that of the proverbial "woman in the pew," the silenced majority. Whereas the experience of God, and more and more also the study of Scripture and theology, is open

to all persons who are religious and call themselves Christians—
and not just to those who are called "religious"—this is not the
case for proclamation. Whereas all the people of God—clergy
and lay, men and women, rich and poor—can experience God's
grace and presence in their lives, proclamation is limited in the
Roman Catholic Church by law to celibate male clergy only. For
all practical purposes women of the past and of the present have
not preached and are in many Christian churches still excluded
from *defining* the role of proclamation in terms of their own experience. In such an ecclesiastical situation the danger exists that
the homily will not articulate the experience of God as the rich
and pluriform experience of God's people, but that the male
preacher will articulate his own experience and will declare and
proclaim his own particular experience as the experience of God
par excellence. What is limited and particular to his experience will
be proclaimed as universal and paradigmatic for everyone. I
would, therefore, suggest that in such a restrictive ecclesial situation the homilist has not just the function to articulate his own
experience of God as a very particular experience but must also
seek to articulate publicly the learning processes and the experiences of the people of God as well, since they are for the most
part excluded from public proclamation. In order to be able to
do so the homilist must become (1) self-critical, (2) attentive to the
experiences of others not like himself, (3) seek the involvement
of those others in the task of preaching and proclamation and (4)
develop dialogical modes and styles of preaching.

(1) Self-critical: To the extent that the homilist is aware of the
hermeneutical circle he will become more and more self-critical.
When he becomes aware of how experiences are embedded
within a tradition, culture and society, the self-critical homilist
will be on the alert not to substitute his own experience for that
of the people of God, but rather seek to uncover the limitations
of his own perspective and standpoint. Quite often I have heard
sermons about the insecurity wrought among the faithful by Vatican II, where it was obvious that the problem was not that of the
congregation but that of the preacher. I have listened, for instance, to sermons attacking the liberality of modern exegesis, especially, e.g., about the visit of the Magi, only to puzzle the
audience, only to accomplish a moralist reduction of the text
rather than a fuller development of its christological importance.
I have patiently listened to diatribes against the desire for power,
the lust after pride; sermons that may reflect male drives and sins
but do not take into account the need of women to take control
over their own lives or to be encouraged in their search for self-
affirmation. I have listened to sermon after sermon denouncing

our consumerist attitudes and self-serving wealth, sermons addressing the upper middle class members of the congregation but not those who struggle for economic survival. A homilist who has just returned suntanned from a vacation in Florida or Arizona is ill equipped to preach against the consumerism of a suburban housewife who has not had a vacation for years.

(2) Attentive to others' experience: One of the best ways of becoming self-critical is to listen carefully to the experiences of others rather than to project one's problems and fears into them. Liberation theology appeals to Scripture in pointing out that God can be found especially among the poor, the disadvantaged, the alienated, among those who do not belong. This does not mean that the poor and alienated are the objects of our charity and pastoral care so that they receive from us out of the superabundance of our goods and wisdoms. But rather it means that we are to listen to their experiences of God, to their analysis of *how* our values, life-style, and pious self-security have led to and may have contributed to their exploitation and powerlessness, to their frustration and alienation, and may be the cause of their alienation from Christian faith and community. The homilist becomes self-critical when in such an attentive learning and listening process he becomes convinced that his own private experience is not the hermeneutical key to the experience of God, or that he, as ordained, is not hermeneutically privileged in regard to the Wisdom of Christ, but rather that this hermeneutical key is to be found with the poor, the disprivileged, and the alienated. Only by becoming attentive to the God-experiences of "others" who are not "like him," the homilist will become capable of relativizing his own stance and of connecting his own experience with the God-experience of others. Only then will he become capable of articulating the God-experiences of the people of God today in a fuller sense.

A recent experience may illustrate this. Just this Christmas I listened to a sermon in a Brooklyn parish in which the homilist complained that today we talk too much about "the brotherhood of men" but neglect to speak about "the Fatherhood of God." Obviously this preacher never listened to women who have become alienated from the Church and from God because of sexist language that erases them as subjects from the public discourse and liturgy of their church. He has never listened to the agony of women who need a whole week to recover their faith and hope after listening to a chauvinistic sermon on Sunday. I am sure that a great number of the women present did not notice or pay much attention to such androcentric preaching. Yet what about the ten or twenty percent who, like my daughter, are very conscious of the sin of sexism and no longer find themselves addressed by, or tolerant of, such male biased language and proclamation?

(3) Involvement of "others" in proclamation: Since no one single person can comprehend the multiform experience of the people of God or do justice to their legitimate religious needs, the homilist must seek to involve others in the move from experience to study to proclamation. Various models exist for such an involvement: Eduard Schweizer, a Swiss New Testament scholar and pastor, invites a group of parishioners to discuss and prepare the homily. Ernesto Cardenal has given us the scriptural dialogues of the peasants in Nicaragua. The *Gospel of Solentiname* teaches us how poor and alienated people can understand the meaning of the Gospel better than many highly trained middle-class exegetes do. This is not surprising because the New Testament Scriptures are rooted in the early Christian counter-cultural movement that was carried on for the most part by poor, alienated and disenfranchised people.

However, all partial involvement of the people of God in the preparation for proclamation does not suffice. The impoverishment of preaching today is not due to the lack of able preachers, but due to a structural clericalism which demands that one, single group of Christians—the ordained—articulate the richness and fullness of all Christians' God-experiences today. What is necessary is that more and more people, with a variety of life-experiences, not only are allowed to study the Scriptures and theology but also to become involved in proclamation. Relinquishment of his prerogatives as a homilist so that others can preach may be for the ordained preacher the best way of proclaiming God in our midst today.

The involvement of the laity in preaching does not just rest on an extraordinary gift of the Spirit or in an extraordinary situation, but is rooted in the God-experience of all the baptized. If ordination traditionally gives the power to preach, today the ordained homilist may be called to relinquish that power for the sake of the fullness of Christian proclamation. While traditionally the power of the ordained was understood as religious power over the laity, today such power must be reconceptualized not as power over others but as enabling power. Such an understanding of power is rooted in the words of Jesus and explored today especially by feminist theology. While the ordained is responsible that the Word of God is proclaimed, such responsibility does not require that he himself always preaches but that he enables others to do so.

(4) The style of proclamation: Such a communal understanding of proclamation as the right of all the people of God calls

into question the "authoritarian one way form" of communication that characterizes preaching today. After lectures we have responses, after press-conferences we have questions, but no one and nothing can challenge and question the proclamation of the homilist. Dialogue homilies that engage the congregation in conversation or communal homilies that engage the congregation in a meditative sharing of experiences and insights are not necessarily "an adding up of zero to zero that equals zero," as someone once suggested, but they are serious attempts to develop a different, more ecclesial rather than clerical style of preaching. We must much more seriously rethink our form and means of proclamation and search for new modes of communication, if the homily should become open to critical dialogue and public discernment of how God can be experienced today in our midst.

II. Interpretation of the Past Experience of the People of God

My emphasis upon the need to be self-critical and to bring to the fore the diversified experiences of others in elucidating the present meaning of the Word of God and the experience of God today can not only be extended to the past, but this model of preaching is derived from the interpretation of the past experiences of God's people in biblical scholarship. Scripture reflects upon and articulates the diverse experiences of God's presence in Israel and among the earliest Christian communities. In order to explore this model of proclamation in Scripture we have (1) to understand the Bible as the formative root-model of Christian faith and community, (2) to ask for the hermeneutical clue to the correct interpretation of Scripture, and (3) positively use the diversity of contemporary scriptural interpretations.

(1) Biblical studies analyzing the diverse literary forms as well as social world studies reconstructing their diverse historical contexts and cultural milieus have shown the pluriformity and the richness of such experiences of the people of God in the past: not just one literary form but diverse literary forms, different social groups, and even conflicting theological opinions come to expression in our biblical texts. The scriptural texts cannot simply be appealed to as if they provided infallible proof-texts, or as if they provided a monolithic viewpoint that would answer our questions or give us doctrinal solutions for our problems. Instead, the biblical texts present diverse theological insights and diverse practical solutions to theological or communal problems. Since preaching in the present does not rejoice in the diversity of the way we experience God and seek to live as Christians today, homilists are often not able to do justice to the diversity of such

faith experiences in the past, expressed in the formative root-model of Scripture. Rather than to adapt Scripture to a monolithic understanding of faith and church, biblical scholarship teaches us to find God in the richness of the diversity and pluriformity of the past.

(2) Yet this pluriformity of the biblical root-model of Christian faith and community raises also a hermeneutical problem. Insofar as Biblical texts reflect diverse experiences in ancient cultures, they are not just liberating texts, but they also codify the oppressive structures and mindsets of these cultures. As one author has put it, the Bible contains not just the "good news" but also some bad news. Or, in other words, the New Testament contains some texts that bring to the fore the Gospel and are given for "the sake of our salvation," whereas other texts express the religious-cultural structures of their times or seek to adapt the early Christian ethos to the societal norms of their times. For instance, in the face of all the destructive powers of modern warfare, the question must be raised whether we still can pray the curses of the Old Testament psalms against the enemies of Israel. Feminist theology queries whether we can repeat today the patriarchal biblical language for God, while political theology doubts that the biblical language which speaks of God as an absolute monarch is still adequate. If one speaks of scriptural truth, one is speaking of biblical meaning throughout Christian history, of the past as well as of the present, and not just of an isolated stage in this history. Conversely, one can show that certain biblical texts, e.g. the Levitical purity laws or the "household-code" texts of the New Testament, have always functioned to legitimate the patriarchal institution of slavery or the second-class citizenship of women.

The question arises then: how are we to interpret and proclaim these potentially oppressive biblical texts? The homilist cannot simply go on to indiscriminately proclaim all biblical texts as if there were no contradictions among them, or as if there was no distinction between those expressing God's liberating Word of salvation and those expressing oppressive and destructive aspects of the biblical world. The homilist must, therefore, explore the alienating and oppressive aspects and elements in the Bible in order not to preach them as the revelation of God, but to show their human oppressive character. I personally have attempted elsewhere to elaborate how Vatican II in its document on divine revelation has provided us with a hermeneutical clue to the correct interpretation of the Scriptures. In *Dei Verbum* the Council teaches that Holy Scripture teaches without error that truth which God wanted to put in them for the sake of our salvation.

It follows Augustine and Thomas in formulating a criterion that limits revealed truth and inerrancy to matters pertaining to the salvation of the Christian and human community. Salvation must, however, not be reduced to a Platonic sense. It should not be understood just as salvation of the soul but must be conceived in biblical terms as total human salvation and full human rights and wholeness. It cannot be limited to the redemption from personal sin, but, as such redemption, it must be understood also as redemption and liberation from structural-social sin, such as sexism, racism or classism.

(3) However, the preacher encounters not only the problem of the pluriformity of biblical texts and the problem of the criterion with which to theologically evaluate this diversity, but he encounters also the problem of diverse, often contradictory, exegetical interpretations of these texts. As is well known but often insufficiently reflected upon, a broad theological-social diversity exists among Biblical scholars. This diversity among biblical scholars is due to the different presuppositions, methods, and questions that they bring to the Biblical text. The danger exists that the homilist will select that exegete who is the most "established" or that commentary that fits best into his own theological world-view and personal experience. But it is only through becoming aware of the diverse presuppositions and methods of biblical scholarship, and it is only by taking seriously those interpretations that conflict with one's own theological and social presuppositions and conditions that the homilist is capable of broadening out the experiential and interpretative basis of proclamation. What applies to the present, the need to take into account the experiences of others, also applies to the interpretations of the past. The homilist, therefore, must challenge exegetes and biblical scholars to reflect upon their own experiences and presuppositions and to articulate how they come to play in their interpretations. The diversity of biblical exegesis must be taken into account and articulated if the homily is not to reflect simply a particular experience that finds its expression in a particular but limited interpretation, yet claims objectivity and universal validity for such a particular interpretation.

III. The Move from Experience to Proclamation

In a last step, I want to illustrate how my emphasis on experience as the primary ingredient in the move from study to proclamation would complement, concretize and broaden Father Burghardt's emphasis on experience and his homiletic suggestions. In his example of how he moves from study to proclamation, he not only carefully describes five steps in the preparation of a homily, but also focuses in the selection of the topic on Mary as the dominating figure of Advent. He informs us that the social location of the homily is the Shrine in Washington and that his choice of the topic was made with a view to the feast of the Immaculate Conception and in the light of a statement of Raymond Brown that three persons, Isaiah, Mary, and John the Baptist dominate the Advent liturgy. Mary reveals, according to him, more remarkably than anyone else how Christians should wait for Christ.

After having selected the topic and studied the Scriptures, Professor Burghardt moves to stage four, that reflects on the details and organization of the homily and the religious response that the homily should call forth. After the study of Scripture and theology, one expects that he connects the topic of the homily with his own or other people's religious experiences. Indeed, in this context he states that he pauses to read Shakespeare, Gerard Manley Hopkins, T. S. Eliot, Tennessee Williams, and to listen to Beethoven, Barber, Tschaikovsky and even to a dash of country music. He listens to the poets and musicians of his culture in order to formulate the details of the homily and to enflesh the topic. Yet I was surprised that he does not think of taking into account the experiences of pregnant women and their sense of self. I wonder whether the male poets and artists he mentions can give his sermon the detail, sensitivity, and insight that he would need for presenting the pregnant Mary of Nazareth as a paradigm of Christian Advent hope. Instead, listening to the experiences of women with pregnancy, their fears, hopes, troubles, and anxieties, their various experiences in giving birth and their exhilaration in touching the newborn child might have illumined and concretized our understanding of Advent waiting. Yet listening to individual experiences does not suffice. One would also need to study feminist analyses, e.g., Adrienne Rich's book on the institution of motherhood in patriarchal society, to learn how the experience of motherhood is structurally and societally mediated and conditioned. One might also listen to single mothers on welfare or to the woman at the checkout counter trying to feed and clothe their children. If the word has to become flesh in the homily, then it must become flesh in the particular experiences of those about whom the homily speaks. And the Mary of Advent is the pregnant Mary, the unwed mother.

This is not to criticize Father Burghardt's way of procedure—indeed if only more sermons reflected such high literary standards and artistic sources. My point is mainly to emphasize the importance of reflecting upon and listening to different experiences, especially those pertinent to the theme of the sermon. Moving from such attentive listening to women's personal and structural experiences with motherhood, the Lukan texts on Mary come to new life. Mary, and not Joseph, is the morally responsible agent in becoming pregnant. The gospel stresses her freedom of choice. She does not remain isolated but seeks support from another woman, Elizabeth. She has to learn that not natural family bonds and the claims of motherhood but the issues of God determine her relationship to her child. Her calling is not just motherhood but creative discipleship. As such a spirit-filled person, the pregnant Mary announces the future of God to the heavy laden and downtrodden in the *Magnificat*. The future of God's salvation and wholeness is not to be awaited passively and without our active involvement, but it is being born among us today from our flesh and blood, from our commitments and our struggles today. It is fashioned and becomes form as the hope for those who are without hope. In short, it is by articulating the pertinent experiences of women as the people of God that this homily on the Mary of Advent can elicit the faith response that the homily intends.

These brief remarks do not mean in any way to detract from the persuasiveness of Father Burghardt's suggestions, but they merely seek to underline how the interpretation of present and past experience demands that the homilist becomes acutely aware that not he himself, and not he alone, but in many cases, others may have the key to what the meaning of the word of God is for us today. It was in this light that I have suggested that an interpretation of Mary's experience during Advent can only take place with references to the personally and structurally reflected experiences of women among God's people. In short, the "silenced majority" must be heard and allowed into "speech" again if the richness and fullness of God's presence with us should be articulated and proclaimed today. The right of the baptized to proclamation is not just charismatic and extraordinary, but it must become the essential ingredient of all preaching, if the experience of God in our midst should be proclaimed in its fullness. While the ordained have the call and duty to ensure that proclamation takes place, all the people of God—ordained or not— are called to proclaim the great and marvelous deeds of God in Christ for our world and church.

6
THUS SAYS THE LORD
The Word Forms the Preacher

Some years ago, two Catholic scholars found themselves at odds in print. The issue was Scripture—specifically, contemporary Catholic exegesis, the historico-critical method. The "concerned" Catholic expressed his displeasure with Catholic exegetes in the words of a distraught Mary Magdalene at the tomb of Jesus: "They have taken away my Lord, and I know not where they have laid him" (Jn 20:13). The unconcerned exegete retorted in the words of angels: "Why do you seek the living among the dead? He has risen; he is not here" (Lk 24:5; Mk 16:6).

That confrontation is not impertinent here. My subhead reads: "The Word Forms the Preacher." Not a question: "Does the Word Form the Preacher?" A declarative sentence. Actually, a declarative that is more like a Greek optative, a mood expressive of wish or desire: "The Word Should Form the Preacher," or "Would That the Word Formed the Preacher!" A tough topic, for all that it seems so self-evident. I propose to address the topic in three stages, moving from the less difficult to the more difficult. First, I shall ask why the scriptural word should form the preacher. Second, I shall cast a glance over my shoulder, to ask how that word formed a particularly impressive gaggle of preachers in the past. Third, I shall ask the most difficult question, the heart of the homiletic matter: How might the scriptural word form the preacher today? In other words, I shall play, in turn, the theologian, the historian, and the prophet.

I

First, why should the word form the preacher? Four succinct definitions will clarify what the question means—the way we operated in a tighter seminary theology. The "word" I take to be the inspired text of Scripture, Old Testament and New. The "preacher" on whom I focus is the homilist, addressing a congregation in the context of Eucharistic liturgy. Not indeed exclusively (other religious situations may be beneficiaries of my bons mots) but primarily. To "form" is to give a particular shape to something or someone, to mold or fashion into a certain shape or condition. To form a preacher is to help shape what a homilist ought to be, how he ought to think and feel and express himself. The verb "should" is here an ought: not simply what is fitting or becoming or expedient, but what is necessary, indispensable, therefore involving moral obligation. My thesis, therefore: To preach effectively in the Eucharistic liturgy, the homilist must be molded in his being and his feeling, in his thinking and his speaking, by the inspired pages of Scripture.

But why? Why can't I mount the pulpit armed with the sword of the Spirit and a manual of orthodox theology, supplemented by pastoral experience and the irresistible attraction of my Brite smile? Because the homily is not just *any* sermon. "Its character," Vatican II insisted, "should be that of a proclamation of God's wonderful works in the history of salvation, that is, the mystery of Christ. . . ." That is why the homily "should draw its content mainly from scriptural and liturgical sources."[1] And so the Council urged the clergy to read Scripture diligently and study it carefully. Such "cultivation of Scripture is required (*necesse est*) lest any of them become 'an empty preacher of the word of God outwardly, who is not a listener to it inwardly,' since they must share the abundant wealth of the divine word with the faithful committed to them, especially in the sacred liturgy."[2]

In a nutshell: We are to preach, above all else, God's wonderful works, and these works are detailed in privileged fashion in the Old and New Testaments. Not all God's works, of course. After all, God did not cease working wonderfully in our midst after the Second Letter of Peter was completed early in the second century. "The world is" still "charged with the grandeur of God."[3] The fifth act in the drama of salvation (the "last age") is being played right now, and we are witnesses thereto, even actors therein; but the first four acts have been played: Eden, Israel, Calvary, and the newborn Church. And the record lies in a book that moves from creation to a final

"Come, Lord Jesus!" (Rev 22:20)—a record that, inevitably couched in words of men, is unique in being the word of God. No other source, no other reference book, can claim that distinction.[4]

No doubt, therefore, that Scripture must not simply season or salt our sermons but shape them. I would not dream of producing a modern *Hamlet* without being saturated by Shakespeare's hero, even though I am not bound to be faithful to the Bard's every genuine word. I can reinterpret a Chopin sonata, but to do so justifiably I had better know Chopin as well as I know myself. A fortiori for Scripture. At the close of my homily I should be able to say "This is the word of the Lord." With some trepidation indeed, some nuancing, and a lower-case w. How can I call this God's word if my sermon is not steeped in Scripture? Not only my sermon but myself.

Precisely how I do this I reserve to my third point. Right now I see no benefit in belaboring a first point which should elicit a speedy amen from every Christian preacher—not only the Bible-thumping TVer but also the sermonizer whose eyes are fixed not so much on yesterday as on the signs of *our* times. Our own signs—the hell of the Holocaust or the hell of nuclear war, the agonizing struggle for justice and the muted cries of the hungry—make no Christian sense unless their context is the age-old story of salvation, God's dealings with His people through every captivity and every exodus. No spoken word without God's written word.

II

Second, a look back into the distant past, to see how one rather well-defined group of preachers were formed by the word. I mean the Fathers of the Church, those ecclesiastical writers of the first six or seven centuries who were distinguished for orthodoxy of doctrine and holiness of life, and have therefore been approved by the Church as witnesses to its faith.[5] These men saw themselves, in Campenhausen's words, "as trained, enlightened interpreters of the Bible, which contains God's saving revelation."[6] A popular current of contemporary thought would have us believe that these writers have little or nothing to offer the 20th century in the realm of the Bible, that their passion for the allegorical and their poverty in the basic tools of biblical research have made them expendable in this area. A more balanced appraisal of the patristic contribution to the Christian understanding of the Bible might well begin with the praise of Pius XII in the encyclical *Divino afflante Spiritu*. Despite inferiority in secular learning and in knowledge of languages, the Fathers still had a God-given gift, "a delightful insight into the things of God and a remarkably keen discernment" which enabled them to penetrate deeply the depths of God's word and bring to light what can help to clarify the doctrine of Christ and assist to sanctity.[7] In somewhat the same vein, but from a different perspective, the first-rate Scripture scholar Pierre Benoit wrote:

> ... We are not merely Westerners; we are moderns, who have passed through the crisis of rationalism and are still imbued with its scientistic positivism. Despite us, in us rational truth has supplanted religious truth. Hence that itch for material precision, that passion for dwelling on the detail of some fact, the while we forget its value as sign—the only thing that ultimately matters. We "strain out the gnat and swallow the camel" (Mt 23:24). This insistence on the critical is useful, but in its subordinate place; it ought not be a myopia which hinders one's view of the horizon. "This must be done, but without leaving the other undone" (Mt 23:23). The sacred writers of old, who saw in everything the problem of God, grasped the inner meaning of history better than we, even though they were not as successful in mastering its exact details. And the Fathers of the Church, Greek and Latin though they were, possessed nevertheless that religious sense which made them go straight to the essential, without being troubled to the same extent by deficiencies that are secondary. It is this feeling for the faith that we must recapture if we too want to understand what the Bible is trying to tell us. Then it will be that many of the false problems will vanish. We shall find in the Bible the truth in its totality, because we shall be searching for it there alone where God put it.[8]

Now I am not advocating a return to the exegetical method of the Fathers, especially the allegorism of the Alexandrians; we have gone beyond it. I am not canonizing their interpretations; they are frequently wild, off the wall—as when they find Christ in every line of Scripture. I am not recommending large-scale priestly plagiarism; it is the rare paragraph that can be transferred bodily from the fourth century to the 20th; our rhetoric, like our people and our problems, is not theirs. I do submit that, for our spirituality and our preaching (they go together, you know), we can with profit appropriate the Fathers' familiarity with Scripture, their love for Scripture, their search for Christ in Scripture, their refusal to cut Scripture up into a set of isolated texts heaven-sent to prove theses, their deep realization that Scripture is God's story of salvation, that

there are depths to Scripture which even the most accomplished exegete will never completely fathom. Their value for the preacher is
a three-pronged principle that bursts forth from the patristic pulpit: It is God's revelation that must be preached; we know this revelation, in unparalleled fashion, from Scripture; and so we should
know Scripture intimately, love it dearly, preach it passionately.
Their preaching, like their theology and their sense of tradition, can
be summed up in four words: Scripture within the Church.

Take Augustine of Hippo,[9] an eloquent preacher who constantly astonished and delighted, though he had a weak voice and
tired quickly. Most of his sermons were more spontaneous than they
seem: delivered first, written down then or afterwards by someone
else. His preparation was prayer or a short meditation. "What he
really did was to improvise on the Bible texts that had just been
read."[10] Nor was orderly construction his forte: "Augustine disre-
garded any need for logical construction and observed only that order which was dictated by circumstances and by his own heart."[11]
He played perpetually on words, punned shamelessly; he was in-
ordinately fond of assonance, alliteration, antitheses. He encouraged reactions from his audience, found applause stimulating,
provocative: "What is there to cheer about? We are still battling with
the problem and you have already started to cheer!"[12] He saw the
sermon as not only education but entertainment: "You must not believe, brothers and sisters, that the Lord intended us to be entirely
without theatrical spectacles of some kind. If there were none here,
would you have come together in this place?"[13]

Now it is not improvisation or disorder that I am commending
to you, unless you are Augustine reincarnate. I do resonate to his
weaving of words, even to his paronomasia; I would love to be in-
terrupted by applause; and I get immoderate pleasure when the
people of God are amused by my pleasantries.

But something far more substantial in Augustine's sermons im-
presses me most. His preaching is essentially biblical in character;
he is proclaiming biblical truth. "As soon as he touches a text it
seems to open up like a flower. And when the text in its turn touches
Augustine, it becomes . . . a stream of living water from the hidden
places of Holy Scripture; for he lives so much in Holy Scripture that
a single associational link suffices to call some unfamiliar word into
life and bring out the sweetness of its meaning."[14] Read his homilies
on each Psalm, on just about each verse of John. You may be
amused or amazed at what he gets out of a Psalm or reads into the
Gospel; you will be touched by the way Old Testament and New

have shaped him. His exposition of the Sermon on the Mount, Pelikan concludes, "shows Augustine as a master of biblical preaching, a converted rhetor who had learned from the living Word that rhetoric could be a snare, but who brought his rhetorical gifts to the service of that Word."[15]

The Donatist Tyconius called the Bible an immeasurable forest of prophecy. Augustine "believed that this forest rustled with one single truth and that every leaf whispered a prophecy for him who knew how to listen. In all its treetops, he said, there rustled but the single word—the Word."[16] The Bible is at once full of riddles and very simple, accessible to all. And in Augustine's theory of knowledge, no man or woman really instructs another; the real teacher is God. And so he planted the word of God from God's word and let God make the twig bear fruit, the leaf burst forth.

On the Greek side, take John Chrysostom. Chrysostom is not his name; it is a description that has replaced his name since the sixth century: "the man with the golden mouth." The 18 large volumes of his works in Migne (MG 47–64) are for the most part sermons. The remarkable purity of his language, the style the classical scholar Wilamowitz-Moellendorff called "the harmonious expression of an Attic soul," and his startlingly direct, down-to-earth applications can make us forget that most of his sermons are exegetical homilies on the Old and New Testaments. An amazing aggregation. You find 76 homilies on Genesis, sermons on 58 selected Psalms, 90 on Matthew, 88 on John, 59 on Acts. Almost half of his homilies are on Pauline epistles, for no one fired his eloquence more than Paul: 32 on Romans, 48 on 1 Corinthians and 33 on 2 Corinthians, a series on Galatians, 24 homilies on Ephesians, 15 on Philippians, 12 on Colossians, 11 on 1 Thessalonians and 5 on 2 Thessalonians, 18 on 1 Timothy and 10 on 2 Timothy, 6 on Titus, 3 on Philemon, 34 on Hebrews.[17] The homilies home in on the literal sense; they invariably extract a spiritual message; and they confront the congregation where the people actually live. Chrysostom can do all this because yesterday's Scripture and today's issues are part and parcel of him, are inextricably intertwined in the one man who is at once preacher and pastor, exegete and shepherd.

III

So far so good: Scripture should form the preacher, and Scripture has formed preachers. The most urgent question remains:

How might Scripture form the preacher today? How do you go about it?

Let me begin with a proposition that at first glance is discouraging. A remarkably articulate Lutheran preacher, Joseph Sittler, published a little book almost two decades ago with the expressive title *The Anguish of Preaching*.[18] Speaking of the preacher as the appointed voice of a community that "came into existence speaking, confessing, praising, reporting," of a community that "continues" and that "continues doing those same things," Sittler goes on to say:

> Disciplines correlative to preaching can be taught, but preaching as an act of witness cannot be taught. Biblical introduction, training in languages, methods of exegesis, cultural and other historical data that illuminate the texts of the Scriptures— these matters can be refined and transmitted in teaching. But preaching itself, the creative symbiosis within which intersects [*sic*] numberless facts, experiences, insights, felt duties of pastoral obligation toward a specific congregation, the interior existence of the preacher himself, this particular man as he seeks for right utterance of an incommunicable and non-shareable quality of being and thought—this cannot be taught. It is, nevertheless, commanded—and not only by custom of the church.[19]

"Preaching as an act of witness cannot be taught." After a decade of being taught homiletics and four decades of homilizing, I tend to agree. I can indeed help you in ways that are not insignificant. I can alert you to useful commentaries such as Brown on John, Fitzmyer on Luke, McKenzie on Second Isaiah. I can urge you to deepen your understanding of theological themes highly pertinent to preaching: Read Dulles on the Church, Cooke on ministry and sacraments, Schillebeeckx and Sobrino on today's Christ, Mc-Cormick on bioethics in a brave new world. I can correct your composition, retool your rhetoric, propel you to project, perhaps even lessen your lisp. All these are important, especially in a context where the long-suffering laity are intolerant of the trivia we dish out, the constipation of thought amid a diarrhea of words, are surprised or scandalized by a dismal style and a vapid vocabulary unworthy of the word we claim to proclaim, and are puzzled by our ability to declaim about the divine without a shred of feeling or emotion.

All true; and still it remains true that "preaching as an act of witness cannot be taught." For here we confront what Sittler called "the interior existence of the preacher himself, this particular man as he seeks for right utterance of an incommunicable and non-shareable quality of being and thought." Here, I suggest, it is the living Christ who is our teacher; more comprehensively, the Father through Christ in the Spirit.

At first blush, frightening; on second thought, encouraging. For it fits fascinatingly into my thesis: It is God's word that forms the preacher. Not exclusively, but in large measure and at the roots. Encouraging because it takes some of the pressure off our native oratorical skills and deficiencies. Preaching is not, in the first instance, a matter of posture and gesture, of assonance and resonance. It is primarily a question of the person—the person who precedes the preacher, the person who *is* the preacher. It is not first the homily that the word must fashion; it is the homilist. Shaped by the word, you are a different person. Different preacher because different person.

But how? God's written word must take hold of you as His spoken word took hold of Isaiah and Jeremiah, of Ezekiel and Hosea; as the spoken word of Christ mesmerized Matthew and Magdalene, captured Simon Peter and the Samaritan woman.

But how? Basically, the word you study has to be the word you pray, and the word you pray the word you live. You recall, I'm sure, how Luther's study of Scripture between 1513 and 1517—the Psalms and Romans, Galatians and Hebrews—transformed his theology.[20] But not his theology alone—his life and his preaching. And still he could recognize and regret how inadequate sheer scholarship soon proves itself. At the close of his Christmas sermon in 1522 he cried out despairingly:

> O that God should desire that my interpretation and that of all teachers should disappear, and each Christian should come straight to the scripture alone and to the pure word of God! You see from this babbling of mine the immeasurable difference between the word of God and all human words, and how no man can adequately reach and explain a single word of God with all his words. It is an eternal word, and must be understood and contemplated with a quiet mind. . . . No one else can understand except a mind that contemplates in silence. For anyone who could achieve this without commentary or interpretation, my commentaries and those of everyone else would not only be of no use, but merely a hindrance. Go to the Bible itself, dear Christians, and let my expositions and those of all scholars be no more than a tool with which to build aright, so that we can understand, taste and abide in the simple and pure word of God; for God dwells alone in Zion.[21]

But even contemplation of God's word was not enough for Luther's theology, not sufficient for his preaching. To become a theologian worthy of the name—and, Luther would surely add, a preacher worthy of that name—you must have *experience* of sin and grace, of life and death. "Consequently Luther's teaching on justification bears the marks of profound, often anguished, moments of personal involvement with deep feeling. Sin and guilt are terrifying in this world of thought, grace and forgiveness liberating and full of delight."[22]

I submit that Luther offers a rich model for the way God's word should shape "the interior existence of the preacher": quiet contemplation of the word in the context of serious study and profound experience. A word on each of the three facets.

For most of us, there is no substitute for *study* of the word. I know that my dear forebear Ignatius Loyola had a single illumination—of God One and Three, the world's fashioning, and the bodying forth of the Son—that outstripped, by his own admission, all he learned or was given by God in 62 years. But *I* cannot count on such a self-manifestation of God. I must have recourse to the source God invented for all of us, the self-disclosure that is His written word. It exists not to while away some disenchanted evening, but to transform me, to turn me inside out, to fashion a new creature. If that is so, then the more I know about it and the deeper I plunge into its depths, the more likely I am to experience its incomparable power.

It's a strange situation, isn't it? The Catholic preacher has at his beck and call the single most significant book in the history of humankind, the most revealing story of human existence, a book we profess to be God's word. And yet, over 32 years I've seen swarms of seminarians study Scripture as simply another course to be passed: This is not where the action is. Unnumbered priests in parish ministry will not touch a commentary: It's just too tough; it doesn't speak to the people, to the ditchdigger and the "bag lady"; there's enough information in some prepackaged "homily hints."

I have news for you, bad news. For all their immediate and practical value, for all their ability to rescue the storm-tossed pastor, "homily hints" are not likely to reshape your spirit, to mold the core of your being. Granted, study alone will not so shape you; but organized, disciplined, methodical searching is a splendid beginning. If nothing else, it tells God and your people that you take Him seriously, take Him "at His word."

Still, Luther was on target: Scholarly tomes and commentaries are "no more than a tool with which to build aright, so that we can

understand, taste and abide in the simple and pure word of God."
The word we study calls for *contemplation:* It "must be contemplated
with a quiet mind." The Bible is not Blackstone's *Commentaries* or
Einstein's theory of relativity; it is a book to be prayed. Not only does
it inform the intellect; it ought to form the whole person. This is
impossible in a classroom; it demands a prie-dieu, forces you to your
knees.

What I am commending to the preacher is a spirituality that is
biblically based—and expressly so. Not simply the *study* of Old and
New Testament spirituality, though this can base the broader life of
the spirit. Rather, a reverent immersion in Scripture such that intelligence is subservient to love. We Christians do fairly well with the
Gospels. My own spirituality continues to be shaped by the Spiritual
Exercises of St. Ignatius, where three of the four Weeks are con-
templations on a living, dying, rising Christ. Nor am I singular in
this regard. Your inner life is surely fed more nutritiously by the
story of Jesus than by any other aliment. This is the way it should
be, and I can only slap your spiritual rump in macho encourage-
ment: Keep it up, baby!

One problem here: Such contemplation is restrictive. To limit
myself to the Gospels, or the Gospels and Chrysostom's beloved
Paul, is like reading only the end of a mystery, the last chapter of
an Agatha Christie. God's story and mine, God's love for the human
family, is much broader. The Christian, particularly the Christian
preacher, ought to be nourished by all that has gone before: by a
God who walked with Adam in the cool of evening and with His
people through the Red Sea; by a God who was Father and Savior
and Lover long before His Son took our flesh; by singers of psalms
and prophets of doom and deliverance; by a special people's journeying to God through faith and infidelity, through wisdom and
purification.[23] Forget not the advice of Paul to Timothy: "As for
you, continue in what you have learned and have firmly believed,
knowing from whom you learned it and how from childhood you
have been acquainted with the sacred writings [the books of the Old
Testament] which are able to instruct you for salvation through
faith in Christ Jesus. *All* Scripture [again, the Old Testament] is inspired by God and profitable for teaching, for reproof, for correction, and for training in righteousness, that the man of God may be
complete, equipped for every good work" (2 Tim 3:14–17).

Good indeed, but not yet enough. The contemplation which
complements study must itself be completed. How? By *experience.* I
mean very specific experiences, analogous to Luther's experience

of sin and grace, of life and death. Let me concretize this with one powerful example: Jeremiah. I borrow it from an essay in biblical spirituality by Carroll Stuhlmueller.[24]

It is the search for vocation in Jeremiah. What developed from that search is a theology of vocation that became the classical biblical model. The Suffering Servant (Isa 49), John the Baptist (Lk 1), Paul (Gal 1:15–16), and Jesus himself appealed in varied ways to Jeremiah's soul-searching attempt to appreciate the meaning of God's call. It is a theology that "exploded from his heart . . . seemingly without structure or order," less a theology than a ferment.

Throughout his long ministry Jeremiah was constantly questing for the meaning of his vocation. The first six years of his preaching (627/626–621 B.C.) were exciting. He was responding to an apostolic opportunity. On the one hand, Babylon's declaration of independence meant a resurgence of Babylonian deities and Babylonian religion; on the other hand, independence for Judah meant a fresh enthusiasm for the God of Israel. High were Jeremiah's hopes and ideals; the future was rich in possibility. Success came speedily; and such success, Jeremiah reasoned, surely proved that God had called him, demonstrated beyond doubt what his vocation should be.

Then ensued a series of reversals. In 621 young King Josiah and some cronies began to *impose* reform on the people. It was so contradictory to Jeremiah's "new covenant" written on the heart, expressing itself spontaneously in an interior knowledge of the Lord (Jer 31:31–34). Then even the dictatorial reform ground to a halt. Now commenced the second period of Jeremiah's life, the "long trek across the dreary plateau of failures." The reign of Jehoiakim, puppet of the Egyptians and then of the Babylonians, was the prophet's way of the cross. Time and again he disputed with God: "You are just, O Lord. . . . Why does the way of the wicked prosper?" (Jer 12:1). To be where God was to be found, he had to search into darkness. And God's answer, when it came, was discouraging: Things will get worse before they get better. Only as he walked deeper and deeper into the shadows of his faith, sustained only by the conviction that God must be there, did the very concept of his vocation come to be increasingly purified. Only at the end of his life could he tell with fair clarity what his calling meant. Only after repeated failure and frustration did he realize that his plans for God were not necessarily God's plan for him. His own dreams, dreams for God, had to crumble before he could lose himself totally in God. Stuhlmueller writes with insight:

At the end of his life when he wrote chapter 1, Jeremiah said that his vocation was to be a prophet to the nations, a prophet to the Gentiles. Jeremiah never was a prophet to the nations. Jeremiah died with that hope which he left to the next generation, picked up by the Suffering Servant and by St. Paul. Jeremiah's vocation was to be the carrier of hopes to the next generation.[25]

The point of this seeming excursion into Jeremiah land? If I, this preacher, am to be formed or reformed to the depths of my existence by God's word, study of Scripture is insufficient, and not just any contemplation will do. Scripture must speak to my experience, my experience to it—an endless oscillation, rhythm, dialogue. Jeremiah is not merely a nifty story from an alien past. Jeremiah is not primarily a rich source for quotable quotes: "Before I formed you in the womb I knew you" (1:5); "I have loved you with an everlasting love" (31:3). Jeremiah is I; I am Jeremiah. Oh, not in every smallest detail; but surely at the level of their deep significance our experiences run parallel. All my life long I too must search for the more profound meaning of what I started out to do; only at the end may I be able to write that meaning.

Old Testament? It is perennially new, ceaselessly fresh—if I pray it. Need I add that contemplation of Christ, this kind of contemplation, contemplation-*cum*-experience, should prove even more formative of the Christian homilist, of the Christian person? If the word that is Scripture is to take flesh in us, the Word that is Christ must be enfleshed in us. I suspect that, in the last analysis, my hope for homilists can be summed up in St. Paul's affecting cry to the Christians of Galatia: "My little children, with whom I am again in travail until Christ be formed in you!" (Gal 4:19). Until Christ be formed in you. . . .

7

IN SEASON AND OUT OF SEASON
What Shall I Preach About?

A number of times over the years, priests have put to me a poignant question: What should I preach about? In less experienced days I thought this a frivolous, if not ridiculous, question. With all the riches of God's revelation, with centuries of theological and spiritual reflection on God's wondrous works in the story of salvation, with two millennia of Church history, of holiness and sin, can a preacher be at a loss for sermon material? Whatever was your seminary all about? But gradually I realized that, for all its truth, such a response is terribly vague, much too broad. The crunch comes when I am faced with specific scriptural readings. What should I do when confronted with this or that excerpt from Ezekiel, this or that passage from Paul, this or that episode in John?

This chapter develops just one approach—an approach I have found highly helpful and have used extensively. I call it the problem approach. In a particular reading or set of readings, I look for a challenge. I find myself confronted by a human and Christian problem, a perplexing question. As I read the texts, I do not know the answer; I may not know the answer when I finish the homily! But it is precisely this problem that racks my preparation; it stretches my mind, harasses my heart. To move from the abstract to the concrete, let me plunge into the Church's year, sketch a dozen challenges, and indicate how I have actually dealt with them.[1]

I

First problem: Advent.[2] One word sums up Advent: waiting. From beginning to end, the liturgy revolves round a tireless refrain: Be ready and waiting. But what are you waiting for? The liturgy trumpets it ceaselessly: You should be waiting for the Lord, for the coming of a saving Christ: "Your God will come and save you" (Isa 35:4).

But isn't this a form of playacting? Isn't this sheer make-believe? After all, the Son of God actually did touch our earth in Bethlehem; God-made-man is present in the liturgical community, is sacramentally present on the altar; he gives himself to us as food; day in and day out he dwells within our whole person. He has come; he is here; he lives with us and within us. What is there to wait for? Apparently only his coming on clouds at the end of time!

The solution lies not in the what but the how. How are you waiting for the Lord? Take three different ways of waiting: a poor old fellow on a park bench; a college student in an airport before Christmas; a pregnant woman in a maternity ward. All three are waiting, but with profound differences. The old fellow doesn't expect very much; he'll be happy if someone, anyone, comes along—someone to talk to, make the hours pass, till it's time to return to a lonely cold-water flat. The student at the airport is excited; the plane *means* something. It's all the difference between school and home, between being stranded on a cold campus and being warmed in love by family or by a Caribbean sun. The mother-to-be: excitement there too, anticipation, tension. But two facts are uncommonly true here. First, "he who is to come" has been there all along—but a hidden presence, at times a bit unreal. At a certain moment the child actually transpires, comes to light, is held in loving arms. Second, a remarkable co-operation: Something is happening to her *and* she is helping to make it happen. Nine months ago it began to happen; now, praying, gasping, pushing, sweating, bleeding, she brings it to completion.

So with Advent. Not the boredom of a park bench; not only the anticipation of an airport; rather, a bringing to light. Christ is actually within you, but perhaps more like an embryo, a fetus. An embryo: You don't experience him. A fetus: more uncomfortable than exhilarating. Advent is a form of parturition; its function is to bring a living Lord to life in your living. Christmas for you is not a given day, December 25; Christmas is when the Child actually transpires, comes to light, is held in your loving embrace, is real to you. But you have to make him real. You too have to pray and gasp, push and sweat and bleed. How? One down-to-earth way: if the faith you speak is a justice you do. Feed the hungry and slake the thirsty, bring love to the unloved, hope to the hopeless; the Christ you comfort is the same Christ who will awaken in you.

II

Second problem: Christmas.[3] I find a paradox in Christmas; some would call it a flat contradiction. One side of the paradox was sung by Christ's angels, his messengers, the midnight of his birth: "On earth peace among men and women with whom [God] is pleased" (Lk 2:14). *Peace*. The other side of the paradox was preached 30 years later by Christ himself: "Do you think that I have come to give peace on earth? No, I tell you, but rather division"— dissension, disunity (Lk 12:51). *Division*. Even the liturgy points up the paradox. On Jesus' birthday all is peace: a child and his mother, drowsy shepherds, caroling angels, kings bent low in adoration. But the very next day the Church sheds the white vestments of peace for robes blood-red. Red for Stephen stoned for Christ; red for the Innocents baptized by Herod in blood; red for Becket murdered in a cathedral; and all but red for the apostle John.

How make sense of the paradox? One way: What does Christmas peace mean? The peace the angels sang is not simply some uneasy truce, a cease-fire among warring nations. And the traditional "men of good will" are not rational animals bubbling over with some manner of good cheer. The peace sung from heaven means "God's peace to God's friends." It is, before all else, peace between the individual and God. It is John the Evangelist's accents of wonder: "All who received him . . . [the Word-made-flesh] empowered to become children of God" (Jn 1:12). The peace the angels sang has rarely been summed up more pithily than by Paul: "He (Christ) is our peace" (Eph 2:14). *There* is the peace no human being can take from you, no human being save yourself: Christ *is* your peace. If, like the Innocents, you can be mistaken for Christ, if you are intimately one with God, then an incomparable peace is yours.

But if in likeness to Christ there is peace, in Christlikeness there is the sword as well. Because they looked like Jesus, the Innocents suffered and died. And the Herods of this world are on the loose again. Human beings are still being hounded, will always be hounded, if they look like Jesus. From the millions of Christians who perished under Hitler's steel boot, through the uncounted faithful who writhe beneath a hammer and sickle, to a Romero murdered in his own cathedral—to live the Christlife is to face an endless wave of hostility and hate. Nor is the sword only on the outside. Believing in Christ, hoping in him, loving him above all else—impossible without anguish of mind and heart. You do not have to pay the price of Christlike living. But you cannot refuse the Christian sword without losing the Christmas peace. You must take the whole paradox, or none of it. If you are to look like Jesus, you may not rest content with the joy thereof; you must bear the bitterness as well.

III

Third problem: Lent.[4] Is Lent for laughing or for crying? We have been brought up to see it as a season of sadness; and yet the first Preface for Lent proclaims "this joyful season." The problem reaches new heights when Holy Week begins. We have two names for that Sunday: Palm Sunday and Passion Sunday. In the procession we pray "Today we honor Christ our triumphant King," but in the Mass we pray "You have given the human race Christ our Savior as a model of humility." In the procession we sing "Hosanna to the King," but in the Responsorial Psalm we sing "My God, my God, why have you abandoned me?" The reading from Paul reminds us that Jesus "emptied himself . . . became obedient unto death," then proclaims that "every tongue should confess that Jesus Christ is Lord" (Phil 2:7–8, 11). The Gospel of the procession cries "Behold, your King comes to you" (Mt 21:5), but the Gospel of the Mass ends "Jesus uttered a loud cry and breathed his last" (Mk 15:37).

The paradox raises two questions: (1) What are we doing in the Lenten liturgy? (2) How should what we are doing in the liturgy affect the rest of our lives? A basic problem is a pervasive misunderstanding of the liturgy. As I grew up, we reproduced in Lent, we re-presented, we lived again the sufferings of Christ, his dying. Why? So that on Easter we could celebrate his rising. Today tragedy, tomorrow triumph. Lent, dying; Easter, rising. Liturgical nonsense. Lent is no more a preparation for the resurrection of Jesus than Advent is a preparation for the birth of Jesus. This is to emphasize the history at the expense of the mystery. There is indeed a history, a chronology: from desert to cross to resurrection. But Lent gets its liturgical meaning from Easter. And what is Easter? Easter is the paschal mystery, and the paschal mystery is a duality:

the dying/rising of Jesus. And the fact is, he has already died and risen; we dare not pretend that he has not. Lent is not the dying of Jesus, Easter his rising. The whole of Lent is a progressively more intense initiation into the paschal mystery, into the twin reality of Jesus dead and risen. Not palms *or* passion; both. Not triumph *or* tragedy; triumph *in* tragedy. Not a dying *or* a rising Christ; a dying/ rising Christ. If we stop at the history, we miss the mystery.

What does Lent say to Christian experience, to our day-to-day living? One obvious relation: The shape of my life should be a cease- less dying/rising. Our own journeying to Jerusalem goes to life through death, and death gives life not only when we breathe our last, but all through our Christian existence. In this journey to life, we die in two ways. Death comes to us from sin; and so our rising to life is a constant dying to the sinfulness in us—not something neg- ative, but a never-ending turning to Christ. And death comes to us from the very shape of the human journey: We have to let go of where we've been. Essential to the Christian journey is a self-emp- tying more or less like Christ's own emptying. Time and again, from womb to tomb, you have to let go. And to let go is to die a little. It's risky, this letting go of yesterday, if only because you cannot be cer- tain where it will lead. But only by reaching out into a shadowed future can you *grow* into Christ, come to be increasingly conformed to his dying/rising. Only by dying, not only to sin but to yourself, can you come fully to life.

IV

Fourth problem: Holy Thursday.[5] The Eucharist is so much a part of our daily or Sunday lives that it risks turning stale. How give it new life? I learned vividly from a published meditation of a French Jesuit, who saw in the Last Supper three challenges to our Lord's love, three problems that confronted him.

Problem 1: He had to go, and he wanted to stay. He had to leave us: It was his Father's will. And yet he wanted to stay with us: Never had he loved his own so intensely as in that hour. Two loves in con- flict. Which would yield? Neither. Jesus cut through the problem with a solution that shocked the good folk of Capernaum. He did go and he did stay, left us and remained with us. He took from us the God-man as Palestine saw him with the eyes of the body; he left with us the same God-man, whom you and I see with the eyes of our faith. The solution? The *Real Presence*. He is present in the Blessed

Sacrament, and his presence is real. "This is my body. . . . This is my blood" (Mt 26:26, 28).

Problem 2: the urgency of love and the tragedy of love. Love's urgency? To give till you can give no more, to lay down even life for the beloved. And Jesus would gladly have died a thousand deaths for us, would gladly have died daily. Love's tragedy? Love cannot die daily, die a thousand times. As Paul put it, "Christ, having risen from the dead, dies no more" (Rom 6:9). Again, a solution that has shocked the ages. Of course Jesus can die but once; but what a revenge he invents for that unsatisfied desire! Each hour of each day, all over the world, a priest brings down on an altar the Victim of Calvary. Not that he dies again; but the Christ who rests on that altar is the same Christ, wounds and all, who died once for all on the cross. The solution? The *Mass*. "Do this in remembrance of me" (Lk 22:19).

Problem 3: the dream of love and the law of Providence. Love's dream? Union—perfect, unending, sensible and sensed, face to face and heart to heart. The law of Providence? Such union is reserved for heaven; it *is* heaven; and Providence will not permit even Jesus to put heaven on earth. The solution? Shockingly simple. He gives himself, but beneath a veil; unites himself, but without making himself felt; a passing thing, but wonderfully real and a daily thing; not heaven, but awfully close. The solution? *Communion*. "Take and eat. . . . Drink of this" (Mt 26:26–27).

V

Fifth problem: Easter.[6] Once more, how avoid the commonplace, the expected, the uninspiring? How keep from parroting "Jesus rose from the dead, and that proves we too will rise"? Perhaps a closer look at "risen Christ, risen Christian"?

What does "risen Christ" say to me? A physical fact indeed: The Jesus who died came alive. He *is* alive. Not merely in my memory; far more alive than you or I. Not only in His eternal Godness, but in the flesh that Magdalene clung to, the wounds he invited Thomas to examine, the humanity he took once and for ever from Mary. But the sheer physical fact takes its profound meaning from two monosyllables: *for me*. He "loved me," Paul proclaims (Gal 2:20). Not that something lovable in my irresistible personality called out to him; it is *his* love that makes me lovable. Why me? The why is buried deep in the mystery that is God—a God who not only loves but *is* Love.

What does "risen Christian" say to me? To begin with, Paul's "If you have been raised with Christ, seek the things that are above" (Col 3:1). What is Paul talking about? My baptism has introduced me "into Christ Jesus" (Rom 6:3); at this moment I am living my life in union with him. "It is no longer I who live, but Christ who lives in me" (Gal 2:20). The risen Christ who lives in me makes possible a risen faith, a risen hope, a risen love. These are some of "the things that are above."

But, at the risk of offending Paul, I would add: "If you have been raised with Christ, seek the things that are below." Oh, not "what is earthly in you: immorality, impurity, passion, evil desire, and covetousness . . . anger, wrath, malice, slander, and foul talk from your mouth" (Col 3:2, 5–8). But to be raised with Christ means, paradoxically, that the risen Christian still lives, for now, on Calvary. I continue to walk my own way of the cross, and I stand beneath countless crosses to which other Christs are fixed with their own nails. This is risen religion. This is St. Paul's "one body" of Christ with many members (cf. 1 Cor 12:11 ff.), where "if one member suffers, all suffer together" (v. 26).

Gathered round the table on which the risen Christ will rest, here is a splendid spot to begin seeking the things that are below. Here we minister to one another, awesomely aware that each of us is a *wounded* healer—risen indeed with Christ, but still frightfully flawed, needing another's touch, another's "Peace!" In healing touch with one another, we can move out from church or chapel— not to Lima or Lesotho, not dreamily to Mother Teresa's Calcutta or Father Ritter's Times Square, but to the acres on which we dance so lightly. For me personally, it is the red-brick buildings that house 80 of my Jesuit brothers, men with gethsemanes I skirt around; a hospital several hundred yards away, several hundred beds, each a beam off Calvary's wood; in-between those two complexes, thousands of youthful Christ figures, all the high spirits and low, all the manics and depressives, all the sin and sanctity, all the love and lust, all the chapel-visiting and pub-crawling that create a college campus. What part do I play in all this, what figure do I project? The self-righteous Pharisee or the compassionate Christ? Or . . . just nothing?

The risen Christ destroyed distance. He made himself present: to devoted Magdalene and doubting Thomas, to two disheartened disciples on the way to Emmaus and seven hungry apostles for a seafood breakfast. And the risen Christian? Too often our distances are not geographic—Cameroon or Kalamazoo; our distances are of our own making. Too often (I've said it again and again) we seek out people the way we select a beer: good body and lots of froth.

Risen with Christ? Then seek the things that are below—where Christ is still on his cross.

VI

Sixth problem: God's providence.[7] It confronts us unexpectedly on the Eighth Sunday of the Year, cycle A. You remember the Gospel (Mt 6:24–34), sheer poetry from Jesus on the Mount. Don't be anxious about food or drink or clothing. Look at the birds of the air: God feeds them. Look at the lilies of the field: God clothes them more gloriously than Solomon. Doesn't He love you far more than the sparrow or the flower? What to eat or drink or wear—why, this is what unbelievers worry about. Seek God first, and all this will be yours as well.

The passage raises a terribly real problem. If Jesus had only said "Don't worry about your basic needs, about food and clothes. Why not? Because worrying about them won't do any good. It will merely irritate your colon, trigger your hiatal hernia, give you heartburn or a headache." Psychologists would nod sagely; non-Christians would see how sensible our Jesus is. But Jesus says more: "Trust in God, make me your only master, and you won't have to worry; you'll get everything you need." And our experience rebels: no, not true! Some get what they need and some don't; you cannot guarantee it. Did Jesus know what he was talking about?

Much mystery here, of course. We are speaking of God, of Mystery in person. The homilist cannot dissipate all the clouds; not his to crack the code of earthly evil. What *I* do is suggest one way of looking at this Gospel that may prove of profit. It means moving back 19 centuries, to the social situation of the early Christians. Then you had relatively small communities, people who cared. Not that they never argued, enjoyed perpetual peace. Still, most were conscious of being a community, the body of the risen Christ. And those who lived the Christian life, who put their trust in God, did experience what Jesus promised: They had enough to eat, to drink; they had clothes on their backs. The community saw to that (cf. Acts 4:34–35).

What I am suggesting is that Jesus was not laying the whole burden on his Father: You set your heart on God, and God will personally feed you. In principle, the God who rained manna on the

Israelites in the desert can ply the poor with sirloin strip and ho-
mogenized milk. In practice, chances are He leaves that to His people, to us (cf. Jas 2:14–17). So then, when I see the homeless in
Thailand and our land, when I watch TV's "Save the Children" programs, when I see bloated bellies and staring eyes, might it not be
time to stop asking questions about a God whose providence we fail
to fathom, and turn my thoughts to the Christian community that
is not really Christian or a community unless it cares? We may argue
till doomsday about God and the problem of evil, but philosophy
should not be a cop-out from the compassion that calls us to play
Christ to our crucified brothers and sisters.

VII

Seventh problem: riches.[8] On the 28th Sunday of the Year,
cycle B, it would be easier to preach on Wisdom 7:7–11, or focus on
the first half of the Gospel (Mk 10:17–30), the rich fellow Jesus
looked on and *loved*. But the crucial sentence has to be faced: "It is
easier for a camel to go through the eye of a needle than for a rich
man to enter the kingdom of God" (v. 25).

Here some biblical background can help the homilist. Why
were the disciples "amazed," "exceedingly astonished" (vv. 24, 26),
at Jesus' words? In part because they were heirs to a powerful Jewish
tradition: Wealth was a sign of God's favor. Not the only tradition,
but a strong one. If you feared God, really loved Him, you would
surely be blessed with the good things of the earth (cf. Ps 34:9–10).

What did Jesus say to that revered tradition? He reversed it
rudely, brutally. Not only did he have "nowhere to lay his head" (Mt
8:20; Lk 9:58); not only did he live off the hospitality of others; he
condemned wealth in harsh terms. It is to the poor that the kingdom
belongs. Ponder some parables: the rich fool (Lk 12:16–21), the rich
man who went to hell (Lk 16:19–31). "Anyone who does not bid
farewell to all he has cannot be a disciple of mine" (Lk 14:33).

Raw language indeed. But there is another side to it. As far as
we know, Jesus never told Lazarus and his sisters to give up all they
had, did not announce to Nicodemus and Joseph of Arimathea that
they were excluded from the kingdom. Especially, remember little
Zacchaeus down from his perch on a tree: "Behold, I give to the
poor *half* of my goods" (Lk 19:8). Jesus' reaction? "Today salvation
has come to this house" (v. 9). Half. . . .

Will the real Jesus please stand up? I fear that Jesus is more

complex than the TV preachers suspect. There is the radical Jesus
and the moderate Jesus—and the liturgy is not the place to har-
monize the paradox, to synthesize Jesus' theology of wealth. Better
to suggest that the very paradox that baffles the Scripture scholar
can speak eloquently to us little folk. On the one hand, absolutely
nothing should take precedence over Christ in my life. But history,
my history, tells me there is a peril in any possession—from a child's
"raggedy Ann" to the power of a president or pastor. The peril?
Simply that it's mine, and it can become the center of my existence,
organize my life, manipulate me, strangle me. Then it is that I do
not hear Christ's invitation or his command: to give it all up or only
half, to care and to share, to let go. The radical Jesus poses a perennial question: What rules my life—the camel or the kingdom?

On the other hand, the moderate Jesus fixes my eye on something splendidly positive: the gift I have in anything I possess.
Whatever is mine is ultimately God's gift. But a gift of God is not
given to be clutched; it is given to be given. Therein lie its Christian
possibilities. Millions or the widow's mite, intelligence or power,
beauty or wisdom, faith and hope and love, gentleness and compassion—the moderate Jesus tells you to use them as he invites or
commands. To some: Give all you have to the poor and follow me
naked. To others: Share what you possess; use it for your brothers
and sisters. Employ your power for peace, your wisdom to reconcile, your knowledge to open horizons, your compassion to heal,
your hope to destroy despair, your very weakness to give strength.
Remember, your most precious possession is yourself. Give it away
. . . lavishly.

To do that, you dare not stare at the eye of the needle, trying
to get your personal camel through it; you may despair. Look at our
Lord. How can you reconcile your possessions with God's command
to let go? "With men and women," Jesus noted, "it is impossible, but
not with God; for all things are possible with God" (Mk 10:27).

VIII

Eighth problem: the beatitudes and the woes.[9] In a sense, this
is kin to the problem of riches, but more extensive still. Blessed: You
are fortunate if you are poor or hungry, saddened or slandered.
Woe: You are unfortunate if you are rich or sated, joy-filled or ap-
plauded. Now why did Jesus promise the kingdom to the former,
the disadvantaged? Not because they were holier, better disposed,

more devoted to God than the prosperous; some were not. Jesus
does not idealize poverty, glorify hunger, canonize tears. In the beatitudes Jesus tells us something about *God*.

The ancient East expected its kings to be protectors of the poor
and oppressed. Not because these were better citizens than the rest,
but because a king would not be a genuine king if he did not show
special concern for the oppressed. In this, the earthly king was mod-
eled on God. For Israel, Yahweh was protector of the poor, de-
fender of the defenseless, not because they were more pious or
trusted in Him alone, but because God owed it to His justice to bring
about a just kingdom.

In the beatitudes, therefore, we have a theology not of human
poverty but of divine justice. The good news is "The kingdom of
God is at hand" (Mk 1:15). In Jesus we glimpse the real nature of
divine kingship, a kingship that seeks not to dominate but to save—
and to save in the first instance those on whom the consequences of
sin weigh most heavily. The Christian stress was indeed to change.
Christians would soon fix their eyes not on God's conduct in estab-
lishing His kingdom, but on our conduct if we are to share in that
kingdom. In this perspective the poor are privileged not by their
oppression but by the qualities of soul that make them profoundly
religious and merit for them the recompense to come. This is suggested by the fourth of Luke's beatitudes: Blessed are you when you
suffer *for the sake of Christ* (cf. Lk 6:22–23).

With that as background, I try to rephrase Luke's beatitudes
for today's Christians. To the 60 million poor in America, to the half
billion starving at this moment, to those who cannot laugh, dare I
say "Blessed are you"? In some ways, yes. Blessed are you because
Christ has a special place in his heart for the oppressed; because
somehow the blessings of God's kingdom will be yours; because
sometime you will laugh and leap for joy. Blessed are you because
now God alone can fill your emptiness. Blessed are you because you
prick my conscience, reveal to me my poverty in God's eyes. Blessed
are you because you are living the crucified Christ I constantly
avoid.

Then I try to turn the woes around. Blessed are you rich—rich
in money or power, in talent or time—because you can do so much
to lift the yoke of the oppressed. But blessed only if you have the
mind of Christ. Only if you realize that you are stewards, that whatever you have you hold in trust—from God for His images. Only if
you are not enslaved to your riches, are ready to lose all you have
for the sake of Christ, for your sisters and brothers.

Blessed are you who are full now, because you are strong enough to feed the hungry. But blessed only if you have the mind of Christ, the mind of the hungry. Only if you do not take your food for granted. Only if you are uncomfortable as long as one brother or sister cries in vain for bread or justice or love. Only if you experience your own profound emptiness—how desperately you need the hungry, how far you still are from God.

Blessed are you who laugh now, because you can bring the joy of Christ to those whose days are woven of tears. But blessed only if you can laugh at yourselves, if human living doesn't revolve around you and your needs, if you delight in all God's creation. Only if laughter means that you let go—let go of all that shackles you to yesterday, imprisons you in your small selves.

IX

Ninth problem: forgiveness.[10] It is the 24th Sunday of the Year, cycle A, and the Gospel is the parable of the Unforgiving Debtor (Mt 18:21–35). My homily begins with the extraordinary meeting, in Rome's Rebibbia prison, between Pope John Paul II and his would-be assassin, Mehmet Ali Agca. As the Pope left the cell, he said: "I spoke to him as a brother whom I have pardoned. . . . "

Touching indeed, but John Paul's forgiveness raises agonizing problems. Are there no conditions that affect forgiveness? Can Israel in good conscience reconcile with the PLO as long as the PLO takes responsibility for bombing women and children and is bent on Israel's destruction? Do not we Catholics expect God's forgiveness in the sacrament of reconciliation only if we are sorry for what we have done and promise to change our lives? Does forgiveness mean we waive punishment, return the rapist to the scene of his crime, simply say "Forget it"? If it does, what happens to justice, to the moral order? How can society survive?

One approach to the problem begins with God, because forgiveness begins with God, "merciful and gracious," who "does not deal with us according to our sins" (Ps 103:8, 10). But what does it mean for God to forgive? It means that He changes me—at the very roots of my being. I have a new relationship with God: I am His friend, one with Him, St. Paul's "new creature" (2 Cor 5:17). But only God can forgive like this—where the very forgiveness *is* a change in the other. If that is so, what is left for man and woman?

It is indeed God who changes hearts, but men and women can

be His instruments. Not by shouting "I forgive you" no matter what is happening out there—the life of a child or a nation, the whole moral order, the City of Man and Woman. What can I do? I can, like John the Baptist, "go before the Lord to prepare His ways" (Lk 1:76). This is what the Pope did: He took the first step. Why? So that God might use John Paul's gesture like the "matter" of a sacrament, like the water of baptism or the bread of Eucharist, infuse it with His own power, make it an instrument of His grace.

Similarly for you and me. Even when sheer earthly realism forbids a simplistic "forgive and forget," we are not helpless. We have to make every feasible effort to be present in love to those who hate, ready to reconcile, to offer friendship, and so to be instruments God can use, like bread and water, to soften hearts hardened by hatred, raw with resentment. What gesture one makes in a concrete situation, no homilist can say. But most of us are not asked to do the impossible. Most of us have only to swallow pride, show ourselves a little more loving than the other, make some gesture God can use to change a human heart.

X

Tenth problem: the Second Coming.[11] How might you handle the 33rd Sunday of the Year, especially cycles B and C? Mark 13:24–32 fixes the eyes of the faithful on the end of the world as we know it, on "the Son of man coming in clouds" (v. 26), on the gathering of all the elect. Luke 21:5–19 predicts a desolation that is frightening: wars and quakes, famine and plague, persecution and betrayal, days of distress and grapes of wrath. One approach to such difficult texts is to focus on (1) liturgy, (2) Scripture, (3) ourselves.

First, liturgy. The liturgy is the whole Church celebrating the story of salvation, not only rereading it but re-presenting it, making God's wonderful works effectively present in us. In Advent we relive a whole world's waiting for its Savior. We welcome the Lord Jesus as he comes to us surprisingly in the flesh of an infant. We grow up with him in his three silent decades, expand with him in Nazareth our experience of human living. We walk in his steps through Galilee and Judea, recapture his dying/rising through Lent and Easter. In him we too ascend to the Father; his Spirit descends on each of us who believes. In the months after Pentecost we capture with our ears and experience in our lives the mission of the Church, share its endless effort to grow into Christ, its living in hope for the final coming of its Savior. And now—now we reach the end of the liturgical year. Next week the peak: We will crown Christ king. Today we celebrate the beginning of that end, live in anticipation what will precede the moment when all creation is subjected to Christ, "when he delivers the kingdom to God the Father after destroying every rule and every authority and power" (1 Cor 15:24).

Second, Scripture. Don't be seduced by the Gospel images, distracted by its descriptions. This is the language of apocalyptic; here you have some science-fiction, first-century cosmology; it is not to be taken with wooden literalism, extreme realism. On the other hand, the Gospel *reality* is not fiction. The kind of existence we are experiencing will not last forever; it will come to an end, and with it will close the story of salvation here below, God's magnificent plan to bring all men and women to Him in endless joy. It will end because it will be time, God's good time, for Jesus to come "in power and glory," for the elect to be gathered into his kingdom. The end is prelude, an overture, important because it will usher in the reign of Christ in its glorious fulness.

Third, ourselves. Here a critical question: If Christ's coming "in power and glory" is mostly a matter of Christian hope, if it may well be a millennium or more away, if I can do nothing to hasten or delay it, isn't it quite irrelevant to my day-to-day existence? On this I like what Reginald Fuller has written: "Christian faith always lives 'as if' the second coming were just around the corner. . . ."[12] If I am convinced that "Christ will come again," that the final moment is the moment to which all of history, including my own, is marching, that this is the climax of Christian yearning, then I will live in its light. I will become now what I want to be then.

How assure that? Jesus' command: "Watch!" (Mk 13:35, 37). Be on the alert! Keep your eyes open! For what? For the constant coming of Christ into my life. Not on a pink cloud or with a jeweled crown. In the preached word; in the Host I cradle in my hand and on my tongue; in the faithful gathered for worship; in each man, woman, and child whose eyes meet mine—especially those who hunger for bread or justice or love (cf. Mt 25:31–40). In Christ's glorious coming is indeed our Christian hope. But it would be tragic if the far horizon blinded us to Christ's daily coming in rags and tatters, lonely, frightened, joyless, sick in so many ways, lost in a strange world that does not seem to care. Here, after all, is our Christian love.

XI

Eleventh problem: a wedding homily. Not a simple task, especially if your ministry is in a conventional parish and you must preach at a score or two of marriages in any given year. Do you fall back on one or two proven pieces? After all, no couple can cry injustice; the homily is first-rate, is perennially pertinent, is hardly likely to have been heard by more than a few hardy wedding-watchers. And how many different homilies can you concoct for a marriage?

In one sense I am fortunate. Theologian-in-residence at a university, I celebrate and/or preach at three or four marriage liturgies a year. But in another sense this makes for problems. From two sources: I preach only for dear friends, and these homilies too are published. In consequence, each homily has to be not only personal, directed to this particular couple. It must be different from every other, take a fresh tack, unfold an aspect of human-Christian existence I have not treated in quite the same way before.

To my surprise and delight, I have been able to do it. *Tell the Next Generation* (1980), a collection of homilies that cover some 15 years, had only one sermon for a wedding,[13] and my prefatory remarks to the reader included two revealing sentences: "I have given this homily a number of times in substantially the same language, and so I have thought it prudent not to insert the names of any couple actually addressed. Let two traditionally popular Catholic names, John and Mary, serve as an appropriate disguise." Two years later *Sir, We Would Like To See Jesus* (1982) contained two new wedding homilies.[14] Two more years and *Still Proclaiming Your Wonders* (1984) included two additional compositions.[15] Less than two years were to pass before *Grace on Crutches* brought forth all of five fresh pieces.[16] And each of these nine homilies addresses two people by name.

The secret? No magic formula. In large measure, I take my stimulus from the biblical texts a couple chooses. To me, these passages are important not only because they are plucked from God's own Book, but especially because they have been selected with care by these two people out of a host of possibilities. They express, therefore, certain values that this man and this woman together hold particularly precious. This compels *me* to confront the same texts, plumb their original meaning, suggest what they might be saying or could say to a bride and groom about to say yes to each other for ever.

Examples? Jane and Remy had chosen Gen 2:18–24, 1 Cor 12:31—13:13, and Mk 10:6–9.[17] Much musing evoked the pertinence of these texts: ". . . they speak powerfully of three basic needs you have: a human person, a divine Person, and a love that links them to you." The Genesis text revealed that, from the opening act of creation, to be a person is to be with and for another. And personhood is more perfect as communion is more complete, a gradual growth in mutual giving that removes aloneness from flesh and spirit. The Marcan text hinted that, for all their shining, sterling qualities, marriage is still too perilous to entrust solely to a man and a woman; our 50% casualty rate is a terrifying testimony to that. They need God: the Father who fashioned them, the Son who died for them, the Spirit who lives in them. Paul's paean to the love that links the human and the divine to bride and groom does not sing of love in its usual understanding, not love in some shadowy sense, not simply the love they enjoy because they are so wonderfully human. It is the love Paul calls "God's love poured into our hearts through the Holy Spirit who has been given to us" (Rom 5:5). The third need is a love at once human and divine. Human because it is bride and groom who love this way; divine because it is God who enables them to love this way. Because it is divine, it is not something they deserve; it is a gift. Because it is a gift, they may never take it for granted; they must ceaselessly thank God for it.

Cathy and Sam had selected a difficult Gospel: "You are the salt of the earth. . . . You are the light of the world . . . " (Mt 5:13–16).[18] I had first to burden the congregation with a bit of learning. How irreplaceable salt was in Jesus' time: to improve the taste of food; more importantly, to keep it from spoiling, from rotting. That is why, in Old Testament times, salt was used to season every sacrifice. It was a sign of a permanent covenant between the Lord and His people, a covenant that would never corrupt. What Jesus was telling us is that this world of ours depends for its moral well-being on the Christian disciple. It is our task to improve the quality of human living, change what we touch, preserve our sin-scarred, tear-stained earth from destruction.

And the light? In the one-room cottage of the Oriental peasant, the small dish-like devices in which oil was burned were indispensable. Not a very bright light; but without it I could not have seen you once the sun went down, could not have read the Torah, could not have walked with sure foot and light heart. What Jesus was telling us is that we who believe in him are not allowed to hide our gifts in a sort of flour bin, keep them to ourselves or for our groupies.

They should attract all manner of people: our faith give pause to the skeptic, our hope lend heart to the disheartened, our love cool the anger of those who hate.

But this is something to which *all* of us are bound by our baptism. Why this Gospel at a wedding? Because from this hour husband and wife will bear an uncommon burden: They are to be salt and light *together*. Together they are to salt and light family life, be a sign to others that love unto death is not an unreal ideal. Such a love makes three demands above all else. First, like the love of God-made-man, their love must take flesh, that is, be lived in a flesh-and-blood world, a paradoxical planet where children of God die for one another and kill one another; where vows are held sacred and vows are sold for silver; where children are accepted and aborted, adored and abused, hugged to life and choked to death. Here it is that their love must give an acre of God's world reason to hope that two can be one, that a family can pray together, play together, stay together. Second, their love, like the God-man's, has to be a crucified love, a love that lives its calvaries as their share in the sufferings of Christ, experiences that are not lost hopes but their role in redemption. Third, their love, like Christ's, will salt the earth if they can flavor it with joy: a deep delight in each other, an openness to fresh ideas, a movement together out to those who have never experienced love such as theirs. In sum, love that takes flesh in the midst of frail humanity, love that lives in the shadow of a cross, love that is charged with joy—such love will lend fresh flavor to others' love, preserve love that threatens to corrupt.

XII

Twelfth problem: a funeral.[19] Surely one of our most difficult tasks, especially if the deceased is someone we know. Here the personal touch can be wonderfully consoling—where it is evident that I too share the grief of those whose hearts have been left empty. But the most profound comfort must come from a monosyllable proclaimed all through the Mass—from the white of the vestments through the liturgy of the word to the Bread that is broken. The sacred syllable is "life"; and this is the syllable we must preach.

I am afraid, however, that too often the life we preach over the dead falls short of the reality. Here the Gospel conversation between Jesus and Martha is highly instructive (Jn 11:20-27). Martha complains: "Lord, if you had been here, my brother would not have died." Jesus consoles her: "Your brother will rise again." Martha responds with an act of faith that strikes us as quite admirable: "I know that he will rise again in the resurrection at the last day." But Jesus himself is not satisfied. Martha does indeed believe in life—but in *another* life. No, says Jesus, that's not the point. "Whoever lives and believes in me shall never die." Shall *never* die.

This is not pious exaggeration, food for feeble Christians, a sop for those who mourn. The pith, the marrow, of John's Gospel is summed up during this poignant dialogue: "I am . . . the life" (v. 25). Jesus not only *has* life; he *is* life—because the Holy Spirit, that Spirit who gives life, is his Spirit; and this Spirit, this life, this Spirit of life, he gives to us. In the perspectives of the Fourth Gospel, in the Christian perspective, I die only if and when the Spirit of life leaves me. At the moment Jesus "bowed his head and gave up his spirit" (Jn 19:30), he was gloriously alive, because the Spirit of life, the Holy Spirit, was still and forever his Spirit, his life.

And so for our "dead." Indeed, there is much to mourn, as there was much to mourn on Calvary. We shall have to wait for "the resurrection at the last day" before we see the smile light up their eyes again, before we feel the gentle pressure of their touch. But the thrilling truth remains: They are alive! Alive with the life of Christ, because even in death the Holy Spirit has never left them. More alive than they ever were before, because every tear is past, every malignant growth, every infirmity of our fragile humanity. In the presence of God, there is only God, there is only love.

Here, then, is one approach to homilies, an approach that finds its springboard in problems triggered by the scriptural readings. I have sketched a dozen examples—but, dear homilist, kindly take note: These sketches are not yet homilies. You have to mull over the problem, pray over it, uncover your own Christian solution; then you must unpack it for your specific community, take it out of its theological wrappings, mold it into language that not only illuminates but ignites, not only presents sound doctrine but helps your hearer to see Jesus. Then, even when mystery remains, the Mystery will transpire.

8
DO THIS IN MEMORY OF ME
The Homily As Liturgy

This chapter confronts in detail a problem at which I have only hinted earlier: How does homily relate to liturgy? Not simply a problem for the liturgical academy; a problem as well for effective preaching, for authentic homiletics. Let me grapple with the question through a series of stages, with a set of affirmations.

I

Affirmation 1: The homily is "part of the liturgical action."[1] This phrase from Vatican II's Constitution on the Sacred Liturgy was not a gratuitous remark, without background or cause. You see, within Roman Catholicism the homily is a special kind of sermon. It is a sermon that takes place within the action we call liturgy—especially, though not exclusively, the Eucharist. But it is not an extraneous activity inserted into something more properly designated as liturgy, interrupting liturgy, akin to the TV commercial, useful for parochial announcements or as a spur to greener giving. The Council was contradicting an attitude that was widespread when the bishops assembled, an attitude summed up in a 1958 article I shall not dignify with documentation: "The sermon is accidental to the Mass, and although it is important, its omission does not affect the integrity of the great act of worship."

Nonsense, retorted the bishops in effect. If "integrity" means substantial fulfilment of a serious Sunday obligation, you may leave the church after the Gospel, rejoin the worshiping community *after* the homily, and afterwards argue persuasively that you have actually attended "the great act of worship." But here "integrity" has to do with wholeness; it concerns the constituent parts that together compose something whole and entire. In this perspective a liturgy without a homily is kin to a man or woman with one arm or one leg or one eye: essentially woman or man, but not the complete being the God of nature designed.

Theologically, the liturgy of the word (including the homily) and the liturgy of the Eucharist make up one unified liturgical celebration. Such was the Lord's Supper from the earliest days of the Christian community, deriving in large measure from the structure of the Jewish Passover meal. The Passover, as Reginald Fuller has pointed out,

> was invariably preceded by the *haggada,* a discourse relating the meal and its elements to the saving events of the Exodus. Before thanks was offered to God for the mighty acts of the Exodus, the participants must have these events brought to mind. Thus the passover would seem to have been a memorial in a double sense— a memorial to man, *and* a memorial before God, the first taking place in the *haggada,* and the second in the *berakoth* or prayers of blessing recited over the elements.[2]

Similarly, Christians could not participate in the Lord's Supper unless they heard what it meant and stood present to share in it by faith. Scripture and homily "recall the saving events of Jesus Christ before the congregation. But this recalling before man is the preliminary to the recalling of the events before God by way of eucharistic recital, so that God in turn may make those events actually present to the participants."[3]

Here, as in so many areas of religious and theological life, I have been instructed and inspired by several of the more remarkable Reformers.

> It was Martin Luther, the great Reformer in Germany, who wrote about the way in which the sacrament of the Lord's Supper was a means for receiving into one's life the reality of 'the Word' preached in the sermon which he wished always to be associated with the sacramental celebration. The two held together as a single action were to be the main Sunday service of worship for every Christian. So also the Swiss Reformer John Calvin wanted to have the regular Sunday service in Geneva a combination of Eucharist and sermon. The English Reformers, in the Prayer

Book which was prepared by Thomas Cranmer in 1549, had exactly the same intention—as is shown by their providing that only at the eucharistic celebration was there to be the collection of alms and the making of parochial announcements.[4]

II

Affirmation 2: The homily is worship. An exaggeration? In actuality, arguable; as an ideal, not at all. Simply recall what worship means. In Gerard Sloyan's pithy definition, "To worship is to be in the presence of God in a posture of awe."[5] And a bit later: "To sum up: preaching is an integral part of the worship act. One speaks in the assembly to facilitate the people's prayer."[6] Here Vatican II was pointed and pellucid: "The two parts which, in a certain sense, go to make up the Mass, namely, the liturgy of the word and the liturgy of the Eucharist, are so closely connected with each other that they form but one single act of worship."[7]

For the Catholic homilist, and for countless other Christian preachers, the primary setting of worship is the Eucharist. It is a setting that should lift or bend a preacher to a posture of awe. I recall a famous paragraph from the pen of Dom Gregory Dix. Jesus, he noted, "had told His friends to do this henceforward with the new meaning 'for the *anamnesis*' of Him, and they have done it always since." He went on in rapturous phrases:

Was ever another command so obeyed? For century after century, spreading slowly to every continent and country and among every race on earth, this action has been done, in every conceivable human circumstance, for every conceivable human need from infancy and before it to extreme old age and after it, from the pinnacles of earthly greatness to the refuge of fugitives in the caves and dens of the earth. Men have found no better thing than this to do for kings in their crowning and for criminals going to the scaffold; for armies in triumph or for a bride and bridegroom in a little country church; for the proclamation of a dogma or for a good crop of wheat; for the wisdom of the Parliament of a mighty nation or for a sick old woman afraid to die; for a schoolboy sitting an examination or for Columbus setting out to discover America; . . . because the Turk was at the gates of Vienna . . . [and] on the beach at Dunkirk; . . . tremulously, by an old monk on the fiftieth anniversary of his vows; furtively, by an exiled bishop who had hewn timber all day in a prison camp near Murmansk; gorgeously, for the canonisation of S. Joan of Arc—

one could fill many pages with the reasons why men have done this, and not tell a hundredth part of them. And best of all, week by week and month by month, on a hundred thousand successive Sundays, faithfully, unfailingly, across all the parishes of christendom, the pastors have done this just to *make* the *plebs sancta Dei*—the holy common people of God.[8]

A thrilling tradition indeed. The error occurs when we recognize worship only from the Offertory through the Consecration to the Communion. No, the community is at worship from the moment it gathers together, even before the "gathering song" brings the congregation to its feet as one corporate person. Nor is it only in a humbling penitential rite or a resounding *Gloria* or a responsorial psalm or a reverently rendered passage from Scripture that the community is at prayer, that the People praises its God, recalls His wondrous works in the drama of redemption, senses His presence, bends low in adoration. Equally part of the "posture of awe" is the homiletic moment. Not only in the pulpit but in the pew. All of which compels a third stage, a further question: What does it mean, in concrete actuality, to say that the homily is worship?

III

Affirmation 3: Word and sacrament are intimately related. But how? For me, one of the most satisfying explanations has come from the pen of that remarkable theologian-in-a-wheelchair, the Dominican Yves Congar, in a short article on "Sacramental Worship and Preaching" which I have swiftly summarized in the chapter "The Word Made Flesh Today."[9] It deserves somewhat more detailed consideration here.

Congar underscores three facets of the need for integration, three links that wed word and sacrament, word and worship. First, Christian worship is an anamnesis. We actualize in memory, we actively re-present, God's saving acts in our regard. Above all, we celebrate the event of Jesus Christ from his incarnation to the Spirit's descent. With the Eucharist as their common central point, all the sacraments refer to the Lord's Pasch and apply it to the decisive moments of our lives.

The problem? The incomparable insights of the liturgy are not immediately obvious. The liturgical forms and texts have been rather rigidly fixed through the ages "for all people and whatever their condition, in festivity or in trouble, in power or suffering oppression, whether they are children or adults, uncouth or refined."[10] What is needed is to transport the age-old symbols to this time, this place, this people. Such is the task, the function, of the homily. It makes "the acts of worship not merely some reality in their own right but acts of living people who feel involved in them."[11] It is the word that must mediate between the fixed forms of the liturgy and the spirit and freedom of a particular people.

Second, Christian worship is a witness to faith, that is, the expression of a conviction about a transcendent but active God who desires a personal relationship with me. It is through faith that I yield to those divine initiatives and touch them to myself. Faith and sacraments or liturgy "are wholly intermingled in a process where faith precedes, accompanies and expresses itself in the celebration, and comes out of it expanded, nourished and fortified."[12]

The danger? The liturgy can be too impersonal, the words and gestures not sufficiently "actual," to rouse the faith it should. Hence the homily. What the rite expresses in a common way, in a general way, the homily personalizes.

Third, Christian worship is a spiritual sacrifice. It means accepting gratefully God's Eucharistic gift and uniting to it my total concrete existence. Oh it's true, the whole range of parish activities can contribute to this linkage of liturgy and life. Still, the homily is singularly suited to this function. It not only comments on the mystery in the light of the liturgical texts; it draws the faithful into the mystery, helps them unite their life to the mystery—life not as "an empty framework of existence, a kind of general and anonymous spiritual life," not "what remains of man's life after everything that really interests him has been eliminated," but "life as filled or crossed by all kinds of events, great or small, a life that is committed to the conditions and tasks of every day."[13] Then it is that the sermon achieves its purpose: to be a word that evokes a response.

Without apparent dependence on Congar, other students of liturgy say more or less the same with different rhetoric. For Dominican John Burke,

> the liturgical homily manifests the present significance of the liturgical act in such a way as to incorporate the worshippers more fully in the act of worship by arousing their faith and the dispositions of that faith appropriate to the liturgical act, so that the effects of the sacrament extend beyond the immediate sacramental celebration into all phases of their daily life and the life of the entire Church.[14]

Seeking the relationship between the service of the word and the service of the Eucharist, Benedictine Campion Gavaler concludes:

> In the service of the Word the risen Lord is present in the priest to speak, and in the people to hear: 1) the proclamation of his saving death and resurrection; 2) the call to believe in the saving event and thank God for it; 3) the invitation to be joined to the saving event in the Eucharist. The purpose of the sermon is to create the awareness of the present moment in sacred history, not only of the past and future.[15]

Gerard Sloyan, insisting that the human situation in which preaching finds itself is one of worship, that "preaching is part of the one, prayerful thing we do publicly," goes on to argue:

> This being so, the homily must above all be an integral part of the worship service. It is not "word"—rational discourse—in contrast to "sacrament"—symbolic, nonrational activity: the comprehensible providing the incomprehensible with interpretation or relief. Homilies, like liturgy generally, are reflections upon, expansions of, the biblical word. They are reasonable exercises because the word of God testified to in scripture is reasonable. The biblical word is not gibberish. It is not speech that transcends human categories, or oracular utterance that gives assurances no other speech can give. The biblical word is a record of the dialogue of believers with God, their report on all that deity has done for them and spoken to them and meant to them. The Bible is a people's speech to and about and with the God no human eye has seen. These holy books help us carry on a conversation with the one who is life and all to us.
> The conversation at its best is lost in wonder. Besides praise there are other, equally valid topics: thanksgiving, questioning, petitioning, complaint, challenge. All these activities the Bible gives tongue to under the rubric "God says." For our speech about God is God's speech to us. The two are one. The homily is a continuation of the conversation. It is Spirit-invested but not, like the Bible, Spirit-inspired.[16]

For Lutheran Robert Esbjornson, preaching *should* be an act of worship in the sense that "preaching is, could be, should be an act ascribing worth to and paying attention to God. . . . "[17] At the close of his article he suggests that St. Paul may well be the classic model for the preacher.

His letters are situational, close to the lives of people and their
struggles. They are full of instruction. They reveal his human
limitations. They are doctrinal. At times they are opaque and
confusing. But somewhere along the line they break loose from
logic, from immediate concerns, from the confines of ordinary
language, to become doxological expressions of the reality of God
and the immensity and wonder of the grace of our Lord Jesus
Christ. So close was he to God that he could not long do anything
without worshiping. The language of exaltation, acclamation, astonishment and wonder break[s] into his discourse.

So preaching is; if it is not, it should be; if it is not yet so for
someone, it can become so. Praise God for that![18]

In a chapter that offers a basically liturgical view of preaching,
Gilbert E. Doan Jr. sums up:

That is to say, liturgy is worship; worship is essentially an act of
adoration; the lesson is provided as an occasion of that act, and
the sermon is provided, as it were, to assure that the worshiper
hears, receives, the lesson. It should be clear that such preaching
offers not only the clarity and power and depth, and the affirmation and integration, which might reasonably be expected
from the proper doing of a piece of good liturgy, but as well, joy,
surprise, remorse and penitence, awe, aspiration, exaltation. And
it should be clear that liturgical preaching accomplishes this not
despite but because of its liturgical integrity—that is to say, because those are appropriate responses to The Story in the text
and to the one to whom the text bears witness: the Lamb of God
and King of Kings.[19]

Finally, a thesis from Robert Lechner, C.PP.S., that takes us
back to 1963:

In general it is the function of the homily to serve as the bond
between the liturgy of the word and that of the bread and cup.
The homily unifies the word in preparation for the sacrifice.
More specifically, it is first of all a faith-nourishing word which
introduces the mystery of the Eucharist. As such it is not primarily kerygma (that is the Gospel), nor simply catechesis (though
elements of this are present); it may perhaps best be described as
spiritual formation.[20]

IV

Now if the homily is part of the liturgical action, if the homily
is worship, if word and sacrament are intimately related, an affir-

mation 4 seems in order: It is the task of the *homilist* to effect this. It does not happen automatically, by sheer movement from altar to pulpit, by an episcopal imposition of hands. Then how does it happen? Here let me move away from the experts, speak more intimately from my own experience, at times dreadfully embarrassing.

First, the process begins at a far distance from pulpit or lectern; it has its roots in a preacher's life. If preaching is prayer, then the preacher must be a pray-er. Not simply that you can count on me for x-number of spiritual activities on any given day: the Morning Offering, a meditation, my breviary, a rosary, an examination of conscience before bed. My whole life must be a prayer. I mean, concretely, that the context, the setting, the framework of all I think and say and do should be a relationship of love with Father, Son, and Holy Spirit.

The point is, a homily is not primarily a performance, a spectacle, a one-act, one-person play. Oh yes, a professional performance is highly desirable. A homily that weds all the persuasive powers, all the force and charm, of classical and contemporary rhetoric, a sermon that is poetry and music and good theatre wrapped in one awesome package—this I commend with all my heart. And still, a homily is not, in the first instance, an exercise in acting, an artistic production. I am not playing a role: Laurence Olivier becoming Henry V, Paul Scofield recapturing Thomas More. When I say "It is no longer I who live, but Christ who lives in me" (Gal 2:20), I am not putting on Christ for the homiletic moment, only to remove the putty and the paint in the sacristy. If I am a consummate actor, I may play the impostor on occasion or for a time, preach effectively even when divorced from the Lord Jesus, fool all of the people some of the time; but I assure you, it will not last. You will grow tired of playacting, ashamed of sham.

I am not saying that before you preach you must be perfect, that effective homiletics demands high sanctity. I do say that for the homily to be worship, the homilist must be a worshiper, habitually; and this calls for talking with God, listening to God, wrestling with God; it calls for "God's love poured into our hearts through the Holy Spirit that has been given to us" (Rom 5:5). It demands the close union of the Christian with Christ expressed in the Pauline "in Christ," "an inclusion or incorporation that connotes a symbiosis of the two."[21]

Second, the preparation of a homily must itself be a prayer. More specifically, a sacrifice, an offering to God of the very gifts He has given me. I still blush to recall how often I have knelt before

Him as a last resort, a homilist in a foxhole, when all the resources of scholarship and human wisdom have failed me. I am not proposing that rosaries *supplant* sweat and blood. I *am* proposing that the sweat and blood be more consciously, more explicitly, an act of worship—a prayer not only of petition but of praise, a doxology, a "glory to God in the highest."

How take this out of the wild blue yonder and make it practical? In my case, preparation became prayer when I began to preach first to myself. It is understandable, I suppose, that in the first flush of priestly preaching the audience in view, my congregation, was purely and simply "out there." It is not quite as understandable that it took decades before Nathan's words to adulterous David came home to me: "You are the man" (2 Sam 12:7). Not that I disregard the faithful who will sit "sheepishly" before me; not that I avoid turning the Good News, or the bad news, in their direction. But before I do that, even in my preparation, I flash the light of the gospel on myself. What does the word of the Lord say to *me*? Not, therefore, "Here is an ideal application for the selfish in the parish, for the lukewarm, for the sex-crazed, for today's entrepreneur, the megabucks addict, the 'me generation.' " No, with the toll collector in the temple, I dare not even lift my eyes to heaven, but beat my breast: "God, be merciful to me *the* sinner" (Lk 18:13).

Third, I must be careful not to project my homily as the absolute high point of the liturgy. A seductive temptation, especially if I preach impressively, if the people respond to me, if *they* find in my homily the cream of the liturgy. The antidote? Surely not a deliberately shabby homily. Rather, an examination of conscience on two counts. (1) What sort of celebrant am I? Is my activity at the altar— voice and bearing, hands and eyes, my body language—a powerful word in its own right? Or am I going through motions, a languid repetition of rote and routine? Do eyes that meet mine at Communion-in-the-hand strike a spark in me, smiles provoke a smile, anguish arouse compassion? Does my joy in liturgy break through, or have I infected "celebration" with a new and doleful virus? (2) Are my homilies keyed to the wider liturgy, oriented to Eucharist, calculated to form a unity with the Sacrifice? Or is my homily an independent unit that stands on its own, in solitary isolation from the Bread of Life?

Fourth, the actual delivery. Here my inner attitude, how I see myself and what I am about, is all-important. When do I experience my preaching most intensely as prayer, as an act of worship? (1) When I am conscious of having been "sent by God." Not puffed up

by it; humbly aware of it. I proclaim the gospel not on my own authority but by the authority of Him who has entrusted to me "the
message of reconciliation" (2 Cor 5:19). "Do this in memory of me"
can be said of the preacher in the pulpit as well as of the celebrant
at the altar. (2) When I am penetrated by the realization that I am
a servant, that my homily is a service, that my task under God is to
enable this people to see Jesus with their own eyes, hear him with
their own ears, respond to him with their own "Thy will be done on
earth." (3) Strangely, when I am a *suffering* servant. In point of fact,
I preach best when I feel worst—physically or psychically or spiritually. Not that my prepared text changes; it does not—not by a single syllable. But somehow suffering—flu or fear, anxiety or dark
night of the soul, diverticulosis or inflamed ileum or hiatus hernia—
charges the selfsame words with fresh power. Paradoxically, in such
circumstances I am thinking less of myself and more of the faithful
before me, am uncommonly aware that of myself I can do nothing,
that if these paltry words of mine are to strike fire, it is the Lord
who must light the flame. It is then that I share St. Paul's experience: "When I am weak, then I am strong" (2 Cor 12:10). Why? Because then I am doing what is perhaps the most difficult thing
Christ asks of me: I am letting go, entrusting my whole self to the
Lord who alone can change hearts through my tongue, who chooses
"what is foolish in the world to shame the wise, what is weak in the
world to shame the strong, what is low and despised in the world,
even things that are not, to bring to nothing things that are, so that
no human being might boast in the presence of God" (1 Cor 1:27-
29). I know it for a fact: I come through differently, more effectively, more passionately when I am in pain; and I do so because
then I am sharing more intimately in the passion of my Lord, in the
passion of my sisters and brothers. Here, in a hundred gethsemanes, the preacher is a pray-er par excellence. Here, in singular fashion, words are transmuted into worship. Here I sing as rapturously
as Aquinas did to his Eucharistic Christ:

> See, Lord, at thy service low lies here a heart
> Lost, all lost in wonder at the God thou art.[22]

When the act of preaching is a prayer, the act of listening is
more likely to be a prayer as well. In the last analysis, a homily that
is a prayer is an act of love—love not only of God but of His images
in front of me. I am reminded of Augustine's psychology of religious instruction, an insight that moves catechesis to the personal

commitment that is its purpose: Love gives birth to love. "For there is nothing that invites love more than to be beforehand in loving; and that heart is overhard which, even though it were unwilling to bestow love, would be unwilling to return it."[23]

On the whole, the faithful in the pews are a pretty perceptive lot, sensitive to their celebrants and their homilists. As they can sense whether I joy in the Eucharist or am going through motions, so can they recognize not only the prepared but the prayerful preacher. Give them this, and the liturgy will come alive for them. The whole liturgy. The homily.

9
LET JUSTICE ROLL DOWN LIKE WATERS
Preaching the Just Word

In May 1979, passions flamed in our nation's capital. Mass was about to begin in St. Matthew's Cathedral—a Mass to mark Argentina's national day. Unexpectedly, the assembled Argentinians—embassy officials, military leaders, others—were addressed from the sanctuary by a priest protester. For six years this missionary had ministered to a Buenos Aires shantytown; he told how he had been imprisoned and tortured, how priest friends had simply disappeared; he wanted the congregation to join him in a prayer for reconciliation. But at that moment "the organist drowned him out . . . the microphone went dead . . . the rector of the cathedral . . . told [him] to move on."[1]

The trouble seemed over; the 40-or-so demonstrators moved from church to street and the liturgy opened. But the preceding was only prelude. The homilist, head of the Spanish Secretariat of the Archdiocese, appeared in symbolic purple. Instead of the usual eulogy, he quoted statements by John Paul II and the bishops of Latin America about repression, torture, and disappearances, about the attempt of governments to justify such activities on the basis of national security. He began to focus on the people who had vanished under the Videla regime and quoted Scripture on Herod's slaughter of the innocents.

At that juncture the congregation (300 or more) stormed angrily out of the church, led by a high-ranking general. Some damned the homilist for "turning a religious event into a political one." Another said "priests have no place in politics. He should have given a sermon on another subject, like the love of God." But the archdiocesan director of communications said "he had no objection to the way the sermon was handled. . . . 'We hope our priests are teaching the truth' he said. 'Whether what they say is offensive and bothers the conscience of some people should not be the issue. The issue should be whether it is the truth.' "

The scene at St. Matthew's provides a stirring context for this chapter; perhaps it will put teeth into it. You see, my subtitle is deceptive. What could be less threatening, more pacifying, than the sleepy subject "Preaching the Just Word"? In point of fact, as the Argentinian incident demonstrates, there are three "sleepers" here: the first is theological, the second liturgical, the third homiletic. The theological question: Does a Church committed to eternal salvation have anything to do with everyday justice? The liturgical question: If the Church has a role to play in the area of justice, how can this possibly affect the liturgy? The homiletic question: If justice does enter the liturgy of the worshiping community, should the preacher preach it—and if so, how?

I

My first question is theological: Does a Church committed to eternal salvation have anything to do with everyday justice? The question is basic; for unless I address that issue, there is no point in my asking the next two questions: How does justice enter the liturgy? How do I preach justice?

To get concrete, should the Church speak out on economic injustice, on the fact that at this moment about 500 million people are hungry? Should the bishops of Chile have criticized their government in 1974 "for violating human rights, creating a climate of insecurity and terror . . . "?[2] Should Bishop Desmond Tutu castigate the South African regime for racial discrimination and repression? Should the Church take a position on the contras in Nicaragua or the rebels in El Salvador, on capital punishment or the Panama Canal, on ERA or Federal aid for abortions?

I give these examples simply as examples, not to debate the merits of any of them; for these are complex issues. My question is broader than any example. Does the Church, precisely as Church, have a mission that includes justice and human rights? Does the Church have a role to play in the social, political, and economic orders?

Many Christians, many Catholics, shout a resounding no. As

they see it, the Church, as Church, has *no* commission to right human injustice. The Church is a spiritual institution, and its mission is sheerly spiritual: it is a channel that links the human person with God. The Church's charge is to help us know, love, and serve God in this life and to be happy with God for ever in the next. Oh yes, poverty and politics, injustice and inhumanity may stand as barriers to God's grace. If they are, then the Church must struggle against them. But not as a direct facet of its mission—only as obstacles at the outer edge of its vocation. The Church's commission is to gather a band of true believers who will prepare themselves by faith and hope for the redemptive action by which God establishes the kingdom at the end of history.

Two concrete examples. A letter from Texas once took Msgr. George G. Higgins to task for his views on the Church and social justice. Christ "did not relieve suffering," the correspondent declared; he simply forgave sins. In consequence, the Church should not be concerned about violations of social justice. Like Christ, it should concentrate on showing us that "it is the hardness of men's hearts that causes our suffering" and that "as long as the angel of darkness roams the world in search of souls and men fail to reject sin, human misery will continue to exist."[3]

Similarly, in a study on Christianity and the world order, a distinguished professor in a British university made the point that the essential thing religion should provide is a "sense of the ultimate worthlessness of human expectations of a better life on earth."[4] For him, "the teachings of the Savior clearly describe a personal rather than a social morality." By nature, Christianity is exclusively concerned with "the relationship of the soul to eternity."

Against such a privatized, me-and-Jesus religion the best of Catholic tradition cries out clearly, at times in anger. Papal pronouncements from Leo XIII's *Rerum novarum* (on the rights and obligations of workers, employers, and the state) to John Paul's address at Puebla, his first encyclical (*Redemptor hominis*), and more recent statements in Canada and the Third World—give the lie to such a thesis.

Oh indeed, the Christian has to avoid two extremes. On the one hand, salvation is not sheer socialization, personality development, liberation from oppressive structures, an end to poverty; it is a divinization, transformation into Christ. The Church's primary task is to see to it that the human person is refashioned in the image of Christ; short of this there is no salvation. God fulfils us by uniting us with God. The essential liberation is freedom from the slavery that is sin. As Pius XII said in a 1956 allocution, "The goal which Christ assigns to [the Church] is strictly religious. . . . The Church must lead men and women to God, in order that they may give themselves over to God unreservedly. . . ."[5]

On the other hand, any program of evangelization is inadequate if the Church does not spend itself to free the human person from every inhuman shackle. Oh yes, the Church has good news to preach even to those whose situation is humanly hopeless; for *the* good news is Jesus—Jesus alive, yearning to make those who are heavy-burdened one with him. Sanctity is possible in poverty-ridden Appalachia, in the political prisons of South Africa, in the excrement of Calcutta. But this does not exempt the People of God from the ceaseless struggle to transform the City of Man and Woman into the kingdom of God—a kingdom of peace, of justice, of love.

This is the vision that emerged from the Second Vatican Council—resoundingly in its Decree on the Apostolate of the Laity:

> Christ's redemptive work, while of its nature directed to the salvation of men and women, involves also the renewal of the whole temporal order. The Church has for mission, therefore, not only to bring to men and women the message of Christ and his grace, but also to saturate and perfect the temporal sphere with the spirit of the gospel. . . . The two spheres [spiritual and temporal], distinct though they are, are so linked in the single plan of God that He Himself purposes in Christ to take up the whole world again into a new creation, initially here on earth, completely on the last day.[6]

This is the vision of the 1971 Synod of Bishops in its message "On Justice in the World": The vindication of justice and participation in the process of transforming the world is "a constitutive element of the preaching of the gospel."[7] This is the vision that emerged from the 1974 Synod of Bishops in a significant statement on "Human Rights and Reconciliation." Said the bishops in common:

> Human dignity is rooted in the image and reflection of God in each of us. It is this which makes all persons essentially equal. The integral development of persons makes more clear the divine image in them. In our time the Church has grown more deeply aware of this truth; hence she believes firmly that the promotion of human rights is required by the gospel and is central to her ministry.[8]

And in 1976 the International Theological Commission (an advisory body serving the pope), in a very carefully articulated examination of "Human Development and Christian Salvation," argued that God's grace should sharpen the conscience of Christians, should help us build a more just world. Not simply by spiritual reformation; not simply by assisting individuals;

> for there is a kind of "injustice that assumes institutional shape," and as long as this obtains, the situation itself calls for a greater degree of justice and demands reforming. Our contemporaries are no longer convinced that social structures have been predetermined by nature and therefore are "willed by God," or that they have their origin in anonymous evolutionary laws. Consequently, the Christian must ceaselessly point out that the institutions of society originate also in the conscience of society, and that men and women have a moral responsibility for these institutions.
>
> We may argue how legitimate it is to speak of "institutional sin" or of "sinful structures," since the Bible speaks of sin in the first instance in terms of an explicit, personal decision that stems from human freedom. But it is unquestionable that by the power of sin injury and injustice can penetrate social and political institutions. That is why . . . even situations and structures that are unjust have to be reformed.
>
> Here we have a new consciousness, for in the past these responsibilities could not be perceived as distinctly as they are now. . . . [9]

That last sentence is highly important. We Christians "have a new consciousness. . . . " Not that the Old Testament and the New are silent on social issues. Those who read in Scripture a sheerly personal morality have not sung the Psalms or been burned by the prophets, have not perceived the implications of Jesus' message.[10]

Take the prophets. Through Isaiah and Hosea, through Amos and Micah and Jeremiah, Yahweh ceaselessly tells Israel that He rejects just those things they think will make Him happy. He is weary of burnt offerings, does not delight in the blood of bulls or lambs. Incense is an abomination to Him. Their appointed feasts His soul hates. Their prayers and the melody of their harps He will not listen to. He does not want rivers of oil, thousands of rams, even their first-born. Then what is left? What can God possibly want? Two things: their steadfast love and that they execute justice (cf. Isa 1:11–18; 42:1–4; Hos 2:18–20; 6:6; Amos 5:18–25; Mic 6:6–8; Jer 7:5–7).

That God should want Israel's love is understandable. But that the second great commandment should be "execute justice" is not what we would expect. Is there not a higher commandment, such as the Lord's demand in Leviticus: "You shall love your neighbor as yourself" (Lev 19:18)?

The point is, the justice God asked of Israel was not an ethical construct. It did not merely mean: Give to each what is due to each, what each person has a strict right to demand, because he or she is a human being, has rights that can be proven by philosophy or have been written into law. What, then, was the justice God wanted to "roll down like waters" (Amos 5:24)? Justice was a whole web of relationships that stemmed from Israel's covenant with God. The Israelites were to father the fatherless and feed the sojourner, the stranger, not because the orphan and the outsider deserved it, but because this was the way *God* had acted with *them*. A text in Deuteronomy is telling: "Love the sojourner, therefore; for you were sojourners in the land of Egypt" (Deut 10:19). In freeing the oppressed, they were mirroring the loving God who had delivered *them* from oppression, had freed them from Pharaoh. In loving the loveless, the unloved, the unlovable, they were imaging the God who wooed Israel back despite her infidelities, betrothed her to Himself for ever (cf. Hos 2:14–23).

Justice, for the Jew, was not a question simply of human deserving, of human law. The Jews were to give to others what they had been given by God, were to act toward one another as God had acted toward them—and precisely because God had acted this way. Their justice was to image not the justice of man but the justice of God. For Israel, the practice of justice was an expression of steadfast love, a demand of steadfast love—God's love and their own love. Not to execute justice was not to worship God.

This is the tradition that sparked the ministry of Jesus: "I will put my Spirit upon him, and he shall proclaim justice to the Gentiles. . . . He will not break a bruised reed or quench a smoldering wick, till he brings justice to victory" (Mt 12:18–20). In harmony with Hosea, he wants not sacrifice but compassion, mercy (cf. Mt 12:7; 23:23). And the just man or the just woman is not primarily someone who gives to another what that other *deserves*. The just man, the just woman has covenanted with God; this covenant demands that we treat other human persons as *God* wants them treated in His covenant plan, treat friend and enemy as He treats them. And how does He treat them? He "makes His sun rise on the evil and on the good, sends rain on the just and on the unjust" (Mt 5:45).

The early Christians seem to have grasped that. If *anyone* is hungry or athirst, naked or a stranger, sick or in prison, it is always Christ who clamors for bread or water, Christ who cries to be clothed or welcomed, Christ whom you visit on a bed of pain or behind bars (cf. Mt 25:31–46). And the First Letter of John is terribly uncompromising: "If anyone has the world's goods and sees his brother in need, yet closes his heart against him, how does God's love abide in him?" (1 Jn 3:17).

For all this remarkable tradition, it still remains true that the Church has grown in its awareness of what Jeremiah's "execute justice" (Jer 7:5) and the gospel of love demand. It is in line with this growth that John Paul II confirmed contemporary magisterial teaching in telling the Third General Assembly of the Latin American Bishops in Puebla: "The Church has learned [in the pages of the Gospel] that its evangelizing mission has as indispensable part (*como parte indispensable*) action for justice and those efforts which the development of the human person demands. . . . "[11]

To my mind, the most remarkable example, within recent memory, of the Church's growth in understanding its proper involvement in the sociopolitical arena was the role played by the bishops of the Philippines in the presidential election of February 1986. Towards the end of that month, despot Ferdinand Marcos left a land he had despoiled for decades, and a Philippines in bondage recaptured its freedom. It recaptured its freedom in large measure because the Catholic Bishops' Conference of the Philippines had declared that "the polls were unparalleled in the fraudulence of their conduct": in the systematic disenfranchisement of voters, widespread and massive vote-buying, deliberate tampering with the election returns, intimidation, harassment, terrorism, and murder. It recaptured its freedom because the same bishops had proclaimed: "A government that assumes or retains power through fraudulent means has no moral basis. We do not advocate a bloody, violent means of righting this wrong. The way indicated to us now is active resistance by peaceful means—in the manner of Christ."[12] It recaptured its freedom because a cardinal called uncounted thousands to the streets to arrest tanks of war with rosaries and marigolds, with orchids and their unarmed bodies.

That cardinal, Jaime L. Sin, 14th of 16 children of a Filipina mother and a Chinese father, told the story with incomparable persuasiveness in a commencement address at Georgetown University, May 25, 1986. The ceaseless theme of his address: The Catholic Church in the Philippines has been accused of interfering in politics. But the Church was simply defending the human rights of the people. It was the state that was interfering with human rights: e.g., people driven off their land by the military; a priest (one of my theology students between 1950 and 1954 at Woodstock Seminary in Maryland) shot through the heart at six inches for championing their cause.

Sin was accused of interfering in politics because he wrote a pastoral letter to his people: Not "Vote for Cory" or "Vote for Marcos," but "Vote honestly . . . according to your conscience!" Because he wrote to his people about bribery: "Do not sell your vote. But if anyone offers you money, take it . . . and vote according to your conscience, according to your heart. Take the five pesos (25 cents). Buy rice for your children, buy fish, buy milk for the baby." How justify taking the pesos? Because "The money is yours anyway; it was stolen from the people."

> Look at these poor people! Twelve in one little room. At night they cannot sleep lying flat, because there is not enough room. They must sleep on their side, or else the twelve will not fit in that one little room. They do not eat properly, even once a day. Some live on food that they salvage from the garbage heaps.

In another pastoral letter Sin pleaded with those in charge of the counting: "Please, do not cheat! Let the votes of the people be counted!" The appeal worked: 30 of the computer operators walked out, "because what they were putting into the computers was not coming out in the official tally."

When Sin asked the people to go out into the streets, to Camp Crame, to get between the 301 anti-Marcos soldiers and the advancing tanks, "They came out! At once! They filled the streets! They met the tanks! They put flowers into the muzzles of the rifles. The nuns knelt in front of the tanks and prayed the rosary. Schoolchildren linked arms and stood in front of the trucks—and the trucks were filled with armed soldiers. It was wonderful!" Was this interference in politics?

> I do not think that it was. If we did not do that, the tanks would have attacked Camp Crame, the planes would have bombed the troops that were besieged, the mortars would have shelled Ramos and Enrile from Camp Aguinaldo—and Manila would be now in a state of civil war. We would have had carnage from Aparri to Jolo. We did what the gospel told us to do. We stopped hatred with love. We stopped violence with prayer, with laughter, with

confidence in the natural goodness of every man. I *knew* that the Filipino soldier would never fire on defenseless women and children. I was *sure* of that! That is why I sent our people out into the streets. . . .

I think that the script for the Philippine elections in February, and the script for our revolution, was written by God. . . .

I agree. I was privileged to write the citation for Cardinal Sin's honorary degree at Georgetown, privileged to close the citation with these words:

In honoring this contemporary "prince of peace," Georgetown recognizes a powerful symbol of Christian reconciliation: ever a mediator with Marcos but never an accomplice, ever the passionate protester but never the reckless rebel, an inspiration to the fearful and the tearful. For reminding us masterfully that authority is service, that politics can be priestly, and that marigolds might be mightier than the sword, the President and Directors of Georgetown University with great pride and admiration proclaim His Eminence Jaime L. Cardinal Sin Doctor of Humane Letters, honoris causa.

II

So far so good: The struggle for justice is an indispensable facet of the Church's mission. But the theological question leads to the liturgical question: Granted that the Church has a vital role to play in the area of justice, how can this possibly affect the liturgy?

On principle, it should. As sacrament of Christian belief, liturgy has a twin function: It should give expression to the faith experience of the Christian people, and it should mold that experience. All "liturgies" express experience and mold it: country music in Nashville, pro and college football, marching bands and the New York City Ballet, the Nazi goose step and the Aztec Two Step. This is what expresses and evokes the joys and frustrations of a people, their anger and violence, their loves and their hates, their pent-up emotions. If we accept the thesis of first-rate liturgiologists that Christian liturgy sacramentalizes what goes on in the rest of our lives, that the liturgical journey ritualizes the human journey, two questions challenge us: (1) In point of fact, does this liturgy express the faith experience of this people? (2) If it does, how Catholic is that expression? The dimensions of this problem, its dangers, were brought home to me some years ago in an article by Brian Wicker:

> [The liturgical] revival [among organized Christians] had a good side—in that it stimulated mature and scholarly thought about the fundamentals of Christianity and an understanding of the depths to which secularization had gone. But it had a bad side too—the side that made it possible in some places for the Christian liturgy inside the church and the fascist liturgy outside the church to coexist, or even at times to cooperate with each other. The liturgical revival was, in its origins, a conservative or even reactionary movement, liable at times to delusions of grandeur. This gave it a certain sympathy for the trappings of fascism and made the essential atheism of the latter hard to nail down. It is perhaps not surprising that those Christians most opposed to Hitler were often those least touched by the new liturgical ideas— either intellectual protestants like Dietrich Bonhoeffer, or simple tridentine-formed peasant-Catholics like Franz Jägerstätter. Neither is it surprising that many post-fascist secular theologies of Europe and America (including those developed under Catholic auspices) have today turned away from liturgy as a source of inspiration or hope, or have even given it up as a bad job altogether.[13]

Does it frighten us that the liturgy in a Catholic cathedral is expected to coexist with, perhaps even co-operate with, the fascist liturgy that is Argentinian repression? Does it bother us that in liturgizing, ritualizing, sacramentalizing a nation's experience, we are expected to limit our symbols to love of *God*?

A challenging book on this very issue appeared in 1979. Its title: *The Eucharist and Human Liberation*.[14] The author, Oblate Tissa Balasuriya, insists that, since Eucharistic worship is at the center of Christian life, the Eucharist must affirm and promote the biblical imperative of human liberation. But, he finds, almost without exception the Eucharist has been a place where the oppressor joins the oppressed with impunity; the Eucharist has been used in co-operation with and support of colonizing powers; even today liberating movements do not find affirmation in Eucharistic worship. Whatever the defects of the book, however utopian its hopes, it compels us to ask a crucial question: How is it possible to celebrate Eucharist if it is not expressing the real oppressions of our people, if it is not molding a faith that liberates from all enslavements?

But precisely here a work of discrimination, of discernment, is imperative. I will assume that Joseph Gelineau's thesis is valid: " . . . the celebration of the risen Christ by the assembly of believers is one of the most effective political actions that men can perform in this world—if it is true that this celebration, by contesting any power system which oppresses mankind, proclaims, stirs up and inaugurates a new order in the created world."[15]

Here "politics" is used to describe "that *exercise of power* which controls public welfare and progress."[16] But how does the liturgy influence public welfare and progress? On the face of it, few actions seem less political than liturgy. Totalitarian regimes hostile to the Church "begin by forbidding Christians any form of self-organized action in society; they then prohibit or supervise religious instruction and preaching; but in general they allow worship as inoffensive."[17] The issue is highly complex; space forces me to simplify, and to simplify is, in a sense, to falsify.

1) Paradoxically, it is not primarily by introducing political themes, by inserting an ideology, that the liturgy becomes a social force. I am not disparaging the Mass of Protest in Latin America or the Mass for Peace in the Roman Missal; I have been moved by liberating readings from Exodus and the prophets, by "prayers of the faithful" that cry to heaven for bread and justice. I mean rather that there is a serious danger in a "celebration which tries to be political but relies more on an ideology than on the paschal dynamics of the Christian mystery"; it "very soon becomes a politicized liturgy: that is, one used for specific political ends."[18] This can mean a form of manipulation at odds with the essential nature of liturgical action. The liturgy does not of itself make Christian Democrats or make for constitutional amendments; it is not a substitute for sociology, economics, or political science.

2) And yet, as George Higgins argues, "it is still the Mass which matters most—even in the temporal order."[19] But the liturgical action effects change above all by its own inner dynamic. Why? Because the temporal order can be changed only by conversion—only if men and women turn from sin and selfishness. And for Catholics the primary source of conversion is the Sacrifice of the Mass, which extends through time and space the Sacrifice of the Cross through which the world is transfigured. The Mass should be the liberating adventure of the whole Church, the sacrament which frees men and women from their inherited damnable concentration on themselves, looses us from our ice-cold isolation, fashions us into brothers and sisters agonizing not only for a church of charity but for a world of justice as well.

In this context, a Jesuit colleague at the Woodstock Theological Center in Washington, D.C., John C. Haughey, recaptured for me several years ago a remarkable insight expressed by government people engaged in a Woodstock project on government decision-making. As they saw it, good liturgy facilitates public responsibility not because it provides principles of solution, not because it tells the people what precisely to think about specific conflicts; rather because a celebrant who effectively celebrates the transcendent puts them in touch with that which transcends all their burning concerns, their particular perplexities. Good liturgy frees them to sort out the issues they have to decide, because it makes them aware of their addictions and their illusions, casts a pitiless light on myopic self-interest, detaches from a narrow selfishness, facilitates Christian discernment. In that sense liturgy is not so much didactic as evocative. Let *God* transpire; let *God* speak.

No, the Eucharistic signs and symbols do not of themselves change social, political, and economic structures, do not speak directly to complex issues of poverty and justice, of statecraft and technology. But they should change millions of hearts and minds, grace them to admit the oppressions of which they are victims and for which they are responsible, inspire them to struggle with others for the coming of a kingdom characterized by peace and justice and love.

This brings me back to the peril of a politicized liturgy. Here the peril I have in mind is not some manifest manipulation of the paschal mystery; such abuse can be recognized and rejected by all save its myopic sponsors. I am rather concerned about situations that are cloaked in ambiguity.

How ambiguous and controversial the use of liturgy can be as a force for social, political, or economic reform was illustrated in July 1986 in Mexico's northern state of Chihuahua. Archbishop Adalberto Almeida y Merino had issued a pastoral letter announcing that his 62 archdiocesan churches would cancel Sunday Masses on July 20, to protest allegedly fraudulent elections two weeks before in Chihuahua: "as a sign of protest, as a loud cry on our part for those whose eyes remain blindfolded or who have been blinded by their own guilt."[20] According to the pastoral, the July 6 Chihuahua gubernatorial and municipal elections—the most bitterly contested state elections in recent Mexican history—were so marred by fraud that they constituted "a social sin." Unexpectedly, John Paul II intervened and ordered the churches to remain open. According to newspaper reports, he did so to avert a confrontation between the Church and the government in a country where, for all the 95% who are nominally Catholic, anticlericalism and tight state control of religious activities force the Church to walk a perilously thin line, especially where intervention is seen as partisan political involvement. For our purposes in this chapter, the most revealing explanation of the Pope's intervention came from the apostolic delegate, Msgr. Jerónimo Prigione. Celebration of the Mass, he declared, "can never be an instrument of politically motivated pressure."

Without taking formal issue with the specific principle reportedly enunciated by the apostolic delegate, I find it at least intriguing that back in 1926, when the Ley Calles banished foreign priests and many bishops, imprisoned clergy and religious, and suppressed all Catholic schools, the Mexican bishops ordered their priests to suspend religious services in churches.[21] Undoubtedly, the episcopal pressure in '26 and in '86 was in a sense "politically motivated." But I suspect that the Mexican bishops, now as then, might argue, as Cardinal Sin did in the Philippines, that the basic issue was human rights, that in defense of human rights "intervention in politics" can be justified, and that the liturgy itself is not necessarily "used" illegitimately in such defense—no more than St. Ambrose abused the liturgy when he told Emperor Theodosius the Great that unless he did public penance for the massacre of several thousand citizens of Macedonia in 390, Ambrose would never offer the Sacrifice in church for him. If I may hazard a conjecture unsupported by direct evidence, I would not be surprised if John Paul II overturned the archbishop's order on solid prudential grounds rather than on the broad liturgical absolute as expressed by his delegate.

To sum up. The primary way in which the liturgy becomes a social force is through its own inner dynamism, by its incomparable power to turn the human heart inside out, free it from its focus on self, fling it out unfettered to the service of sisters and brothers enslaved. More specific "uses" of the liturgy, in concrete social, political, and economic situations, call for a collective discernment by the faithful and their leaders. Here, I suggest, two extremes should be avoided: on the one hand, manipulation of the Mass in the interests of ideologies; on the other, a perilous conservatism that would make the liturgy utterly inoffensive, a peaceful Sunday service where oppressed and oppressor can escape from the furies and passions of the week, simply praise God for His wonderful works.

III

So much for the theological question, so much for the liturgical question. The struggle for justice is an indispensable facet of the Church's mission, and the liturgy should express and mold this facet of human experience. Now for the stickiest issue of all, the homiletic question: Should the preacher preach justice—and if so, how? Is the pulpit an appropriate place for justice issues—and if so, is it possible to lay down a *modus operandi?*

The more general question—*Should* I preach justice?—ought not detain us, much less paralyze us. The specific function of the homily, as pointed out earlier, is not only to explain the liturgical mystery, but to bring the faithful into the mystery "by throwing light on their life so that they can unite it to this mystery. When this happens, the sermon is truly a word which prompts a response."[22] The liturgy's insights are rarely obvious; liturgical texts and forms tend to get fixed and rigid, are not much different in Buenos Aires than in Boise, Idaho. What the homily does is extend the immemorial symbols to a particular time and place, a particular people.[23] And so I must speak to this people's needs, this people's hungers. If they need to act justly, or if they hunger for justice, a liturgy which expresses and molds their faith experience forbids me to keep silent. To say nothing is to say something.

But what do I say? How concrete dare I get? For some, the priest simply preaches the gospel, the word of God, teaches what Jesus taught. Preach the word of God and parishioners will make the right decisions in the moral order. In a word, you limit yourself to general principles.

I'm afraid it will not wash for at least two good reasons. First, such limitation betrays a glorious tradition in the Church. It forgets how Ambrose of Milan, ordered by the Empress Justina to surrender a basilica to the Arians, *preached* a resounding no. "I am commanded," he declared to Justina's son, the Emperor Valentinian, " 'Hand over the basilica!' I reply: 'It is not right for me to hand it over; nor will it profit you, Emperor, to receive it. You cannot legally violate the home of a private citizen; do you think you can take away the house of God? . . . You may not have it. . . . ' "[24] It forgets that John Chrysostom, royally hated by the Empress Eudoxia, opened his homily on the feast of John the Baptist by crying: "Again Herodias raves; again she rages; again she dances; again she asks for the head of John upon a charger."[25] It will not square with John

Paul II's homily at a Mass in Santo Domingo's Independence Plaza on January 25, 1979:

> Making this world more just means, among other things, . . . to strive to have a world in which no more children lack sufficient nutrition, education, instruction; . . . that there be no more poor peasants without land . . . no more workers mistreated . . . no more systems which permit the exploitation of man by man or by the state . . . no more who have too much while others are lacking everything through no fault of their own . . . no injustice or inequality in administering justice; . . . that the law support everyone equally; that force not prevail over truth and rights . . . and that the economic and political never prevail over the human.[26]

At the beginning of his journey to Latin America, John Paul was not mouthing pious abstractions; he was addressing actual life-and-death issues. And thus has he preached wherever his travels have confronted him with social, political, or economic injustice.

Second, homilies that avoid concrete applications risk saying nothing. The Old Testament and the New are indeed our Bible, the privileged source of our faith and our morality. But if I mount the pulpit with "Scripture alone" in my hands, if I limit my preaching to the broad biblical imperatives, if I simply repeat scriptural slogans like "Man does not live on bread alone," "My peace I give to you," "Seek first the kingdom of God," "Love your neighbor as you love yourself," "Wives, be subject to your husbands," hungry stomachs will stay bloated, the arms race will escalate, dissidents will rot in political prisons, blacks will return to their slavery, and women will continue to be second-class citizens in much of the world. After all, it is not only the heathen who are responsible for oppression. The oppressors, large and small, often break Eucharistic bread with us. In fact, who among us is not, by act or silence, an oppressor of our brothers and sisters?

No, the gospel must be touched to concrete human living. And remember, the Church grows—the whole Church, pope as well as peasant—in its understanding of what the gospel demands. For example, in its efforts to construct a livable, viable social order, the Church has consistently stressed three facets of human living: truth, justice, and love. Only within recent times have these principles of social order been finally rounded out with a fourth principle indispensable in our days. I mean freedom. It is the growing realization that truth, justice, and love are not enough, are not really there, if the man and woman they serve are not free.

It is this that must be preached—our fresh understanding of what the perennial gospel demands or suggests in the context of our time and space. The magisterium does it (see *Mater et magistra* and *Populorum progressio*); the institutional Church need not, should not, and does not regard itself, in Karl Rahner's words, "solely as the doctrinaire guardian and teacher of abstract principles which become ever increasingly abstract and are liable to carry within themselves the danger of a terrifying sterility. . . . "[27] The Church has and should have the courage for concrete imperatives, concrete directives, "even in regard to socio-political action by Christians in the world."[28] This same courage, for concrete imperatives, concrete directives, the preacher must carry to his pulpit.

But the neuralgic problem remains: How concrete dare I get? First the bad news: There is no simple solution, no all-purpose push button to activate the answer. Each issue calls for discernment; some call for blood, sweat, and tears.

At times the issue is clear. In 1964 I simply had to endorse the Civil Rights Act; there was no alternative, save the enslavement of a race. But few political and socioeconomic issues are that clear-cut. Once you get beyond the general principles—the right to live and eat and work, the right to education and health care, the right to decent housing—it is difficult to locate the evil, to identify the villain, to pinpoint the solution. I can indeed proclaim from the pulpit today what the United Nations World Food Conference proclaimed from Rome in 1974: "every man, woman, and child has the inalienable right to freedom from hunger and malnutrition. . . . " But the causes are confoundingly complex. Is nature the villain—"acts of God"? Is it people—the world growing too fast? Is it productivity—lack of agricultural know-how? Is it our international economic order—a whole web of unjust relationships between rich and poor countries?[29] Experts, men and women of good will, disagree.

Now for the good news: Disagreement need not strike me dumb. It can only render me mute if I see the pulpit as the podium for eternal verities alone, defined dogma, the very words of Jesus. Beyond that, our delicate, indispensable task is to help form consciences. Not force them, form them. *There* is the crucial phrase, with each word of high significance: Help form a Christian conscience. I am not an expert on world hunger and defense budgets, but without playing partisan politics I can at least wax as indignant as World Bank President Robert S. McNamara when he denounced an arms race that then cost the nations more than 400 billion dollars a year, while over a billion men, women, and children were living in inhuman degradation, condemned to stunted bodies, darkened minds, shortened lives.[30] I do not know the political solution; I cannot fashion a budget; but I do know that those horrifying figures add up to a moral evil. Given that moral evil, how can I fail to echo the cry of HEW Secretary Joseph A. Califano Jr. at Notre Dame's 1979 commencement: "Of all the judgments of history and God we should fear, it is their judgment on our continued failure to use the means at hand to end the hunger of the world that we should fear most"?[31] This much at the very least God's people can expect of me: in the midst of my mind's chaos, a cry from the heart.

But what if I am convinced I do have the answer? The answer to the arms race is unilateral disarmament; to abortion, a constitutional amendment; to the parochial-school crisis, tax credits; to capital punishment, life imprisonment; to feminine enslavement, the ERA; to migrant-worker injustice, a boycott of grapes and lettuce; to Pretoria, economic sanctions. These are indeed moral issues; but may I preach my own solution in the name of the gospel? Of all homiletic mine fields, this may well be the most perilous. I shall move quickly and warily, aware that each step could trigger an explosion.

1) I do not see how you can bar the controversial from the pulpit simply because it is controversial. After all, I cannot be content with glittering generalities; I must move the gospel to this age, to this people; but the meaning and demands of the gospel today are chock-full of complexity. And the more complex an issue, the more open to controversy.

2) With Peter Henriot and George Higgins, I submit that "the pulpit, as a general rule, is not the proper forum in which to pontificate on complicated and highly controversial political and socioeconomic issues."[32] Here the crucial word is "pontificate." On such issues, in a short span of time, with no room for counterargument, I dare not speak in dogmatic fashion, as if I alone am the trumpet of the Lord.

3) If I dare not dogmatize, I may still raise the issues, lay them out, even tell the people where I stand and why. Not to impose my convictions as gospel, but to quicken their Christian conscience, to spur them to personal reflection.

4) I may not take unfair advantage of a captive audience, especially since the expertise in the pews often exceeds my own. Inasmuch as the suffering faithful, however sorely provoked, are

expected by immemorial custom to hold their tongues as I empty my quiver against ERA, I should provide another forum—parish hall, smaller discussion groups—where controversial issues may be properly debated, where all who wish to speak their piece may be heard. You see, I must guard against a persistent priestly peril, where I see the ordained minister as alone bearing the burden of Christian guidance, of pastoral counseling. Here Vatican II was clear, concise, and compelling: "Let the laity not imagine that their pastors are always such experts that to every problem which arises, however complicated, they can readily give a concrete solution, or even that such is their mission."[33] No, all of us are in this together; all of us, pope included, belong to an *ecclesia discens,* a church that is learning.

5) In line with that realization—we are one body, animated by the same Spirit, and all of us need one another—many a priest must reappraise his attitude toward the people who must listen to him. Some years ago an Irish layman rapped our homiletic knuckles sharply:

> I am afraid that too often our preachers entirely ignore what we, the silent faithful, expect to hear in a sermon. . . . They address us as rebels whom they must subdue; as idlers whom they must shake up; as hardened sinners whom they must needs terrify; as the proud who require to be humiliated; as the self-satisfied who need to be disquieted. . . . [They] are never done telling us of our duties and of our neglect of duty. . . . But if you come to examine it, there is really nothing easier than to put forward a person's duty; and to hand out reproaches costs nothing either. . . . The thing which is really difficult, which is actually divine, is to give us a taste for our duties, and to awaken in us a wish to do them and to be generous in the doing. And another name for a taste for duty is love. Beloved preachers, then, make us love God, or rather, help us to believe in his love for us.[34]

Those striking words have troubled me from the moment I discovered them. Especially the last several sentences: The divine thing "is to give us a taste for our duties . . . help us to believe in [God's] love for us." This does not mean that, in harmony with the Argentinian I quoted at the outset of this chapter, we preach an abstract, bloodless "love of God" utterly unrelated to the situations that deface God's human image. It only means that we should not "beat on" our people indiscriminately, cut a wide and savage swath across a congregation. It means that we see before us a believing community that, like the Israelites of old, needs to be led rather than driven on its tortuous pilgrimage to the Promised Land.

Very recently, in a quiet moment between addresses on preaching in the Diocese of Rockville Centre, Long Island, a permanent deacon of the diocese lent me a useful suggestion from his long years in the advertising game. If preaching is to be effective, he noted, especially in troublesome areas of social justice that divide a community (e.g., the U.S. bishops' pastorals on peace and the economy), it can learn much from the approach of the advertiser—on TV and radio, in newspapers and magazines. Know your audience: what turns them on or off, their hang-ups, their backgrounds and social situations, the influences on their living and thinking. Don't pontificate or browbeat; use all the arts of persuasion, the arts that sell millions each day on products they never suspected were essential to human living. "The children of this world are shrewder . . ." (Lk 16:8).

6) My final point has to do with a principle I have stressed earlier in this volume: Ultimately, *I* am the word, the word that is heard. Ralph Waldo Emerson insisted that "The preacher should be a poet." He meant that "a man's sermon should be rammed with life."[35] That is why, in the midst of a famous iconoclastic address at the Harvard Divinity School on July 15, 1838, he railed at the junior pastor of his grandfather Ripley's church in Concord:

> I once heard a preacher who sorely tempted me to say I would go to church no more. . . . He had lived in vain. He had no one word intimating that he had laughed or wept, was married or in love, had been commended, or cheated, or chagrined. If he had ever lived or acted, we were none the wiser for it. The capital secret of his profession, namely, to convert life into truth, he had not learned. Not one fact in all his experience, had he yet imported into his doctrine. . . . Not a line did he draw out of real history. The true preacher can always be known by this, that he deals out to the people his life,—life passed through the fire of thought.[36]

It is understandable that our people hear no one word from us intimating that we are married or "in love." It passes understanding that our people rarely sense from the homiletic word that our hearts are in anguish because Christians are murdering Christians in the north of Ireland, because ten million Americans go to bed hungry each night, because human rights are bloodied in South Africa, because 200,000 homeless humans have to defecate at curbstones in

Calcutta, because on my street there are people who are lonely or hungry or scared. Can they feel that I get angry, that I cry, that I beat my fists against a wall in frustration, that I shout out to God against His own seeming injustice? Or do they feel that in my case "the just word" is just a word and nothing more?

And so, what I put to preachers most urgently on preaching the just word goes beyond the word that is preached. I phrase it in two questions. (1) Do you *live* the just word you preach? Are you, as St. James puts it, a "doer" of the just word, "a doer that acts" (Jas 1:22–25), or do you simply speak it? Does your just word leap forth from some experience of our sorry human condition? Is it your life that passes through the fire of your thought? (2) How do you *celebrate* the just word, the Word who *is* Justice? Do the faithful sense that it is *your* body too that is being offered for them, *your* blood too that is being shed for them? From your celebration of transcendence, do they experience the God who enables them to "execute justice"?

10
OF THEIR RACE IS THE CHRIST
How To Preach about the Jews

At first blush, a puzzling chapter—perhaps even arrogant. Who asked me to preach about the Jews? Not the Jews themselves, who would surely have the highest stake in such a gamble.[1] Why not leave them alone? From Chrysostom and his forebears to Luther and beyond, hasn't the Christian pulpit done enough injustice to the Jews?

Good questions all, but the answer is not as obvious as it seems. The solution is not a respectful silence anent the Jews. Even if I never center a single sermon on the Jews of yesterday or the Jews of today, the single most significant source of my preaching is Scripture. And what is the Old, or Hebrew, or Prior Testament if not the story of God's shaping of a special people? And are the Gospels abstract theological theses or not rather the enfleshed Son of God face to face with "the house of Israel"? And how long can we preach the Pauline epistles before we run afoul of Paul confronting Rome's Christians with "the Jewish problem" (Romans 9–11)—the same Paul who "spoke out boldly" to the Jews in Antioch of Pisidia: "It was necessary that the word of God should be spoken first to you. Since you thrust it from you, and judge yourselves unworthy of eternal life, behold, we turn to the Gentiles" (Acts 13:46)? And in these our days, when reconciliation is a byword and Christian-Jewish dialogue is a continuing must, is it practical or even possible to exclude the Jews from our homilies, to ghetto them in chambers marked "theologians only"? I say no. This much granted, I suggest that the problem "how to preach about the Jews" may be fruitfully faced if we focus on (1) the Old Testament, (2) the New Testament, and (3) the signs of our times.

I

In harmony with the Catholic theology of the 30s and 40s, the Old Testament was presented to my untutored Jesuit ears on two different but related levels. First, with a deep bow to St. Augustine, the New Testament was seen to be hidden in the Old, the Old come to light in the New. Second, the Old Testament offered proof-texts for many of our theological theses: striking examples, Gen 3:15 for Mary's immaculate conception, Isa 7:14 for Jesus' virginal conception. On both levels we were heirs to a centuries-long tradition. There was the effort of early Christian Alexandria, Origen in particular, to find Christ throughout the Hebrew Scriptures. There was the famous medieval distich that enshrined so much of the exegesis of the first Christian millennium:

> Littera gesta docet, quid credas allegoria,
> Moralis quid agas, quo tendas anagogia.[2]

Four scriptural senses. (1) Scripture gives us actual facts (*gesta*), the story of God's interventions in the story of humanity. This is the first thing to be learned, the foundation of all the rest. (2) Allegory here is the doctrine, the very object of faith, the "mystery," the ensemble of truths concerning Christ and his Church, prefigured everywhere in the Old Testament, presented in the New. (3) Morality is not just any moral instruction, but that which flows from the dogma, from the mystery. The whole Bible is then a mirror, where I learn to know myself with my misery and my sin, and the perfection to which God destines and calls me; in the facts of Scripture we find the inward drama of the soul. (4) Anagoge is the eschatological sense, that of the last things, the celestial realities which are no longer the symbol of something else. The classic, all-inclusive example is Jerusalem, which is (1) the historical city of the Jews, (2) the Church, (3) the Christian soul, and (4) the heavenly Jerusalem, the Church triumphant.

The stress on spiritual senses has seen its biblical and theological day. The modern emphasis rests on the literal or primitive and primary sense of the author(s), complemented by a typical and/or fuller sense rigorously controlled, in the first instance by Scripture itself. And still, Vatican II could declare: "God, inspirer and author of the books of both Testaments, has wisely arranged that the New Testament be hidden in the Old and the Old be made manifest in the New."[3] And a bit more fully: " . . . the books of the Old Testament with all their parts, caught up in the proclamation of the gospel, acquire and disclose their full meaning in the New Testament . . . and in turn cast light on it and explain it."[4] As a Christian, therefore, I must, and I do, see the word of God reaching a definitive climax in Christ. I dare not downplay or conceal this conviction in my preaching, but is this the sum total of what I preach? Is this all I see when I open the Hebrew Bible? Does it make sense for me to try to understand the Old Testament "on its own terms"? May I claim, with an imprisoned Bonhoeffer, that it is not really Christian to want to get to the New Testament too soon and too directly?

It is not my task or within my competence to settle a still unsettled question: What precisely is the unity of the two Testaments? How in detail do they relate? I intend rather to suggest a broader approach to the Old Testament that may help the Christian homilist, an approach that does not deny but does move beyond the sheer "Novum in Vetere latet, Vetus in Novo patet."

First, an admonition that may not be as impertinent for the preacher as it seems at first glance: It is unchristian to treat the Old Testament as if it were simply superseded or even diabolical. Ours not the position of second-century Marcion, who repudiated the Old Testament as devoid of any revelation of the Christian God. Ours not the posture of Harnack: "The early Church was quite right to keep the Old Testament in the beginning, but she should have jettisoned it very soon. It was a disaster for the Lutheran reform to keep it in the 16th century. But for Protestantism to cling to it as a canonical document in the 20th century is a sign of religious and ecclesial paralysis."[5] Ours not the Nazi postulate of the 30s against which Pope Pius XI protested with flaming phrases: "Whoever wishes to see banished from church and school the biblical history and the wise doctrines of the Old Testament, blasphemes the name of God, blasphemes the Almighty's plan of salvation, and makes limited and narrow human thought the judge of God's designs over the history of the world: he denies his faith in the true Christ. . . . "[6] Ours not a simplistic opposition between law and gospel, as if Torah were divorced from love of God or of His images on earth. I must remember that, for Jesus, Scripture, the word of God, was purely and simply the Old Testament. On this he was spiritually nourished; this he came to "fulfil" (Mt 5:17). Even when he pronounced his startling "You have heard . . . but I say to you" (Mt 5:21 ff.), he was moving a morality he respected to a level arguably a bit higher.

Second, and more constructively, the Old Testament incarnates values which John McKenzie has persuasively divided into universal, Christian, and theological.[7] Among the universal values you find a ceaseless insistence on one only God, splendidly personal, with no room for gross superstition. You find an unparalleled insight into the human person and the human condition, an unrivaled vision of man and woman in history, a precious presentation of the common, universal experience of suffering. You find a striking sense of history's unity: "God originated history, and God will bring history to a term."[8] Over against the Greek specter of destiny, you find a rich record of inner freedom: Despite the Hebrew confession of divine sovereignty, human history is what humans make it to be. There is a good, and I can achieve it; God wills me to achieve it; and history is so directed that I should achieve it. You find an infectious joy in living. Oh yes, the Old Testament is touchingly aware of peril and pain, of temporality and mortality; and still it delights in the sheer pleasure of breathing and moving, of integration with nature and with one's fellows, relishes work as well as play, laughs at the incongruous and joys in achievement. Ambivalent on an afterlife, God's most ancient Book makes it clear that mere survival is not an absolute, that life is not worth living if the price is moral integrity, that human dignity at times demands a yes to death and its darkness.

Besides such universal values, the Old Testament enshrines Christian values. To find Christian values in the Hebrew Bible is not to Christianize it, to impose upon a text anachronistically a meaning it did not have. I do not tell the Jews how to read a Book that is peculiarly theirs. I mean what McKenzie expressed so well:

> When the Word becomes flesh, a man is born; this man is a member of a particular human community and of a particular generation of mankind by nativity. Much of what he is has already been determined by the place and time of his nativity. The Word could not become universal man; he is qualified by those adjectives which we use to distinguish one human group from another. Jesus was a Palestinian Jew of the 1st century of our era; he neither lacked nor sought to escape the determinations that this historical fact laid upon him. It follows that he cannot be known unless these determinations are known. We do not imply that he

cannot be known at all; we do imply that he can be known better
if he is known in his historical reality.[9]

If I am to preach Jesus as the apostolic Church did—the Messiah of Israel—it behooves me to understand the complex of beliefs
and hopes that "Messiah" signified in Judaism. Jesus transformed
the title, but he did not create it. "He asked for faith in something
that they could recognize; otherwise they could hardly have been at
fault in withholding belief. He spoke directly to them in terms of
the traditions that he shared with them. Can one approach him if
one is an utter stranger to those traditions?"[10]

If I am to preach the reign of God as Jesus did, I cannot preach
it in utter abstraction, divorced from the people of God to whom he
preached it. I must share the varied traditions Jesus inherited about
Yahweh as king.[11] He is supreme Lord, Israel's redeemer and savior. He leads the dispersed of Israel back to a glorious restoration.
His rule will extend to all nations. It is a rule of justice through Yahweh's judgment against the impious and in favor of Israel. It means
political independence from Israel's neighboring enemies. The future kingdom will be established through some kind of cosmic catastrophe. And yes, God's dominion over His people has one
primary purpose: to raise man and woman to communion with
Him.

Now the kingdom Jesus proclaimed was not created in a vacuum; it was to fulfil what had begun in Israel. For all its newness,
Jesus saw "the kingdom after the fashion of the prophets and
psalmists: as the gratuitous, personal intervention of God into the
course of history in order to make His will prevail among men and
to destroy the empire of Satan."[12] Daniel and Deutero-Isaiah, Ezekiel and Jeremiah—without them I risk preaching a bloodless kingdom—perhaps a bloodless Jesus.

If I am to preach the Fatherhood of God as God Himself disclosed it, I may not see it as a creation of Jesus, to replace an Old
Testament despot. The Father Jesus preached was recognizable to
his compatriots: the same Yahweh they worshiped, the God who
saves by judging and judges by saving, the Lord whose faithful love
monotonously challenged Israel's infidelity. The triune God intimated in the New Covenant does not displace the fatherly God who
could reassure Israel in an unexpected image:

> Can a woman forget her sucking child,
>   that she should have no compassion

on the son of her womb?
Even these may forget,
   yet I will not forget you.
Behold, I have graven you on the palms of my hands.
                     (Isa 49:15–16a)

Almost every important religious word in the New Testament was employed with a specific traditional meaning. "The Christian transformation of these ideas presupposes and rises from the tradition."[13] There is a significant message here, not only for scholars of the text but for preachers of the word.

Theological values are, obviously, not a category neatly distinguishable from Christian values. I use "theological" here, as McKenzie does, to suggest what we can learn from the very human discipline that presupposes Christian belief and ideally should nourish it. Under this heading I simply submit that traditional Catholic theology has much to learn—and in recent years has learned much—from the Old Testament approach to God and the human person. It is a crucial lesson for homiletics as well. We are so accustomed to rationalizing; since Descartes, the perfection of knowledge is the clear and distinct idea. For the Old Testament, to know God is to experience Him. And to experience Him not in the timeless realm of the abstract, of the general, but in the personal encounter that is history. God does not encounter man, does not encounter woman.

He encounters Abraham, Moses, David, Amos, Isaiah [and, I would add, Ruth, Judith, the mother of the Maccabees]. He encounters Israel at a determined date and place, at a concrete moment of history that will never be repeated. The response of men is equally concrete and definite; it is a response made in a particular situation, and it must reflect that situation. The response of one is not the response of another, for the demands of one situation are not those of another. Each one responds according to the needs and the possibilities that are his when he is called; and if his response does not reflect his personal situation, if the revolution does not occur in the real life in which he is engaged, it is not a genuine response. It is the response of the Athenians to Paul's discourse: "We will listen to you about this some other time." The response is action, immediate and radical. . . . [14]

There is all this in the Old Testament, all this for us, all this and so much more: an incomparably candid self-criticism, together with a constructive criticism of the world that is ultimately an utterance of God's word to living people;[15] books like Job and Qoheleth that raise enduring questions, psalms and prophets that challenge our self-sufficiency, our pride, our infidelity;[16] Abraham's exemplary faith, seen down into the Christian era as a prototype of our own, a total commitment to the living God;[17] commandments that give life, boundary markers that stake out the territory of God's dominion and still allow for free development within their borders;[18] a progressive pedagogy, an *aggiornamento* that "renews the covenants and clears the ground of institutions as decrepit as they are venerable."[19]

For my own part, I have preached some of my most effective sermons on Old Testament themes: on a bewildered Job,[20] on a recalcitrant Jonah.[21] Even more frequently, I have constructed my homily on an Old Testament foundation: for the 50th anniversary of Johannes Quasten's ordination, the wise man and the wise woman of the Hebrews;[22] for the beatitudes, the "poor" in Israel;[23] for a Thanksgiving sermon, thanks and praise in the Old Testament;[24] for the feast of the Dedication of St. John Lateran, Solomon's prayer at the dedication of the temple in Jerusalem;[25] for riches and the kingdom, the Old Testament tradition of wealth and God's favor;[26] for forgiveness, the Hebrew experience of a forgiving God;[27] for love of God and neighbor, Deut 6:4–9 and love in the Torah;[28] for Matthew's three servants entrusted with their master's money, the ideal wife of Proverbs;[29] for Advent, the Exile;[30] for the First Sunday of Lent, biblical repentance;[31] for the Fifth Sunday of Lent, Isaiah's God "doing a new thing";[32] for Passion/Palm Sunday, Isaiah's Suffering Servant;[33] for wedding homilies, Gen 2:18–24,[34] Gen 1:26–31,[35] and Tobit 8:4–9.[36] And so on and so forth.

An important observation. I am convinced that in such homiletic use of Scripture I am not doing violence to the inspired text; I am not reading the New Testament into the Old; I am trying to see clearly and express faithfully what the Old Testament is saying on its own terms. As a Christian, I do indeed acknowledge an intimate unity between the two Testaments. Nevertheless, instructed by the vagaries of Christian exegesis and theology in this regard, I make every effort not to ape the excesses of my dear Origen, while still persuaded that the Prior Testament is a pedagogue to Jesus Christ.

II

If the Old Testament tempts the unwary Christian to minimize or misinterpret its rich values, the New Testament has its own special pitfalls where the house of Israel is concerned. Space permits me to approach only two of the problems that should give pause to the preacher. I mean (1) anti-Semitism and (2) the Pharisees.

Anti-Semitism

A small section in a single chapter within a book about preaching is hardly suited to discussing, let alone solving, the issue of anti-Semitism in the New Testament. Such is not my purpose. I propose simply to alert Christian preachers to the problem and suggest where especially we should walk warily and talk thoughtfully.

The problem itself is real, not artificial. On the one hand, uncounted Christians dismiss out of hand, a priori, any intimation of anti-Semitism in the New Testament. Anti-Semitism is a sin, and the New Testament is God's inspired word, divinely protected against sin and error. On the other hand, Jews as a whole find the Gospels and Paul obviously biased against "the Jews," scandalously unjust in their accusations, the source of most of the anti-Semitism that has cursed the earth from the earliest Christian communities through the medieval ghettos down to the gas chambers of Dachau and Auschwitz. What to say in brief?

First, a general statement of homiletic policy and a strong resolution: I shall no longer preach from ignorance. If I am to preach the gospel, I must know the Gospels. This calls not only for prayerful contemplation but for careful study. Oh I know that unless he is a Scripture scholar like Myles Bourke of Corpus Christi in New York City, the harried pastor can hardly be an expert on the Evangelists and the Jews. I myself am not, despite a lifetime in the patristic era. What to do? Begin with a good recent book. I have been enormously aided by John G. Gager's *The Origins of Anti-Semitism: Attitudes toward Judaism in Pagan and Christian Antiquity*.[37] Gager's first two chapters suggest where scholars sit at the moment, for he summarizes the significant literature stimulated by the Jewish experience in World War II.[38]

Specifically, Gager shows me the French historian Jules Isaac inaugurating a new era of research in 1948 with his *Jesus and Israel*. When his wife and daughter were murdered by the Nazis in 1943, Isaac started, aged 66, two projects that would end only with his death 20 years later: the Christian origins of anti-Semitism, and Jewish-Christian co-operation. One of his main theses: The Jews of Jesus' time neither rejected him nor crucified him; and Jesus did not reject Israel. "The net effect of Isaac's work has been twofold: (1) to lay the blame for anti-Semitism squarely at the door of Christianity; and (2) to buttress the argument that anti-Semitism, while exclusively a Christian product, results from a misinterpretation by Christians of their own scriptures and founder, and stands in fundamental opposition to the historical origins and basic tenets of Christianity."[39]

Gager shows me Marcel Simon's *Verus Israel*, which dominated the postwar era till quite recently. Although Simon faults Isaac for failing to distinguish adequately between anti-Semitism and anti-Jewish apologetic, he agrees with Isaac fundamentally in recognizing "that there is no clear line of separation between anti-Jewish polemic and anti-Semitism and that systematic hostility toward Jews is to be found from the very beginnings of Christianity."[40]

Gager shows me the most telling research after Simon. There is the French scholar F. Lovsky, arguing that "With the possible exception of the Gospel of John, anti-Semitism as such is not to be found in the New Testament." He attributes "the increase of anti-Semitic views in Christian circles of the second, third, and fourth centuries to the impact of popular anti-Semitism throughout the Greco-Roman world."[41] There is Gregory Baum, convert from Judaism, at first distinguishing "sharply between the legitimate, theological anti-Judaism of the New Testament and modern, racial anti-Semitism,"[42] then, in his introduction to Rosemary Ruether's *Faith and Fratricide,* citing her work "as one among several factors that had forced him to abandon his earlier attempts to defend the New Testament against the charge that its writings reflect a fundamental hostility toward Jews and Judaism."[43] And there is Ruether herself, who "not only embraces [Isaac's] basic position on the Christian sources of modern anti-Semitism but moves beyond it on the issue of the inseparability of anti-Semitism and early Christianity."[44] Isaac and Simon, Baum and Ruether, these scholars I had read in part; what Gager did was enable me to see post-Holocaust scholarship in its living movements and its vital relationships.

This is not the place to rehearse Gager's own theses and arguments, much less to provide an evaluation at second hand. My point for the preacher is simply this: I dare not disregard the serious scholarship that attempts to plumb the earliest Christian attitudes toward the Jews—the communities, the Evangelists and Paul, Jesus himself. And with a dash of courage and imagination I can do it.

Not to bog down in generalities, I submit that the Christian preacher must be intelligently aware of a handful of specific trouble spots in the New Testament: Luke's use of "the crowds" where Matthew and/or Mark specify the authorities; John's expression "the Jews" in clearly hostile contexts; "the mob" at Jerusalem in the Passion accounts. And there is the confrontation between Paul and Diaspora Judaism: What went so tragically wrong that, despite some Jewish acceptance, Paul turned from "the Jews" to the Gentiles? No room for discussion here; but the Christian preacher should know, for example, that a careful analysis of the evidence has led a good Catholic biblical scholar to conclude: "the oft-repeated statement that the Jews rejected Jesus and had Him crucified is *historically* untenable and must therefore be removed completely from our thinking and our writing, our teaching, preaching, and liturgy."[45] That conclusion preceded by several months the strong affirmation of the Second Vatican Council:

> True, authorities of the Jews and those who followed their lead pressed for the death of Christ (cf. Jn 19:6); still, what happened in his passion cannot be blamed upon all the Jews then living, without distinction, nor upon the Jews of today. Although the Church is the new people of God, the Jews should not be presented as repudiated or cursed by God, as if such views followed from the holy Scriptures. All should take pains, then, lest in catechetical instruction and in the preaching of God's Word they teach anything out of harmony with the truth of the gospel and the spirit of Christ.[46]

Pharisees

A second problem for the preacher: the Pharisees. We begin with a built-in bias. The word has entered our everyday vocabulary. You are pharisaical, Webster's unabridged second edition (1958) informs us, if you are "addicted to external forms and ceremonies; outwardly but not inwardly religious; formal; hypocritical; self-righteous and censorious of others' manners and morals." Something like an adjective that makes Jesuits bristle: You are jesuitical if you are "designing" or "crafty." Moreover, we tend to identify all Pharisees of Jesus' time with the Pharisee in Luke's parable, the Jew who stood in the temple and prayed: "God, I thank you that I am not like other folk" (Lk 18:11).

Well, why not? Didn't Jesus himself reserve his choicest maledictions for the Pharisees? Alongside Matthew 23, Webster is dreadfully dull:

> Woe to you, Pharisees, hypocrites, because you shut the kingdom of heaven against men. . . . Woe to you, for you make [a proselyte] twice as much a child of hell as yourselves. . . . Woe to you, for you have neglected the weightier matters of the law, justice and mercy and faith. . . . Woe to you, for you cleanse the outside of the cup and of the plate, but inside [you] are full of extortion and rapacity. . . . Woe to you, for you are like whitewashed tombs, outwardly beautiful, but within full of dead men's bones and all uncleanness. . . . You serpents, you brood of vipers, how are you to escape being sentenced to hell?
>
> (Mt 23:13–33)

Softly now! This is not quite what history reveals. Much that we know about the Pharisees evokes respect.[47] Their lifeblood was the law of Moses: not only the written Torah but the oral as well, the tradition ascribed to Moses and the elders, interpretations of the written Torah propounded since postexilic times. A Jew would be saved, the nation made holy, only by knowing the law thoroughly and following it exactly: Sabbath and feast days, ritual purity, tithing, dietary laws—all 613 imperatives. The code may repel you, but in fairness never forget that what the Pharisees were trying to codify was love, loyalty, compassion; they wanted to make of them inescapable religious duties, in this way to fashion an intimate relationship between a Father who cared and the children He cared about. (Isn't this the way Catholics are expected to see the Code of Canon Law—all 1752 canons?) Remember, too, that the Pharisees believed firmly and fixedly in human freedom under the control of providence, in bodily resurrection, angels, the coming of a Messiah, the ingathering of Israel and its tribes at the end of time.

If this be true, how does the preacher handle Matthew 23—and more generally, the Gospel texts on "the Pharisees"? This chapter is not an essay in exegesis or biblical theology; still, a suggestion or two may be wafted toward the pulpit. First, to speak of "the Pharisees" indiscriminately is no more justified than to speak of "the Jews" without distinction. Or of "the Jesuits"! Some Pharisees warned Jesus that Herod was thirsting for his blood (Lk 13:31). The Pharisee Gamaliel told a council of Jews who wanted to kill the apostles: " . . . let them alone; for if . . . this undertaking is of men, it will fail; but if it is of God, you will not be able to overthrow them. You might even be found opposing God!" (Acts 5:38–39). And St. Paul, Paul the Christian, cried out to a council of Jews: "I am a Pharisee, a son of Pharisees" (Acts 23:6).

Second, and more importantly, you must understand that not every Gospel sentence prefaced by "Jesus said" reports exact words that fell from the lips of the Master. Should this strike you as heresy, read the Pontifical Biblical Commission's 1964 *Instruction on the Historical Truth of the Gospels*.[48] That significant document insisted that, if you want to understand what is transmitted in the Gospels, you must "pay diligent attention to the three stages of tradition by which the doctrine and the life of Jesus have come down to us."[49] What are these three stages? (1) What the Jesus of history did and said— say between the years 1 and 33 A.D. (2) What the apostles and disciples preached about him and his message—the years 33 to 65. (3) What the Evangelists recorded as they selected from and synthesized that preaching and explicated it in four different literary compositions—between 65 and 95. In that third stage, the Commission explains,

> from what they had received the sacred writers above all selected the things which were suited to the various situations of the faithful and to the purpose which they had in mind, and adapted their narration of them to the same situations and purpose. Since the meaning of a statement also depends on the sequence, the Evangelists, in passing on the words and deeds of our Saviour, explained these now in one context, now in another, depending on (their) usefulness to the readers. Consequently, let the exegete seek out the meaning intended by the Evangelist in narrating a saying or a deed in a certain way or in placing it in a certain context. For the truth of the story is not at all affected by the fact that the Evangelists relate the words and deeds of the Lord in a different order, and *express his sayings not literally but differently*, while preserving (their) sense.[50]

With that last sentence in mind, move from 1964 to 1984, from the Biblical Commission's *Instruction on the Historical Truth of the Gospels* to the same Commission's document *The Bible and Christology*.[51] Speaking of "the disputes in which Jesus was involved with groups of Pharisees espousing stricter discipline [the pietist current]," the Catholic scholars "admit that the Gospel accounts could have described more harshly than was right the original state of affairs."[52]

Take Matthew. We know he was writing in a situation where he had to show his community that it was "no longer a sectarian group within Judaism but had become an independent movement separate from Jamnia Pharisaism and rooted in Jesus Christ."[53] To do this, he stressed the Jewish Messiah Jesus in tension with the scribes and Pharisees.

> Matthew's anti-Pharisaism reaches its climax when Jesus teaches his disciples and the crowds how their behavior should differ from that of the scribes and Pharisees, then denounces his enemies as hypocrites and blind guides, and finally laments over Jerusalem (23:1–39). . . . True followers of Jesus . . . are to humble themselves and take on the role of a servant (23:8–12). Such a stark contrast would enable the Matthean community to understand how their behavior is to be patterned after that of Jesus rather than that of the Jamnia scribes and Pharisees.[54]

But what does this third stage of the tradition do to the first stage? If the Evangelists do not necessarily reproduce the Master word for word, how can we get back to what has always seemed of supreme importance, the *ipsissima verba Iesu*—what Jesus actually said? This is a critical task for biblical scholarship, and the results are frequently frustrating, often controverted. For preachers, it calls for an awareness that here we walk amid land mines. Gospel truth, specifically "Jesus said," is not tied to some fundamentalistic literalness. As the 1964 *Instruction* insisted:

> From the results of the new investigations it is apparent that the doctrine and the life of Jesus were not simply reported for the sole purpose of being remembered, but were "preached" so as to offer the Church a basis of faith and of morals. The interpreter (then), by tirelessly scrutinizing the testimony of the Evangelists, will be able to illustrate more profoundly the perennial theological value of the Gospels and bring out clearly how necessary and important the Church's interpretation is.[55]

In the first century the Church was already interpreting the words of Jesus, was already telling Christians what Jesus *meant*, was already, in the Gospels it was writing, applying his words to new situations. And it was doing so under God's inspiration.

A fresh burden for a preacher? Undoubtedly. I struggle mightily with the Gospel parables, to uncover what is literally of Jesus and what stems from the apostolic Church. I sweat blood over Matthew

23, to distinguish the original confrontation of Jesus with Pharisees from a later community's encounter with its own Pharisees. Is it worth the struggle, the sweat? Yes indeed! If only because my preaching is now more Christian. I do not play games with history, do not downplay Jesus' conflicts with Pharisees, do not minimize the risks in Pharisaism. But "Pharisee" has ceased to be a dirty word; I even use the disparaging adjective "pharisaical" less frequently than you might use . . . "jesuitical."

III

My third point stems from a thrilling fact: God did not cease speaking early in the second century, when the Second Letter of Peter closed the scriptural canon. God still speaks to His people, and one way in which He speaks to us, preachers included, is through the "signs of the times." This is not gossamer rhetoric. By "signs of the times" I mean events, situations, movements that at given moments, at certain times, reveal to us what God wants of us. Not always easy to diagnose, to translate, to interpret; but at the very least they compel us to stop and think, to look and listen. Such was the rebellion of the blacks a quarter century ago, a nonviolent "We shall overcome" that forced us to face a revolutionary fact: At this point in the evolution of humanity and society, to define the human as "rational animal" is not existential enough; you are not human if you are not free. Such too, I suggest, is the feminist movement of today: Our eyes are opening to a centuries-old global sin, Adam's ceaseless rape of Eve. Here and elsewhere we must listen for God's voice; else we are in terrible danger of human folly. Folly? Historian Barbara Tuchman defined it for us: "persistence in ignoring the signs, the refusal to draw anything from the evidence."[56]

Holocaust

For Jewish-Christian relations, for the Christian preacher, several signs of the times are critical. By far the most awesome is the Holocaust. In the march of human folly, some say the Holocaust never happened. But it did; dear God, it did. What does it say? For some Jews, it says that "God died in Auschwitz"; for other Jews, how can you *not* believe after Auschwitz? What might it say to the Christian, especially to the Christian preacher?

First, it should raise questions about Christian preaching in the past. Consorting with the Fathers of the Church for half a century, I have been regularly embarrassed, dismayed, shocked by so many of their sermons against the Jews. I do not mean their anti-Judaism, their negative reaction to Judaism on theological grounds, their understandable confrontation with Jews, for example, on the issue of Jesus as Messiah. I mean a fair amount of out-and-out anti-Semitism that has its roots in the theological but goes far beyond it in day-to-day hostility. To Chrysostom, for one, the Jews are sensual and voluptuous, avaricious and possessed by demons; they are drunkards and harlots, breakers of their very law; they are the people who murdered the prophets, murdered Christ, murdered God. Take one segment from a sermon to the Christians of Antioch, probably in August 386:

> Many, I know, respect the Jews and think that their present way of life is a venerable one. This is why I hasten to uproot and tear out this deadly opinion. I said that the synagogue is no better than a theater and I bring forward a prophet as my witness . . . : "You had a harlot's brow; you became shameless before all" (cf. Jer 3:3 LXX). Where a harlot has set herself up, that place is a brothel. But the synagogue is not only a brothel and a theater; it also is a den of robbers and a lodging for wild beasts. Jeremiah said: "Your house has become for me the den of a hyena" (cf. Jer 7:11 LXX and 12:9 LXX). . . . God is not worshipped there. Heaven forbid! From now on it remains a place of idolatry. But still some people pay it honor as a holy place.[57]

Even if, as has been persuasively argued, these discourses "were delivered in a Christian church to a Christian congregation with few, if any, Jews actually present,"[58] the prince of patristic preachers is painful to read here. Neither the circumscribed setting of the sermons nor the Judaizing tendency among Christians lessens their defamatory character or excuses their anti-Semitism.[59] And such preaching can have staggering consequences, not only on the day of delivery but for centuries thereafter. In this connection I recall the recollection of Rabbi Marc Tanenbaum at the University of Notre Dame two decades ago:

> . . . one must confront as one of the terrible facts of this period [Nazism] the conversation that took place between Adolf Hitler and two bishops in April, 1933, when they began raising questions about the German policy toward the Jews and Hitler said to

them, as reported in the book, *Hitler's Table-Talk,* that he was simply completing what Christian teaching and preaching had been saying about the Jews for the better part of 1,900 years.[60]

Tanenbaum went on to recall an incident in Buenos Aires in June 1963, when members of a Neo-Fascist group of young Catholics kidnaped a Jewish girl on her way home from the university and carved a swastika in her breast. The chaplain of the movement "has claimed that he bases his 'ministry' to these students . . . on the fact that the tradition of St. John Chrysostom's views toward the Jews and Judaism and those who have repeated that tradition, represent the authentic view of the Church toward the Jewish people and to Judaism."[61]

Protestant preachers, for their part, would do well to keep before their eyes the (in this instance) less than shining example of Martin Luther. Early on (about 1513–23), Luther frequently condemned persecution of the Jews and recommended greater tolerance. As time went on, however, he grew more and more hostile. In pamphleteering (e.g., "On the Jews and Their Lies," 1542) and/or preaching (e.g., "Admonition against the Jews," 1546, shortly before his death) he complained about their diabolical stubbornness, subjected them to vile abuse, even suggested specific anti-Jewish action: forced labor, deportation to Palestine, burning of their synagogues, expropriation of their books, including the Bible. Although we can agree with Roland Bainton that Luther's "position was entirely religious and in no respect racial,"[62] the fact remains that "many of the Protestant rulers of the times relied on Luther's political advice" and so "his attitude resulted in the expulsion of the Jews from Saxony in 1543 and the hostile *Judenordnung* of Landgrave Philip of Hesse in the same year."[63] Theological anti-Judaism can trigger practical anti-Semitism—especially if you are a popular preacher.

Rome and the Jews

A second "sign" stems from the Catholic side. I mean a 1985 document from the Vatican's Commission for Religious Relations with the Jews, on the correct way to speak of Jews and Judaism in our preaching and catechesis.[64] The "Notes" should be read in their entirety; here I select a handful of affirmations of special concern for the preacher.

1) The Commission repeats Pope John Paul II's striking affir-

mation in Mainz on November 17, 1980, to the Jewish community of West Germany: " . . . the people of God of the Old Covenant, which has never been revoked."[65]

2) On the basis of Jesus' assertion that "there shall be one flock, one shepherd" (Jn 10:16), the Commission concludes: "Church and Judaism cannot then be seen as two parallel ways of salvation, and the Church must witness to Christ as the redeemer for all. . . . "[66]

3) Christians must be educated "to appreciate and love [the Jews], who have been chosen by God to prepare the coming of Christ and have preserved everything that was progressively revealed and given in the course of that preparation, notwithstanding the difficulty in recognizing in him their Messiah."[67]

4) As for the relationship between the two Testaments, we Christians do indeed "read the Old Testament in the light of the event of the dead and risen Christ" and "on these grounds there is a Christian reading of the Old Testament which does not necessarily coincide with the Jewish reading."[68] But our typological reading "should avoid any transition from the Old to the New Testament which might seem merely a rupture,"[69] and it "should not lead us to forget that [the Old Testament] retains its own value as revelation that the New Testament often does no more than resume (cf. Mk 12:29–31)."[70]

5) If we underscore "the eschatological dimension of Christianity, we shall reach a greater awareness that the people of God of the Old and New Testaments are tending toward a like end in the future: the coming or return of the Messiah." In this way we shall see more clearly that "the person of the Messiah is not only a point of division for the people of God but also a point of convergence. . . . "[71]

6) Both peoples "must also accept our responsibility to prepare the world for the coming of the Messiah by working together for social justice, respect for the rights of persons and nations, and for social and international reconciliation."[72]

7) "Jesus was and always remained a Jew" who "extolled respect" for the law while "he showed great liberty toward it."[73] "An exclusively negative picture of the Pharisees is likely to be inaccurate and unjust. . . . [I]f Jesus shows himself severe toward the Pharisees, it is because he is closer to them than to other contemporary Jewish groups. . . . "[74]

8) In line with the three stages of Gospel tradition, "it cannot be ruled out that some references hostile or less than favorable to the Jews have their historical context in conflicts between the na-

scent Church and the Jewish community. Certain controversies reflect Christian-Jewish relations after the time of Jesus. . . . All this
should be taken into account when preparing catechesis and homilies for the last weeks of Lent and Holy Week. . . ."[75]

9) " . . . Christians should never forget that the faith is a free
gift of God . . . and that we should never judge the consciences of
others."[76]

10) "The catechism of the Council of Trent teaches that Christian sinners are more to blame for the death of Christ than those
few Jews who brought it about—they indeed 'knew not what they
did' (cf. Lk 23:34) and we know it only too well. . . ."[77]

11) Israel's history has "continued, especially in a numerous
Diaspora which allowed Israel to carry to the whole world a witness—often heroic—of its fidelity to the one God and to 'exalt Him
in the presence of all the living' (Tobit 13:4), while preserving the
memory of the land of their forefathers at the heart of their
hope. . . ."[78]

12) "The existence of the state of Israel and its political options
should be envisaged not in a perspective which is in itself religious,
but in their reference to the common principles of international
law."[79]

13) "The permanence of Israel (while so many ancient peoples
have disappeared without trace) is a historic fact and a sign to be
interpreted within God's design. We must in any case rid ourselves
of the traditional idea of a people *punished,* preserved as a *living argument* for Christian apologetic. It remains a chosen people. . . ."[80]

14) "Religious teaching, catechesis, and preaching should be a
preparation not only for objectivity, justice, tolerance but also for
understanding and dialogue. Our two traditions are so related that
they cannot ignore each other. Mutual knowledge must be encouraged at every level. There is evident in particular a painful ignorance of the history and traditions of Judaism, of which only
negative aspects and often caricature seem to form part of the stock
ideas of many Christians."[81]

Sounds quite progressive, doesn't it? Not to the International
Jewish Committee on Interreligious Consultations.[82] Although it
conceded some positive features to the "Notes," it found certain formulations "a retreat from earlier Catholic statements." Not only was
the document "published without prior consultation with the Jewish
community." It defines Judaism "not in terms of its own self-un-
derstanding . . . but only in terms of Christian categories" which
seem "triumphalistic." Formulations about Jews and Judaism, about

the Holocaust and the meaning of Israel, appear "regressive." The Vatican "Notes" on the genocide and the state "are totally inadequate in providing Catholics with sufficient guidelines on how to teach, preach, and understand these major events that have so decisively shaped the way Jews define themselves." The Vatican "Notes" do *not* remedy the "painful ignorance" of Christians about Jewish history and traditions; these are seen not as having independent value, but simply as preparatory—and that alone is why Catholics should "appreciate and love Jews."[83]

Current Catholic Questioning

A third "sign" is a growing Catholic theological uneasiness with traditional doctrine on the role of the Jews in the history of salvation. "How many Christians," asked Paulist Father Thomas Stransky, "still regard Jews not for what they are but only for what they could become—'potential Christians'—and Judaism not as having permanent salvific validity in God's promise but only as a preparatory religion on the way?"[84] That question reminds me of a moving plea for a new Jewish-Christian relationship put forward almost two decades ago by the Lutheran Scripture scholar Krister Stendahl:

> It is clear to me that Christian theology needs a new departure. And it is equally clear that we cannot find it on our own, but only by the help of our Jewish colleagues. We must plead with them to help us. And as far as we are concerned, it is not a dialogue we need; we are not primarily anxious to impart our views as they impart theirs. We need to ask, in spite of it all, whether they are willing to let us become again part of their family, a peculiar part to be true, but even so, relatives who believe themselves to be a peculiar kind of Jews. Something went wrong in the beginning. I say "went wrong," for I am not convinced that what happened in the severing of the relations between Judaism and Christianity was the good and positive will of God. Is it not possible for us to recognize that we parted ways not according to but against the will of God?[85]

Though I cannot agree "it is not a dialogue we need," I do agree that we need a fresh theology. This is not the place to present a new approach, even were I competent to do so. For our immediate purposes, I simply suggest to Christian preachers several interrelated questions—issues that are crucial, issues that must be studied, issues that should at least give us pause in our preaching.

First, a broad Christological question: In what sense is Jesus Christ our Savior? Must we hold, with the most rigorous of conservatives, that a man or woman can be saved only through explicit personal knowledge of and commitment to Jesus as the Christ? Most Christians would find such rigorism unchristian. Shall we say then that salvation is indeed attainable only through the grace of Christ, *but* the grace of Christ is offered and available to all? Such a position is widely held in theological circles; you recognize it in explanations like "anonymous Christian," "latent Church," "supernatural existential." But can we go further and affirm that, though Jesus Christ is the normative way to God and to salvation, he is not the exclusive mediator for all humankind? That he is central but not unique? Finally—a stance that will not commend itself to the right or the center or the slightly left of center—is it conceivably Christian to claim that there are many mediators of salvation and Jesus Christ is one of them?[86] The pertinence of your answer for the issue of Jewish salvation is unmistakable. But the answer is not to be uttered lightly; it can come only from a wedding of serious study, profound contemplation, and extensive experience.

Second, a specific question that concretizes the questions we have just asked: Granted that, with rare exceptions, the Jewish people, through no fault of their own, have been unable and will be unable to accept Christ as their Savior, why should the instruments of salvation established for them by God in the Prior Testament not remain valid *for them* now? Is it existentially realistic, does it make theological sense, to say that, if they are saved, it is because they are anonymous Christians?

Third, how shall we understand Romans 9–11? Here is a people whose gifts and call are "irrevocable" (Rom 11:29), and yet "a hardening has come upon part of Israel, until the full number of the Gentiles come in, and so all Israel will be saved" (Rom 11:25–26). This *plērōma* of the Gentiles, does Paul mean all the Gentiles there are and will be? Or simply the elect among the Gentiles? And when they "come in," will all Israel be converted to Christ?[87]

11
SO SARAH LAUGHED
Humor in the Holy of Holies?

In the famous Abbey of Lérins, on an island off the southeast coast of France, there is an unusual sculpture. It may go back to the 12th century, and it has for title *Christ souriant,* "the smiling Christ." Jesus is imprisoned on the cross; his head is leaning somewhat to the right; his eyes are closed—in death, I think; but on his lips there is a soft, serene smile.

The smiling Christ—here is my springboard for this chapter. If you prefer Scripture to sculpture, I give you the Sermon on the Mount, Jesus in Ash Wednesday's Gospel: "When you fast, do not look gloomy, like the hypocrites" (Mt 6:16). Not a proof-text; more like an epigraph, an apposite quotation totally out of context. It simply serves to introduce a not inconsequential problem: Is there room for humor in the homily? Two stages to my development. First, a look at Jesus: Did he really smile? Second, a look at the homilist: Dare he laugh?

I

First then, a look at Jesus: Did he really smile? Did he actually laugh? One tradition is enshrined in some fourth-century monastic rules of St. Basil the Great: "So far as we know from the story of the Gospel, he never laughed. On the contrary, he even pronounced those unhappy who are given to laughter (Lk 6:25)." Oh yes, he had "joy of spirit," he had "merriment of soul." But as for its "outward expression," as for "hilarity," no. Such a one would not be "master of every passion," would not be "perfectly continent."[1]

159

True, the Gospels never say that Jesus smiled or laughed, as they twice testify that he wept—over Jerusalem and over Lazarus, over his city and his friend. But I do not understand how one who was like us in everything save sin, who inherited our physical and psychological make-up, could have wept from sorrow but not laughed for joy. How could he fail to smile when a child cuddled comfortably in his arms, or when the headwaiter at Cana wondered where the good wine had come from, or when he saw little Zacchaeus up a tree, or when Jairus' daughter wakened to life at his touch, or when Peter put his foot in his mouth once again? I refuse to believe that he did not laugh when he saw something funny, or when he experienced in the depths of his manhood the exhilarating presence of his Father. Too often Christians have been so aware of Jesus' divinity that his humanity became somewhat unreal, artificial, a kind of playacting. Or we conclude that since he was perfect man, there could be nothing spontaneous, unpremeditated, unplanned about his actions and reactions. Tell me, before Jesus wept over the City, did he retire to the hills, consider his options, and make a conscious decision to cry? No, he was like us. Better indeed, but not a different breed.

I do not say that Jesus smiled when his fellow townsmen tried to throw him over Nazareth's hill. I do not pretend that he laughed in Gethsemane. I do not know if he died with a smile on his lips. There are moments when none of us can possibly smile, when it makes no sense to laugh. But that is not the point. The point is: Here is a man whose whole life was an inexorable movement to a cross, a man who cried out that he was in anguish until his death should be accomplished—and still he moved through life very much as we do. He attracted not only fishermen and centurions but children, simple folk, women like Mary of Magdala—and he could hardly have done so with thunderbolts, if he had only spoken "with authority," if his face wore ever the stern mask of a judge and did not crease into a smile or break out into merry laughter.

I have been happy to find my aprioristic arguments confirmed by religious writers and scholars who have studied the Jesus of history specifically for his humor. Over two decades ago, the respected American Quaker Elton Trueblood, professor of philosophy at Earlham College in Indiana, wrote a small book on *The Humor of Christ*.[2] The opening paragraph is entrancing:

> The germ of the idea which has finally led to the writing of this
> book was planted many years ago when our eldest son was four

years old. We were reading to him from the seventh chapter of Matthew's Gospel, feeling very serious, when suddenly the little boy began to laugh. He laughed because he saw how preposterous it would be for a man to be so deeply concerned about a speck in another person's eye, that he was unconscious of the fact his own eye had a beam in it. Because the child understood perfectly that the human eye is not large enough to have a beam in it, the very idea struck him as ludicrous. His gay laughter was a rebuke to his parents for their failure to respond to humor in an unexpected place. The rebuke served its purpose by causing me to begin to watch for humor in all aspects of the life and teachings of Christ. Sometimes this did not appear until the text had been read and reread many times.[3]

As examples of Jesus' humor, Trueblood discusses his dazzling paradoxes (e.g., calling unstable Peter "Rocky"), his deliberately preposterous statements to get a point across (e.g., the rich man and the needle's eye), his irony (his most common type of humor: e.g., what the Jews might have expected to see in John the Baptist, Lk 7:24–26), his dialogue with the Canaanite woman, and his parables (although I cannot agree with his conviction that the only hypothesis that cuts through all nonsensical interpretations of the parable of the Dishonest Manager or Unjust Steward is that Jesus was joking). Trueblood closes his book with an appendix: 30 humorous passages in the Synoptics.

In the same vein, but more scholarly, is Joseph A. Grassi's *God Made Me Laugh: A New Approach to Luke*.[4] To recapture the paradox of the living Jesus for our time, Grassi chooses Luke-Acts, partly "in order to have a better picture of comic eschatology, where Jesus is often seen as a 'jokester' presenting new and humourous contrasts between God's views of the kingdom and the ordinary expectations and models of many people, especially religious leaders."[5] By "comic" Grassi means "that this eschatology is accomplished in such a strikingly different way from ordinary human expectations that it becomes a matter for surprise, wonder and laughter, when people realize the extreme paradox."[6]

As Grassi sees it, Luke finds the roots of comic eschatology in the Old Testament, where God's plans operating through weak humans seem so surprising, so impossible, that people laugh in astonishment. The prime example? Isaac, "the child of laughter." This theme Luke applies to Zechariah and Mary (virginal conception, a new temple and a new ark in human flesh). Grassi's chapters focus on the unexpected in Luke, the paradoxical: e.g., the contrast between John, gaunt figure of repentance, and "the Nazarene clown" preaching an exiciting new age, a sparkling new wine; the reversal of the included and excluded, the clean and unclean; banquet scenes as "feasts of fools"; the Sermon on the Plain as "crazy discipleship"; Luke's feminine orientation; the sign of Jonah, comic prophet; paradoxical parables; the kingdom as child's play; a forgiveness foolish by human standards; the entrance into Jerusalem on an ass; death turned into life, end as beginning.

This is not to suggest that Jesus was just "one of the boys," a happy-go-lucky, slap-you-on-the-back, belly-laughing, "This Bud's for you" type. There was surely a dignity, a gravity, in his bearing, in his movement, in his speech that set him off not only from a spontaneous, sputtering Peter but even from the more reflective, more elegant John. But this is hardly incompatible with the risibility which some claim distinguishes the human animal from the subhuman, our ability to recognize the ridiculous, the incongruous, the absurd and to laugh aloud or smile gently in reaction. The world's most effective communicator did not exclude from his repertory the humor which lends even God's word an added attractiveness.

Actually, it is Presbyterian preacher and novelist Frederick Buechner who first expressed for me persuasively what he calls "the gospel as comedy."[7] As Buechner sees it,

> The tragic is the inevitable. The comic is the unforeseeable. . . . How can Charlie Chaplin in his baggy pants and derby hat foresee that though he is stood up by the girl and clobbered over the head by the policeman and hit in the kisser with a custard pie, he will emerge dapper and gallant to the end, twirling his invincible cane and twitching his invincible moustache? . . . Who could have predicted that God would choose not Esau, the honest and reliable, but Jacob, the trickster and heel, that he would put the finger on Noah, who hit the bottle, or on Moses, who was trying to beat the rap in Midian for braining a man in Egypt and said if it weren't for the honor of the thing he'd just as soon let Aaron go back and face the music, or on the prophets, who were a ragged lot, mad as hatters most of them and dragging their heels to a man when they were called to hit the sawdust trail. . . .
>
> And, of course, there is the comedy, the unforeseeableness, of the election itself. Of all the peoples he could have chosen to be his holy people, he chose the Jews, who as somebody said are just like everybody else only more so—more religious than anybody when they were religious and when they were secular, being secular as if they'd invented it. . . . [8]

The high point of the gospel as comedy, of course, is the Christ who was "a stumbling block to Jews and folly" to everyone else. Buechner sees Christ's whole life as a kind of comedy: "the king who looks like a tramp, the prince of peace who looks like the prince of fools, the lamb of God who ends like something hung up at the butcher's."[9] Not black comedy but white, "the high comedy of Christ that is as close to tears as the high comedy of Buster Keaton or Marcel Marceau or Edith Bunker is close to tears—but glad tears at last, not sad tears, tears at the hilarious unexpectedness of things rather than at their tragic expectedness."[10]

Besides the very person of Jesus, Buechner highlights the comedy of the word he speaks and its most characteristic form, the parable. He is convinced that the parables "can be read as jokes about God in the sense that what they are essentially about is the outlandishness of God who does impossible things with impossible people."[11] His prime example is the parable of the Prodigal Son (for Buechner, the most remarkable parable of them all, at once the most comic and the saddest). Read how he retells it in today's idioms and images, and you are likely to agree that the parable is "a joke about the preposterousness of God," with the sequel on the elder brother "a joke about the preposterousness of man."[12] Briefly, the gospel as comedy is

> the coming together of Mutt and Jeff, the Captain and the Kids, the Wizard of Oz and the Scarecrow: the coming together of God in his unending greatness and glory and man in his unending littleness, prepared for the worst but rarely for the best, prepared for the possible but rarely for the impossible. The good news breaks into a world where the news has been so bad for so long that when it is good nobody hears it much except for a few. And who are the few that hear it? They are the ones who labor and are heavy-laden like everybody else but who, unlike everybody else, know that they labor and are heavy-laden. They are the last people you might expect to hear it, themselves the bad jokes and stooges and scarecrows of the world, the tax collectors and whores and misfits. . . . [13]

But just as I am about to shout a resounding amen to tragedy as the inevitable and comedy as the unforeseeable, Buechner turns it all around. If you look at the reality with the eyes of God, it is the tragic that is not inevitable, the comic that is bound to happen. What is inevitable is "the comedy of God's saving the most unlikely people when they least expect it."[14]

II

Suppose we turn now from Jesus to the homilist: Dare he laugh? By God, he'd better! For his own salvation and for the redemption of his congregation. Here I apply to preaching what an insightful spiritual writer, Jean Leclercq, has recommended more broadly for Christian existence: "an asceticism of humor" and "a diaconate of humor."[15]

For the preacher personally, individually, an asceticism of humor—a fresh form of self-denial, a fresh face of the cross. A young lady once said to me: "Why are you so hard on yourself?" It was the only self-denial I knew: Keep that rebellious flesh under control, and be intolerant of imperfection—mine and everyone else's! To preachers anxious to live the cross they preach, I suggest that they give up something sweeter than Lady Godiva chocolates, smokier than Kents, perhaps more destructive than sin. I mean an absorption in myself—where I take myself all too seriously, where the days and nights revolve around *me*, my heartache and my hiatus hernia, my successes and failures, my problems and frustrations. For an asceticism of humor, I must distance myself from myself, see myself in perspective, as I really am. I mean a creature wonderfully yet fearfully made, a bundle of paradoxes and contradictions. I believe and I doubt, I hope and I despair, I love and I hate. I am exciting and boring, enchanted and disillusioned, manic and depressive. I am "cool" on the outside and I hurt within. I feel bad about feeling good,[16] am afraid of my joy, feel guilty if I don't feel guilty. I am trusting and suspicious, selfless and selfish, wide-open and locked in. I know so much and so little. I am honest and I still play games. Aristotle defined us humans as rational animals; I suggest we are fallen angels with an incredible capacity for beer!

If it is the incongruous, what does not fit, that makes for humor, I can indeed smile at myself. So, I must let Christ the harlequin, the clown Christ, into my spiritual life. I am not laughing sacrilegiously at him; he is poking gentle fun at me—through tears.[17] St. Ignatius Loyola had a splendid rule for his Jesuit sons: Our "whole countenance should reflect cheerfulness rather than sadness. . . . "[18] And my smile will turn to lusty laughter if I only realize how lovable I am—not because of anything I have made of myself, but because God loves me, because the Son of God died for me, because Trinity lives in me . . . now.

But an asceticism of humor dare not remain a private joke. Humor, someone has said, good humor is basically looking at the world, at others, with eyes of love—being in love without restriction. An asceticism of humor must move out into a diaconate of humor: I must deacon, minister, the smiling Christ to others. Not that I paint on a false smile or bellow for ever with laughter. Simply that, with my new-found Christian delight in myself, I go out to my sisters and brothers as I am and wherever they are.

Christianity calls for risen Christians, men and women like the hero of Eugene O'Neill's play *Lazarus Laughed*—the lover of Christ who has tasted death and sees it for what it is, the man whose one invitation to all is his constant refrain:

> Laugh with me!
> Death is dead!
> Fear is no more!
> There is only life!
> There is only laughter![19]

And O'Neill tells us: Lazarus "begins to laugh, softly at first," then full-throated—"a laugh so full of a complete acceptance of life, a profound assertion of joy in living, so devoid of all fear, that it is infectious with love," so infectious that, despite themselves, his listeners are caught by it and carried away.

So should the Christian preacher be shaped. In this connection a book little known among Roman Catholics has been highly instructive to me: Helmut Thielicke's *Encounter with Spurgeon*.[20] Thielicke, German university professor and Lutheran theologian, experienced a surprising kinship with Charles Haddon Spurgeon, self-educated Victorian Baptist preacher, "who to this day remains a 'prince among preachers' in the English and American tradition."[21] Listen to Thielicke as he finds in Spurgeon one characteristic of the how of preaching—its cheerfulness.

> Because it is cheerful and humorous, it accomplishes the relaxation of stiffness we spoke of above. Here cheerfulness is not an extra, placed like a *donum superadditum* at the disposal of grace by a happy mental constitution. Rather this cheerfulness is something like a manifestation of grace itself. For it is a sign of that detachment and overcoming of the world which grace bestows. So Spurgeon's cheerfulness is not evidence of his having the natural charism of "a good sense of humor"; his humor rather bears witness to the grace that is at work in him.
> Naturally, this humor is also a gift of nature, which grace presses into service as the sphere of its secondary causes. . . . But

it is precisely service into which this nature is pressed! We have the opposite example in those preachers who, though they likewise have at their disposal in their natural constitution a "sunny humor," let it come out only at a cocktail party or a merry wedding celebration; whereas in the pulpit all they have to operate with is the sound-effects of thunder and the gloomy hues of apocalypticism. . . .

Spurgeon's humor is a mode of redemption because it is sanctified—because it grows out of an overcoming of the world and therefore itself represents this overcoming of the world in process. So here it is representative of the extent to which the how of our preaching can be a witness. No wonder, therefore, that he took this humor into the pulpit and that the congregation—as in the blessed seasons of "Easter laughter" in the church, the so-called *risus paschalis!*—joined resoundingly in the laughter. But no wonder either that many people took offense when he broke through the accustomed solemn rites of the high church . . . and suddenly the kingdom of God popped up not only in men's hearts but also in their diaphragms, laying hold upon even this part of nature. In other words, the Word became utterly and radically flesh . . . even in *this* region of the anatomy. Only he to whom nothing is alien can credibly proclaim the incarnation of God. . . .

When Spurgeon was cheerful and humorous in the pulpit, he was putting himself into his preaching; he was entering into the sermon with his whole nature. . . . One who is himself engaged attracts others into engagement. The being-in-it-oneself is the essential evidence of that credibility that is empowered to call others to faith. And this is precisely why the "how" of preaching is itself preaching.

Should we not then, Spurgeon would probably ask in the face of the deadly seriousness with which the business of the church is pursued today, should we not see that lines of laughter about the eyes are just as much marks of faith as are the lines of care and seriousness? Is it only earnestness that is baptized; is laughter pagan? We have already allowed too much that is good to be lost to the church, and cast many pearls before swine. A church is in a bad way when it banishes laughter from the sanctuary and leaves it to cabaret, the night club, and the toastmasters.[22]

I agree. Humor is not merely permissible in the pulpit, a stranger given reluctant Christian hospitality. It houses there by divine and human right—because in taking our flesh the Son of God assumed, transformed, sanctified not only our souls and our senses but even our diaphragms. Yes indeed, lines of laughter can be marks of faith, can bear witness to the grace at work in us, can be signs that in Christ the preacher is overcoming the world.

So much for abstract principle. In the concrete, in Sunday reality, how might a preacher use humor effectively? Not like a TV emcee or an after-dinner speaker: to warm an audience up or provide a moment of comic relief. Homiletic humor should be part and parcel of the homily, woven into its warp and woof. If I am preaching on the Eucharist, it might be amusing but is surely inappropriate to begin with a quip attributed to Bishop Fulton J. Sheen: "An atheist is someone with no invisible means of support." In a farm-belt sermon, on the other hand, I might be excused for defining a cow as "a beast of Borden." But these are, at best, incidental flashes of humor, calculated to render the listeners what traditional rhetoric called *dociles*—not so much slavishly submissive as freely teachable. Homiletic humor should be built into the substance of the sermon. Once again Buechner has a masterful example when speaking of Old Testament Sarah and her husband Abraham.

The place to start [the gospel as comedy] is with a woman laughing. She is an old woman, and, after a lifetime in the desert, her face is cracked and rutted like a six-month drought. She hunches her shoulders around her ears and starts to shake. She squinnies her eyes shut, and her laughter is all China teeth and wheeze and tears running down as she rocks back and forth in her kitchen chair. She is laughing because she is pushing ninety-one hard and has just been told she is going to have a baby. Even though it was an angel who told her, she can't control herself, and her husband can't control himself either. He keeps a straight face a few seconds longer than she does, but he ends by cracking up, too. Even the angel is not unaffected. He hides his mouth behind his golden scapular, but you can still see his eyes. They are larkspur blue and brimming with something of which the laughter of the old woman and her husband is at best only a rough translation.

The old woman's name is Sarah, of course, and the old man's name is Abraham, and they are laughing at the idea of a baby's being born in the geriatric ward and Medicare's picking up the tab. They are laughing because the angel not only seems to believe it but seems to expect them to believe it too. They are laughing because with part of themselves they do believe it. They are laughing because with another part of themselves they know it would take a fool to believe it. They are laughing because laughing is better than crying and maybe not even all that different. They are laughing because if by some crazy chance it should just happen to come true, then they would really have something to laugh about. They are laughing at God and with God, and they are laughing at themselves too because laughter has that in common with weeping. No matter what the immediate occasion is of either your laughter or your tears, the object of both ends up being yourself and your own life.[23]

One way, then, to season the substance of a sermon with wit, with humor, is to retell a Scripture story in today's idiom. Not unexpectedly, Buechner does it extraordinarily well. After all, he is a craftsman, a novelist, a storyteller, an artist of uncommonly rich imagination. But you need not be a Buechner to make an age-old, familiar story come alive with a smile. At the risk of disproving my thesis, I reproduce the first point of my homily for the Third Sunday of the Year (B), "Each of You Is Jonah."[24] The first reading was taken from Jonah, but only six verses (3:1–5, 10). I thought it high time to recapture, for myself as well as for the congregation, the significance of that brief biblical book for the Christian of today. My journey into Jonah land involved three stages: the man, the meaning, and the message. Who was Jonah? What was his importance for Israel? What might he say to us now? I foist on you the first stage.

> First, the man. Who was Jonah and what was he about? For those of you who are skeptical about living conditions inside a big fish—lack of oxygen, raw seafood diet, toilet service—relax. The story is just that: a story. A short story: about 1300 English words. It's fiction, but fiction for a purpose, fiction with a message. A drama in two acts.
> Act 1. The Lord orders Jonah to go to Nineveh, capital of Assyria. Preach repentance to the Ninevites, "for their wickedness has come up before me" (Jonah 1:2). But this vocation brings no joy to Jonah. Preach penance to pagans, announce salvation to non-Jews? Uh-uh, not for Jonah. He flees as far from the Lord as he can, buys a ticket on a freighter bound for southern Spain. The Lord raises up a storm, and the ship threatens to break apart. The pagan sailors draw lots to discover who has brought them bad luck. Who else but Jonah? A good fellow at heart, he asks them to toss him overboard. They oblige; the sea settles; the sailors are converted to Israel's God. As for Jonah, a big fish, with instructions from above, swallows him whole. After three days, at the bidding of the Lord of the sea, the fish vomits him up. End of Act 1.
> Act 2. The word of the Lord comes to Jonah a second time: Get thee to Nineveh! Jonah still dislikes the assignment, but this

time he goes. How argue with a God who got you out of a "fishy" situation? He preaches; the people are converted; God spares the city. But Jonah is angry: Pagans the beneficiaries of God's pardon? He blows his stack, tells God to put him out of his misery: "It is better for me to die than to live" (4:3). He sulks outside the city, shaded from the sun by a plant God provides. Then God gets a worm to wither Jonah's sunscreen, and the sun beats down on his unprotected head. Jonah protests, is again angry enough to die. Now God lets him have it with both barrels: "You pity the plant, for which you did not labor, nor did you make it grow, which came into being in a night, and perished in a night" (4:10). And you resent my pitying 120,000 men and women "who do not know their right hand from their left" (4:11)? With that harsh question the Book of Jonah ends.

A second way to season the substance of a sermon with humor is to introduce a bit of wit into your homiletic theology. In preaching on 1 Corinthians 12:4–7 for the Second Sunday of the Year (C), I had argued that the remarkable charism that is each of us is an integration of human gifts and God's self-giving. In my second point I wanted to stress that this "new you" stems from the Holy Spirit.[25] I said in part:

> You see, there are two unchristian errors at large in our land, two extremes. At one extreme, Pelagianism; at the other, pessimism. The Pelagian is the incurable optimist: He can lift himself to heaven by his bootstraps. No original sin, no need to be reborn; free will can save him, with an occasional nudge from God—your Christian example or a three-point homily. . . . Hogwash! We reach God by God's gracious, uncompelled mercy. Even the clergy do—if they do. . . .
>
> The pessimist sins in her own way. She feels she has nothing to offer the community. She is homely or has blackheads; she is shy, insecure, stutters; she can't sing or disco, isn't particularly smart, can't hold her Michelob; blacks scare her and blood makes her throw up. She doesn't like herself. Don't add community to her problems!
>
> A word from your favorite counselor: All is not yet lost. What makes you an effective Christian is the Holy Spirit. Oh yes, personality can be a blessing; it's great if you warm instinctively to people; it could help if you're a "ten." But more importantly, the Spirit works through you as you are; all He asks is that you be open to His whispering. . . . You may still need therapy or a skin cream to make you utterly whole; but whoever you are, whatever your infirmities and imperfections, it is the Spirit alone who can

make you a means of redemption, a channel of grace, an instrument of God's peace. It is He who changes your water into wine.

A third area of potential playfulness, I find, is my customary third point—where I usually ask what the biblical and theological reflections that have preceded might say to us at this moment, in our (dare I so speak?) existential situation. Preaching on the Fourth Sunday of Easter (A), focusing on "life" as the word more expressive of Easter than any other, I asked three questions: What does being alive say to you? What does it mean to be alive in Christ? How alive are you? The third question, I suggested, is the most difficult of the three.[26]

> We all know people who, while not dead, are only half alive. The Nazi Rudolf Hess, now in his eighties, "living" out his fourth decade in a German jail. Workers on an assembly line, doing the same monotonous thing over and over again. Students putting in time until they graduate, until they get into the "real" world. Two people "living" out their marriage together, but in dull routine, in a rut.
>
> Similarly for the life of the spirit, for life in Christ. What agonizes me is the large number of Christians who have God's life in them but are barely alive. They do everything they have to do, stay out of serious sin, have little if anything to confess. But the Christ within them does not thrill them, gives them fewer goosepimples than Starsky and Hutch. Jesus' death bothers them less than John Lennon's. They look for something else to "turn them on": yoga, rock 'n' roll, the Redskins, a kibbutz in Israel, Star Wars, Lawrence Welk. And so many Christians are in despair because they lack some essential ingredient of contemporary commercial existence, from hair curled with Clairol to a body free of human smell. . . .
>
> The paradox is, life can be full and still be spotted with pain. The proof stares you in the face, from Christ to Casals, from the mother of Jesus to every mother among you. But to live Christ's passion with Easter joy, it is not enough to *have* life, even God's life. You must *live* life, feel it, open up to it, let it sway you and have its way with you. Life's real enemy is not pain, not even death; life's enemy is boredom.
>
> My friends, I recommend to you my own Easter prayer: "Lord, let me never get bored!"

I admit, this is not the brand of humor that evokes a belly laugh, the punch-line joke that (as my young student friends would say) knocks you out of your socks. It is more akin to Spurgeon's "cheerfulness," the absence of "deadly seriousness," the "lines of laughter" about our eyes. But whether it is a gentle smile I evoke or a sonic boom from the diaphragm, the results are much the same. The gospel makes an unbloody entrance (now and again); bodies relax and tensions dissipate; time-conscious folk forget to check their Timex; people begin to feel good about the Good News.

Here, I suggest, is a facet of "faith healing" analogous to what Norman Cousins experienced on the medical level. This well-known littérateur, editor of the *Saturday Review* for more than 30 years, was found to have a crippling, painful disease. The connective tissue in his spine was disintegrating. Chance of recovery? One in 500. His personal road to regeneration and healing? Massive doses of vitamin C and . . . laughter. This is not the place to argue or extol vitamin C, but Cousins' experience with laughter is pertinent indeed.[27] A systematic program was introduced, beginning with amusing films—replays of Allen Funt's TV "Candid Camera," old Marx Brothers movies—supplemented by humor books, in particular E. B. and Katharine White's *Subtreasury of American Humor* and Max Eastman's *The Enjoyment of Laughter*. Not only did Cousins make "the joyous discovery that ten minutes of genuine belly laughter had an anesthetic effect" and gave him "at least two hours of pain-free sleep" (not advised as preparation for a homily). Even more importantly, laughter had a salutary effect on his body's chemistry. Sedimentation-rate readings taken just before and several hours after the laughter episodes revealed each time "a drop of at least five points. The drop by itself was not substantial, but it held and was cumulative. I was greatly elated by the discovery that there is a physiologic basis for the ancient theory that laughter is good medicine."[28]

Laughter is good medicine not only for the body but for the spirit as well. More accurately, good medicine for that complex creation of God's high imagination we call the human person. To banish laughter from the pulpit is to forget that what distinguishes us from the beast is not only the power of analytic reasoning; we alone are genuinely able to laugh. Not grin—like a baboon or a Cheshire cat. Laugh.

I close this chapter on a somber note, a discouraging problem for the preacher with a sense of humor, of gospel humor. Many, if not most, Catholic congregations are not ready for homiletic humor. Oh yes, they appreciate a joke or story clearly labeled "funny." But the more subtle humor, Buechner's "gospel as comedy," the humor that is part and parcel of a sermon's structure, all-pervasive, this tends to get lost. It is not that our people are incapable of such understanding. After all, they cluck and chuckle through films, plays, and TV programs interlaced with delicate humor. The reason is rather, in large measure, that we priests have not led them to expect it of the pulpit, have not ourselves recognized the "preposterous meeting" of sin and grace, of God's absence and presence, "as the high, unbidden, hilarious thing it is."[29] Our people take us all too seriously in the sermon, because we take ourselves all too seriously, preach the gospel grimly. And excessive seriousness is not only soporific; it keeps the gospel from coming through as good news, the best of news, a preposterous God preposterously saving His preposterous image.

12

WHAT SHALL A MAN GIVE IN EXCHANGE?
The Cost of Preaching

Most Christian preachers have heard of Dietrich Bonhoeffer, the German Lutheran pastor who was hanged in 1945 for conspiring to overthrow Hitler. Many are aware of his remarkable work *The Cost of Discipleship,* first published in 1937. It is here that we first encounter a phrase that would echo through much of the Western world: "cheap grace and costly grace."

Bonhoeffer was troubled by a puzzling problem: How could it be that the Church and the preacher were using so ineffectively the most precious gift they possessed, the word of the nearby God Himself? How explain the chasm that yawned between the Church's mandate to preach the word publicly and the dismaying absence of credibility in the preacher and his preaching? He looked for, struggled for, renewal of the word's authority not through a fresh doctrine of ministry but through discipleship alone. And renewal of discipleship meant a renewed concentration on a root Reformation principle: *sola gratia,* "grace alone." Not cheap grace . . . costly grace.

Cheap grace means grace sold on the market like cheapjacks' wares. The sacraments, the forgiveness of sin, and the consolations of religion are thrown away at cut prices. Grace is represented as the Church's inexhaustible treasury, from which she showers blessings with generous hands, without asking questions or fixing limits. . . . The essence of grace, we suppose, is that the

173

account has been paid in advance; and, because it has been paid, everything can be had for nothing. . . . What would grace be if it were not cheap?

Cheap grace means grace as a doctrine, a principle, a system. It means forgiveness of sins proclaimed as a general truth, the love of God taught as the Christian "conception" of God. An intellectual assent to that idea is held to be of itself sufficient to secure remission of sins. . . .

Cheap grace is the preaching of forgiveness without requiring repentance, baptism without church discipline, Communion without confession, absolution without personal confession. Cheap grace is grace without discipleship, grace without the cross, grace without Jesus Christ, living and incarnate.

Costly grace is the treasure hidden in the field; for the sake of it a man will gladly go and sell all that he has. It is the pearl of great price to buy which the merchant will sell all his goods. It is the kingly rule of Christ, for whose sake a man will pluck out the eye which causes him to stumble, it is the call of Jesus Christ at which the disciple leaves his nets and follows him.

Costly grace is the gospel which must be *sought* again and again, the gift which must be *asked* for, the door at which a man must *knock*.

Such grace is *costly* because it calls us to follow, and it is *grace* because it calls us to follow *Jesus Christ*. It is costly because it costs a man his life, and it is grace because it gives a man the only true life. It is costly because it condemns sin, and grace because it justifies the sinner. Above all, it is *costly* because it cost God the life of his Son: "ye were bought at a price," and what has cost God much cannot be cheap for us. Above all, it is *grace* because God did not reckon his Son too dear a price to pay for our life, but delivered him up for us. Costly grace is the Incarnation of God.[1]

I am convinced that within the Catholic Church preaching remains at a low ebb, is by and large ineffective, primarily because we preachers either see the sermon as a product that comes cheap or, recognizing its high cost, are reluctant to pay the price. Effective preaching, preaching that moves hearts and changes minds, is costly because, like grace, it costs me my life. Literally. An outrageous thesis? Hardly. I preach at a great price, because preaching costs me my mind, costs me my spirit, costs me my flesh and blood. Let me consider these costs in turn.

I

First, preaching costs me my *mind*. Here I limit "mind" to the intellect's capacity to reach reality and truth through reason (informed indeed by revelation), as distinguished from the power I possess to feel, to will, even to imagine. Preaching demands of me every component of that power, forces me to stretch the power to its breaking point. Why? Because I must come to grips with one of the most profound, exciting, sobering, even misleading phrases in the Christian vocabulary: "the word of God." In point of fact, God does not use words; God does not "speak." (Oh yes, the Son of God did, but we are careful to point out that He spoke "in His human nature"; precisely as God, He does not have lips or a tongue or a glottal stop.) What we really mean is that God communicates with us, makes His mind known to us, through the words of humans: through Moses and Micah, through Isaiah and the son of Sirach, through Jesus. That is why, as Raymond Brown noted perceptively, the translation of Jean Levie's book title *Parole humaine et message de Dieu* ("Word of Man and Message of God") as *The Bible: Word of God in Words of Men*[2] "is tautological. Only human beings use words; and so, when one has entitled divine communication 'word of God,' one has already indicated that the divine communication is in human words, and therefore that the communication is in a time-conditioned and limited form."[3]

The point of these remarks? In my role of preacher, I am inescapably confronted by two crucial facts: (1) God has indeed communicated with men and women, with the Hebrew people and the people of the Christian covenant; but (2) this communication is conveyed in words, in human language, in words and language that God does not, cannot, personally employ. Hence the preacher's predicament: how to grasp accurately a divine mind translated by syllables that are not divine and are conditioned by time and culture.

Does this seem dreadfully abstract to you? Then look at the oldest of the writing prophets. Amos begins: "The words of Amos" (1:1); Amos ends: "Thus says the Lord your God" (9:15). Add to this the hypothesis that the closing section of Amos (9:8–15) is an addition by a redactor unhappy with the pessimism of many of the other "Thus says the Lord your God" passages in Amos—"one saying of the Lord God correcting another in the same book."[4] Take two different books. To Isaiah the word of the Lord says: "They shall beat their swords into plowshares, and their spears into prun-

ing hooks" (Isa 2:4); to Joel, a contradictory word: "Beat your
plowshares into swords, and your pruning hooks into spears" (Joel
4:10; *RSV* 3:10).

> One may argue whether God changes His message according to
> circumstances, but it is hard to deny the likelihood that in con-
> veying a divinely received insight to a new generation one
> prophet has deliberately taken the words of another prophet and
> used them in a contrary way. The prophets leave no doubt that
> they thought that God had communicated with them, but they
> may have been more subtle than is often suspected about the ex-
> tent to which the words they uttered came from God.[5]

Or take Jeremiah's complaints that "the word of the Lord" he has
spoken does not come to pass (Jer 17:15–16) and that he has been
deceived (15:18; 20:7, 9). Take, especially, the Ten Commandments, in Hebrew the "Ten Words" of God.

> In theological tradition these have had a special place as reflect-
> ing the essence of what God demands of His people, and in mod-
> ern biblical study they have been spoken of as the basic
> stipulations of the covenant between God and Israel. Are they
> really the words of God spoken (externally or internally) to
> Moses, or are they human formulations of a less specified reve-
> lation of divine moral demand? The modern biblical critic would
> be inclined to the latter answer simply from a comparison of the
> two different forms of the Decalogue (Exod 20:1–17; Deut 5:6–
> 21), especially since the *later,* Deuteronomic form of one com-
> mandment, separating the wife from the chattel and slaves, may
> represent a development of moral sensitivity.[6]

For Catholic preachers, "the word of the Lord" tends to take
on greater urgency when we are confronted with the Gospels. Here
we must face up to what the Biblical Commission in 1964 called "the
three stages of tradition by which the doctrine and the life of Jesus
have come down to us."[7] The first stage focuses on the *ipsissima verba
Iesu,* "the very words of Jesus," on what he actually said, and what
he really did. The second stage has to do with the preaching of the
apostles: "just as Jesus himself after his resurrection 'interpreted to
them' (Lk 24:27) the words of the Old Testament as well as his own,
they too interpreted his words and deeds according to the needs of
their listeners."[8] The third stage is that of the Evangelists, the au-
thors of the four Gospels: "from what they had received the sacred

writers above all selected the things which were suited to the various situations of the faithful and adapted their narration of them to the same situations and purpose."[9]

Now a pulpit is not a classroom; a homily is not a lecture on form criticism. And still, the more profoundly I penetrate that expression "the word of God," "the word of the Lord," the richer, the more exciting, my preaching is likely to be. One illustration, from the 28th Sunday of the Year in the A cycle: the royal marriage feast in Mt 22:1–14.[10]

Here is another parable to puzzle us, a parable that seems implausible. Royal wedding invitations to which *all* the invited respond "no." When the king insists, his messengers are killed. The king retaliates: His troops destroy the murderers and burn their city. To fill the dining room, the king pulls in people off the streets, the nice and the not-so-nice. One poor fellow doesn't have a wedding garment; out he goes on his tush. And the whole thing ends with a vague, disturbing warning: "Many are called, but few are chosen" (Mt 22:14). Couldn't the master of parables do better than that?

To make sense out of this parable—to preach effectively thereon—the preacher should be aware of two pertinent facts not mentioned by Matthew. First, the parable is really two parables.[11] The first parable (vv. 1–10) ends with the wedding hall filled; and so it ends on a happy note, with the rabble, the ragtag, the riffraff hoisting one to the king and singing the equivalent of "For he's a jolly good fellow." That's the parable of the Great Banquet or Wedding Feast. The second parable is the Guest without a Wedding Garment, a fellow from the streets who did not find the time or take the trouble to wash his clothes clean. You find this only in Matthew, not in Luke's version (Lk 14:16–24). Luke ends with the house about to be filled with outcasts and underprivileged; the "beautiful people" originally invited have not been killed, but they are not to taste of the banquet. End of parable.

Now why did Matthew take another parable of Jesus, an independent parable, and insert it here? Once the parable of the Great Banquet was applied to the Christian community, it ran the risk of being misunderstood. Did the life of the community have nothing to say to the sinner? Did Jesus' invitation not call for change, conversion, clean clothes? Were the baptized free of moral responsibility? The evil were as welcome as the good, and could stay evil? It doesn't matter whether you're good or evil—just eat up? No. The second parable told the community: You don't have to buy a tux, but whatever you wear has to be washed, has to be clean. You have to change.

A second fact significant for "the word of the Lord." It's clear enough what the king's dinner is all about: salvation—the salvation of the world. But to grasp what this means, you have to understand the situation in which Matthew wrote his Gospel. Don't think of Matthew lounging at the Sea of Galilee, trying to put down exactly what Jesus had said. No. He was writing for a community in transition, a community in process of change.[12] They were largely Jewish-Christians, Jews converted to Christ. It was about the year 85, somewhere in Palestine or Syria. The community was confused, in tension and conflict, bewildered by false prophets. They had been profoundly affected by the destruction of Jerusalem and the temple by the Romans. Rooted in Jewish tradition, they had to ask themselves: In the context of postwar Judaism, what does it mean to be a Christian? Are we to continue as a special sect within Judaism? Who are we? They were being persecuted by non-Jews; there was in-house betrayal and hatred; widespread wickedness was causing love to grow cold.

In response to all this, Matthew retold the story of Jesus from his conception till after his resurrection. He stressed four themes for his community: (1) Though originally sent to Israel, you must give yourselves to the wider Gentile mission. (2) You are no longer a sect within Judaism; you have a separate identity. (3) Forgive and love one another, for your mission will fail if you cannot live with your own divisions. (4) When Christ returns, he will judge not only you but the Gentiles to whom you are sent.

Within this historical situation the parable makes sense. Jesus' own parable was shorter and simpler. He was taking aim only at his opponents and critics: You spurned the invitation to salvation, and so God has called the publicans and sinners. Matthew applies it to the whole mystery of Jews and Gentiles. Now it becomes an allegory of salvation, an outline of God's plan for redemption, from the appearance of the prophets, through the fall of Jerusalem, to the Last Judgment.

The feast, the great evening banquet, is salvation. The first servants sent out are the Old Testament prophets, those men who were called by God to speak in His name, to say "Thus says Yahweh." The guests first invited to the marriage feast of Yahweh's Son are the people of Israel. They reject His call. The second group of messengers are the apostles and missionaries sent by God to Israel. Their message too is rejected; some of them are put to death. The city the king burns is Jerusalem, destroyed in 70. The mission to the streets is God's invitation to the Gentiles: All peoples are now called to the feast of salvation. The entry into the wedding hall is baptism, entry into the community of salvation. The inspection of the guests by the king is the Last Judgment. The "outer darkness" is hell.

Now what I have been saying about the Old Testament and the New did not strike me like a bolt from the blue. This, and so much else about our unique Book, is not infused knowledge. It draws blood, wrings sweat, exacts tears. This is the kind of knowledge that makes a bloody entrance. Simply, I have to study; I must research, read, listen, discuss. Only through such intellectual discipline can most of us, people without extraordinary charisms, become effective preachers.

Three reasons among many. First, it is through disciplined study that I increasingly comprehend what I ought to understand when I proclaim "This is the word of the Lord." Despite the fundamentalists, it does not mean that every sentence I declaim from Scripture is God's revelation, that every set of syllables which makes sense is God's honest truth. There are books in the Bible where it is difficult to find any revelation at all. And still I can speak of this vast, precious collection as simply "the word of God." Why? Because, as the First Vatican Council declared, the books of Scripture "are considered by the Church sacred and canonical . . . in that they were written under the inspiration of the Holy Spirit and therefore have God for author."[13] We are indeed far from a totally satisfying theory of scriptural inspiration, but I find it reassuring and exciting that whatever I read or announce from Genesis 1:1 to Revelation 22:21 is there because, for His own good reasons, God wanted it there and, in His own mysterious fashion, the Holy Spirit arranged that the human writer(s) put it there.

Second reason: It is largely through disciplined study that I can preach a genuinely biblical homily. Not a homily that "uses" a Scripture phrase as superficial springboard or to bolster ideas already elaborated. Rather, a homily that moves seriously (though not without humor) and credibly (though not without risk) from what the text meant then to what it might be saying now. It was through disciplined study that my homily on Mt 22:1–14 could take the turn it did, could focus unexpectedly on . . . community. Matthew's version of the parable(s) came struggling out of his community experience. His community was torn: infighting, lack of love, especially the agonizing question of Christian identity: Who are we? Now the worldwide community called Catholic has for two decades been experiencing parallel problems, and many of our local communities are dreadfully divided. At times we Catholic cats claw at one another with a savagery that must make Christ weep.

Much that Matthew said to his community, I suggested, he would surely adapt to our situation. First, you do have an identity, a Catholic identity. In part, it is an identity you share with other Christians. With them, you confess Jesus as Lord and Savior; like them, you are united to the Father and to one another through Christ in the Spirit. In part, you are different; for you express your commitment to Christ through a body of beliefs, a system of sacraments, an order of authority that other Christians cannot totally share. Despite our theological battles "religiously" reported in *Time* and *Newsweek,* you should know, and I sense that you do experience, what it means to be a Catholic Christian.

Second, Matthew would say: You have a wider mission than to your own local community. The danger in any well-knit group—academic, military, political, social, spiritual—is narcissism. Like the beautiful youth Narcissus in Greek mythology, you risk falling in love with your own reflection. It is indeed an impressive image you project: warm, open, generous, accepting, enthusiastic. You are a community of love, alive with and for one another. In this context you have felt compelled to ask: Is your mission locked into this Georgetown quadrangle? Absolutely not! The world is your parish. Where precisely? Thailand or 14th Street? Appalachia or your office? The corridor you live on or the streets you walk? No homilist knows. The encouraging thing is that as a community we have begun to feel uneasy; we sense that, grateful as we are for all our blessings right here, we may be wrapping them up in Georgetown napkins and clutching them tightly to our happy little bodies.

Third, Matthew would repeat: Whatever your mission is, it will fail if you cannot live with your divisions. The Catholic Church is hurting. Not for the first time; and only those ignorant of history think of today as the nadir, the pits, of Catholic existence. But we do hurt; countless divisions rend us. The point is, the hurts that tear us must be made redemptive. Whether in our tiny chapel or in our diocese (yes, *our* diocese) or in the Church at large, we all have wounds to bind—our own and others': fears and tears, frustration and anger, loneliness and lovelessness, bitterness and envy, even the frightful feeling that in this royal hall I no longer experience, no longer "taste," the banquet of salvation.

Enough from my homily on Mt 22:1–14. Granted, I could preach powerfully on community without going back to the Bible;

I could begin and end right there in the local parish. Why, then, all this intellectual sweat over Matthew and his troubles? (1) Because, all other things being equal (which, John Courtney Murray used to say, they never are), the closer the word of Burghardt to the word of Scripture, the more likely I am to preach the word of God. (2) Because I have good reason to believe that what the Holy Spirit inspired for written transmission centuries ago was intended for me in my captivity as well as for the Jews in Babylon, for the worshipers in Washington's churches as well as for Peter's audiences in the Acts of the Apostles. (3) Because, more often than not, the historical context that frames the naked liturgical readings is exciting, absorbing, makes sense out of an isolated snippet, lends insight into selections that have been dulled by repetition or are just plain unintelligible.

A third reason for disciplined study: It will help me to lay hold of the Church's authentic tradition—I mean, see "Scripture within the Church." Here I recommend two instructive paragraphs from Vatican II:

> And so the apostolic preaching, which is expressed in a special way in the inspired books, was to be preserved by a continuous succession of preachers until the end of time. Therefore the apostles, handing on what they themselves had received, warn the faithful to hold fast to the traditions which they have learned either by word of mouth or by letter (cf. 2 Thess 2:15). . . . Now what was handed on by the apostles includes everything which contributes to the holiness of life and the increase in faith of the People of God, and so the Church, in her teaching, life, and worship, perpetuates and hands on to all generations all that she herself is, all that she believes.
>
> This tradition which comes from the apostles develops in the Church with the help of the Holy Spirit. For there is a *growth in the understanding* of the realities and the words which have been handed down. This happens through the *contemplation and study* made by believers, who treasure these things in their hearts (cf. Lk 2:19, 51), through the intimate understanding of spiritual things they experience, and through the preaching of those who have received through episcopal succession the sure gift of truth. For, as the centuries succeed one another, the Church constantly moves forward toward the fullness of divine truth until the words of God reach their complete fulfillment in her.[14]

This Church of Christ we preachers represent "constantly moves forward" in its quest for God's truth. I have been singularly blessed throughout my years of priesthood; for I have been privileged to study intimately how the Church has grown in understanding: understanding of itself, of its mission, of its message. I am a theologian. But my theology was unreal until it became a search—a search for God and His human images through systematic reflection on experience. My experience indeed, for it is I who am searching. But not experience in some narrow sense, as if my latest eructation is the breath of the Spirit. No, the Catholic experience must be catholic, must include the community experience that spans ages and continents. And so I have felt the Hebrew experience of Sinai and the desert; the New Testament experience of God's breakthrough in the flesh of His Son; the conciliar experience from Nicaea I to Vatican II; the experience of theologians from Origen through Aquinas to Rahner, mystics like Tauler and Teresa.

I have shared the experience of non-Roman Christian communities, their pens and pews and pulpits; and there I have found Christ, heard the whispering of his Spirit. I have discovered the Hindu Bhagavad Gita, the "Song of the Lord," with its four ways of achieving oneness with the Lord: for the predominantly intellectual, the way of intuitive wisdom; for the meditative, the way of consciously practiced mental concentration; for the predominantly emotional, the way of devotional self-giving; for the active, the way of service in the spirit. I have listened to the Spirit speaking through the Jewish community as it alternately affirms and denies that "God died in Auschwitz." My theology has been leavened by the arts—from Tchaikovsky's *Swan Lake* ballet, through Peanuts' latest reflection on reality, to Samuel Beckett's frightening "Two times anything equals zero" and *Godspell*'s glorious "God is dead; long live God!" I have come to agonize over the experience of living man and living woman, as they cry to me that they cannot discover God in my abstractions, as they stand mute before an immutable God who does not weep when they bleed, as they insist that, if they are to find God at all, they must somehow find Him in woman and man.

To do theology this way is to sweat profusely and to risk frightfully; for I am wrestling with God and I am wrestling with His human images—yes, I am wrestling with myself. In consequence, much of my life resembles Nikos Kazantzakis' *Report to Greco:* "the red track [to Golgotha] made by drops of my blood, the track which marks my journey among men, passions and ideas."[15] I am often lonely; for despite the dialogue and collaboration, my deepest reflection takes place alone. I often wonder whether it's all worth doing; for I am explaining the Evangelist John on loaves and fishes while ten thousand of the world's hungry die each day; I argue abstract love over Budweiser or Burgundy while Arabs and Israelis are locked in hate; I try to recapture the meaning of "presence" while waves of Washingtonians are experiencing God's absence. I frequently feel frustration; for to hard questions there are no easy answers, pop theology is an illusion, and at times I must rest content if I uncover not the answer but the question. Increasingly I hurt; for to wrestle the way I do is at times to wrestle with Rome, and to wrestle with Rome is to hear the hounds baying in the States—and they can be savage indeed.

Now I do not expect the parish priest to be a professional theologian; but I do expect him to continue, to intensify, the struggle he initiated in the seminary. I mean an ongoing effort to grow with the Church, to grow in understanding. It will not be easy. Your enemy is time. Your enemy is the explosion of knowledge—in Scripture, in history, in theology. Your enemy is the complexity of today's human issues, from world hunger through genetic engineering to the morality of nuclear war. And still you dare not abandon the struggle to understand; for to forsake it is to risk condemning your preaching to sterile abstractions, far removed from God in His heaven and from people on earth. It is to settle for "cheap grace."

II

Yes, effective preaching lays a heavy cost on my mind. In the second place, preaching costs me my *spirit*. Here I am making a distinction—not total but partial, what scholasticism termed an inadequate distinction—between mind and spirit. Remember, in my first point I limited mind to the intellect's capacity to reach reality and truth through reason. By spirit I understand my whole intellectual nature. It includes, therefore, not only reason but my imagination and my emotions, my creativity and my affections. I mean not only my ability to fashion or grasp an idea, but also the power I have to feel, to will, to imagine.

Let's begin with the imagination. I have detailed this in an earlier chapter, where I spoke of the imagination as our capacity "to make the material an image of the immaterial or spiritual." It reveals itself, I said, in vision and ritual, in story and symbol, in the fine arts. It is indeed a form of knowing, but in a special way: not reasoning, not induction or deduction, not systematic movement from premise to conclusion. It is a way of illuminating bare facts, of looking for the holes in the world, of listening to the space between sounds. It does not so much teach as evoke. As in the parables of Jesus, the image is more open-ended than the concept, more susceptible of different interpretations; it says different things to different people.

Here, I have insisted, is preaching at its best. Not that finely honed concepts are unimportant, Cartesian clarity a vice. Rather that the homily has for primary purpose not to *recall* God's saving works but to make them present and active within us, not to *remember* the mystery that is Christ but to help the hearers to see him with their own eyes, not to convey a truth from one mind to another but to evoke a religious response. And the most effective approach to this purpose is not reason but imagination. Before you say "stuff and nonsense," read my reasoning in the chapter "Sir, We Would Like To See Jesus: Preaching As Imagining."

All right, then; let's suppose that preaching *is* imagining. Why is this, as Milton would say, "dearly to my cost"? Because, for most Catholic preachers, imagining takes more effort, induces more spiritual sweat, demands more courage than the clear and distinct idea. In our philosophy and theology the imagination was an intruder; it took David Tracy to title a book on Christian theology *The Analogical Imagination*. And until Vatican II our preaching was largely a matter of instructional sermons. We were trained to present Catholic doctrine clearly, unambiguously. Not indeed unattractively, not without stories and images; but all such devices were servants of the clear and distinct idea.

I am not suggesting that Christian clarity is by definition divorced from struggle. Not when you are dealing with mystery. Like Maria in *The Sound of Music*, "how do you catch a moonbeam in your hand?" Nevertheless, an instructional sermon is not a class in theology. The preacher does not supplant the professor. A sermon on the Trinity cannot enter into processions and relations; a sermon on Good Friday does not recapitulate various theories of redemption; a sermon on abortion does not distinguish between fertilization and implantation. Sufficient for the day is putting into generally intelligible language what dogma and theology express in the jargon of Rome and the schools. Not a simple matter (good translation never is), but hardly comparable to the labors of Hercules.

Imagination is something else again. Once I start saying "The kingdom of heaven is like . . . ," once I break through the surface to the reality beneath, once I plunge into the world of intuition and wonder, of festivity and play—and all this not for its own sake but to share with other spirits what it means to "feel" God—I'm in C. S. Lewis' Narnia. I like it, I revel in it, this kingdom of the imagination. But for all its fascination, for all its delight, there is a recurring insecurity here. It's like walking on the moon; you're never quite sure what lies ahead. When you start imagining, you open all sorts of doors, open yourself to the unexpected; and the unexpected can be startling, even frightening.

It makes preaching somewhat easier, but at the same time a good deal more difficult. Easier because I no longer approach the podium or mount the pulpit with a hatful of answers; I do not address the laity with pointed solutions to every problem of faith or morality. Remember Vatican II's unforeseen admonition: "Let the laity not imagine that their pastors are always such experts that to every problem which arises, however complicated, they can readily give a concrete solution, or even that such is their mission."[16] But despite such magisterial comfort, preaching assumes added anguish. I must shape my homily in such fashion—so carefully, so artistically, so imaginatively—that my congregation sees not so much me as Christ Jesus, that my listeners listen to what the Lord is saying to each individually. Not that Catholic truth has suddenly been relativized; rather that God speaks not only through encyclicals and pastoral letters but directly to hearts that plead with Him in their perplexity and confusion. Orthopraxis can be more complex than orthodoxy.

One example.[17] Back in 1981, I was preaching at Georgetown University to a congregation that comes together from Virginia, Maryland, and the District of Columbia to worship each Sunday in Dahlgren Chapel. It was the 24th Sunday of the Year, cycle A. The Gospel retold the parable of the Ungrateful Debtor (Mt 18:21–35), the servant whose king forgave him a debt of about ten million dollars, the servant who proceeded to choke and jail a fellow servant who owed him perhaps 20 dollars. In my first point, I sketched the obvious lesson of the parable: "You had better forgive your brothers and sisters; otherwise God will not forgive you, will put you away till you pay the last penny you owe Him." It was summed up in the day's reading from Sirach: "Forgive your neighbor the wrong he [or she] has done, and then your sins will be pardoned when you pray" (Sir 28:2).

My second point suggested what lies beneath the surface of the story, something wonderfully positive. It tells us more profoundly why we should forgive, tells us something about God. "In short, the more important lesson of the parable, the lesson that stems from

Israel's history and touches our own, is surely the question put by the king to the unforgiving servant: 'Should not you have had mercy on your fellow servant, as I had mercy on you?' (Mt 18:33). As I had mercy on you. As God had mercy on us."

My third point was an effort to open the parable to the congregation's own Christian imagining.

> I say "your own" because it is not my task to tell you precisely what to do, how to lead your individual lives, whom to forgive and how. It is not mine to say to a survivor of Auschwitz: Forgive the Nazi who gassed your parents. Not mine to counsel a rape victim: Forgive and forget. Not mine to insist that you sit down and cancel every debt owed you. A homily, like a parable, has different lessons for different listeners, different strokes for different folks. In fact, the conclusion of today's parable, "So also my heavenly Father will do to every one of you, if you do not forgive your brother from your heart" (v. 35), is probably Matthew's own application, may well reflect his "legalistic tendency." My function is to help you to see Jesus—not with my eyes but with yours; to open your ears to his voice, to what *he* is saying to you. And this, believe it or not, Jesus does not clear in advance with the homilist!

I went on to stimulate my listeners' own imagining, their personal response to Christ. In one direction: Each of us should be merciful primarily because each of us has received mercy, not because our debtors merit mercy. Oh yes, the human in anyone should strike a spark in us. But in the last analysis we are bid to forgive because we are bid to mirror God; we are commanded to be merciful because God has shown us mercy. We owe God. This calls not for guilt but for gratitude. And our gratitude will be genuine if we are compassionate as our heavenly Father is compassionate.

> How? Again, different strokes for different folks. For Mother Teresa, it's the skeletons in Calcutta. For some Georgetown students, it's the refugees in Thailand. For Franciscan Father Bruce Ritter, it's the sewers of Times Square. In a single year 12,000 kids ask his help—scared kids, burned, pimped and prostituted, overdosed and angel-dusted.

For most of us, however, compassion is not so dramatic. Our task is to control a common tendency: doling out our love (including our forgiveness) to those who can prove they deserve it, those who say "thanks," those we can count on to return the six-pack. No, without any merit of our own, we have experienced God's forgiveness. Should we not carry His compassion to our sisters and brothers?

Now this sort of approach can rack the preacher's spirit. It is not enough to be logical: God has forgiven us, therefore we must forgive others. I have to move beyond logic in two directions. My presentation has to be so carefully contrived, so imaginatively molded, that (1) while I indeed suggest a potentially fruitful line of reflection, (2) those who hear my voice are led to listen to the Lord, who alone knows just what He wants them to do in their concrete circumstances. This means I must retell God's love story in a contemporary idiom—Karl Rahner's insistence that in preaching I must translate. And it means I must in some sense tell my own story. Not a relentless, repetitive first person singular; and still it is I who must come through to the people as one struggling not only to compose this homily but to live it. This twin storytelling calls for "costly grace." Such creativity involves agony of spirit—hour after hour, sometimes deep into night. You do not tell God's story or your own story lounging on pink clouds.

In this context, imaginative preaching takes a related toll: on my emotions. I am glad that most (not all) of my homiletic preparation takes place in relative solitude: at my typewriter or in a library nook, in the twilight of a chapel or on a lonely stretch of beach. To see me in action is to shake your head in wonder. I have a love-hate relationship with each homily. From the first phase of mulling to the final phrase of text, I am a man possessed. It reminds me of a sentence in the preface of Richard Bach's delightful allegory *Illusions: The Adventures of a Reluctant Messiah:* "once in a while there's a great dynamite-burst of flying glass and bricks and splinters through the front wall and somebody stalks over the rubble, seizes me by the throat and gently says: 'I will not let you go until you set me, in words, on paper.' "[18]

I love it because preaching calls into play just about everything I have studied and taught, experienced and been graced with, through more than half a century of Jesuit existence. Classical studies and history, foreign languages and English literature, philosophy and theology, Scripture and patristics, spirituality and prayer, community living and extensive traveling, Hollywood and Broadway, music and the dance, dialogues Jewish and Lutheran, friendships with all manner of folk from teen-agers to the aging, hobnobbing with hierarchy and disporting with dissenters—all this and so much more is grist to my homiletic mill. I could not ask for a richer set of resources. All of these are caught up into this moment, this hour, these weeks—instruments of beauty and goodness and truth ready to be shaped into a singular symphony.

Perhaps it is excessive to speak of hate; frustration may be more accurate. As "spirit in the world" (dear Karl Rahner again), I am constantly torn between the promise and the fulfilment. As I confessed in an earlier chapter, I frequently feel what St. Augustine felt: "For my part, I am nearly always dissatisfied with my discourse. For I am desirous of something better . . . ; but when I find that my powers of expression come short of my knowledge of the subject, I am sorely disappointed that my tongue has not been able to answer the demands of my mind."[19] Conceiving mystery correctly and expressing it in language acceptable to the Congregation for the Doctrine of the Faith is painful enough, laborious, exacting. More frustrating still is the task of translating the technical truth, molding it in such a way that, without offending against orthodoxy, a fresh vision of God and His Christ takes hold of minds theologically untrained, of hearts yearning to be stirred, of eyes pleading to see Jesus.

In consequence, I wrestle with words. At my right elbow is Webster Unabridged, thumbed as often as the Oxford *RSV* at my left elbow. For several reasons. I must be sure that the word I am using actually means what I think it means; and if it does, whether it has other meanings that might play havoc with what I intend. I need synonyms that give color to my abstractions, that express my thought more vividly, more strikingly. I have to increase my vocabulary, so as not to bog down in an unimaginative, predictable diction that cannot possibly fire or inspire.

But even when I have done all this, I am still frustrated. For words thrown to the winds do not come back as they went forth. Some who hear me will misunderstand what I say; others will find it incomprehensible, foreign to their experience. At this point I must remember two realities. First, what poet Paul Claudel said of St. Francis Xavier, so often an apparent failure, to the very last failure off the coast of China: "He did what he was told to do—not everything, but all he was able to do."[20] Second, what St. Paul preached to the Christians of Corinth: "God chose what is foolish in the world to shame the wise, God chose what is weak in the world to shame the strong, God chose what is low and despised in the world, even things that are not, to bring to nothing things that are, so that no human being might boast in the presence of God" (1 Cor 1:27–29). I simply do all I can—really, agonizingly, all I am able to do; the rest, the effect, the grace, this I leave to a wise and strong God.

A word here on other emotions besides love and hate. As I stew and sweat over a homily, at times anger and rage flood my spirit. Anger and rage over starvation in Somalia, over bombs in Beirut, over segregation in South Africa, over a world's war on the womb. When I type out on a cold page "Of the 122 million children born in 1980, the International Year of the Child, 12 million are dead— one in every ten—almost all from a needless, heedless poverty," tears of compassion splotch the keys. The point is, I should not, I cannot, compose a homily the way I stucco a wall—completely calm, cool, and collected. Not if I am to come through to my hearers as a central actor in this pivotal act of the ritual. Central not because I wrote the piece and speak it trippingly, but because I am intimately one with what I am saying. I am preaching in the first instance to myself; the homily is *I*. It bursts not merely from my brain but from my whole being, from this total person.

III

This leads quite naturally into the third great price that preaching exacts: It costs me my *flesh and blood*. The toll is taken primarily at three stages: while I prepare, for some hours before delivery, and after all has been said and done.

I am not disembodied spirit. In consequence, the anguish my spirit endures in the days and weeks of composition is reflected in my flesh. Not only do I tire; my body tenses, my muscles tighten, my nerves give me fits—almost literally. An idea that will not jell murders sleep. Not constantly, of course; such torment hour after hour, day after day, might well crush the human spirit. But enough of it to make homily preparation significantly different from my research into the Fathers of the Church. Here, too, I struggle in the effort to understand, to make a person or a period or a problem come alive; but the effort is ordinarily more pacific, more tranquil. I am hardly harassed by a clock; I can set my own pace; I am not aware of men and women whose relationship to God and to their fellows may be altered by my research. Weariness, yes; perplexity, often; anxiety, at times; but spasms of the colon, acid in the esophagus, rarely.

The hours before delivery can be, in very truth, nauseating. Especially if the congregation is entirely new to me, or my appearance a one-shot affair, or the occasion uncommon, even somewhat awesome. Georgetown's Dahlgren Chapel at 12:15 and Washington's

Holy Trinity Church at 5:30 are wonderfully familiar. The worshipers love the liturgy; they expect and want a good homily; they know me, appreciate my subtleties, laugh and groan at my humor. Yes, even here my insides betray me; I fret and stew, can do little else save focus on my manuscript, avoid people as I would the plague. But nothing like the singular situation, the "one-night stand," the sea of unfamiliar faces. The Sunday sermon to total strangers in a different city, to good Christians who have not experienced my rhetoric, are unaccustomed to humor that is part and parcel of the message, do not respond visibly and audibly the way Dahlgren and Trinity do. A baccalaureate homily on Georgetown's campus before ten thousand assembled from a hundred countries. A unique homily on the island of Guam, celebrating the recent beatification of Blessed Diego of the Marianas. Here the colon and the hiatal hernia have a field day, and the hours of darkness preceding are a night of the loose bowel. Fortunately, once I begin to preach, the flesh is as willing as the spirit.

I cannot speak for others, but my own thorn in the flesh does not cease to be active once the homily is over. Particularly when the preparation has been unusually protracted and perplexing, the aftermath can be brutal. Once I relax totally, once I sit down with a grateful and satisfied "aaah," it is like a signal for the flesh to take revenge. All energy may vanish, stomach spasms strike with devilish regularity, food refuse to sit comfortably within the system.

Why this physical toll? Perhaps it is a natural price perfectionists must pay. At times I have asked myself whether a less than Christian pride plays a role in all this. In striving on each and every occasion for the perfect homily, am I motivated by human ambition, by a thirst for the world's applause? If I had a more profound trust in God, if I were seeking His glory alone, would "the slings and arrows" I endure be less "outrageous"? Possibly—I simply cannot say yes or no with any conviction. But this I do know: The effectiveness of my preaching often seems directly proportionate to the agony of mind, spirit, and flesh I endure. When I read that a certain first-rate actor throws up before most performances, I can resonate. No doubt, our yearning for approval gets in there to some degree; but I suspect that more powerful still is our anxiety to get inside this audience, lift living people out of a routine existence, inspire a fresh vision—and we are psychically and physically sensitive to the possibilities of mucking it.

I am not recommending to aspiring homilists a recurring colitis or a sickening migraine. I *am* saying, from my own experience and that of uncounted others, that it is difficult for most humans to shape a work of art with hands alone or tongue. The whole man, the whole woman, must be absorbed into the creation. Not with serene objectivity, like a zoologist peering through a microscope. More like Welsh poet Dylan Thomas, "alternately ecstatic and morbid," obsessed "with death, religion, sex, and the sound of words," high-spiritedly in love with life.[21]

How sum it up? In the Christian paradox first enuntiated by Jesus and ever since experienced by devoted disciples: If you lose your life for him, you will find it. In fact, *only* if you lose your life will you find it. Effective preaching is costly because it costs me my life: my mind, my spirit, my flesh and blood.

13
LORD, TO WHOM SHALL WE GO?
Masters Who Just Might Help

It is not my intention to compose a complete, or even a fairly extensive, annotated list of effective preachers through the Christian centuries. Not indeed a bad idea, but not pertinent to my purposes or even congruent with my competence. Let me simply offer you a large handful of speakers whose pulpit skills have influenced *me* in varying ways and differing degrees, and suggest why it might be helpful to read what they have preached. Since a sermon is shaped for speaking, only an audiovisual can recapture it—voice, face, body, gestures, personality. Still, a text can be useful, especially when complemented by knowledge of and insight into the person.

JOHN HENRY NEWMAN

The first, and at that time quite remote, influence on my preaching came more than a half century ago, in a Jesuit juniorate—two years of classical studies (Latin, Greek, English) on a college level. We read "The Second Spring," a sermon preached by John Henry Newman, then a convert of seven years, as the second session of the First Provincial Synod of Westminster opened at St. Mary's College, Oscott, July 13, 1852.[1] Two years before, Rome had restored a diocesan hierarchy to an England whose Catholic situation had been remarkably transformed for the better in the seven decades preceding. Preaching before Nicholas Cardinal Wiseman, the bishops of England, and a number of distinguished children of the Oxford Movement and descendants of the English martyrs,

Newman had his listeners in tears as he sketched the glories of the ancient Catholic Church of England, its death, and its second life only then beginning. It was a historic moment, even though the sanguine hopes of the preacher and his congregation for the rapid conversion of England did not materialize. A historic moment, and a remarkable sermon, which merits study and meditation as a piece of homiletic art.

Fortunately, Newman has shared with us his theory of preaching. His 1855 paper on "University Preaching"[2] claims that "the one thing necessary" for a preacher is earnestness—in the sense of "an intense perception and appreciation of the end for which he preaches, and that is, to be the minister of some spiritual good to those who hear him." (In fact, one of his sermons has for title "The Salvation of the Hearer the Motive of the Preacher.") And the spiritual good has to be definite: "Definiteness is the life of preaching. A definite hearer, not the whole world; a definite topic, not the whole evangelical tradition; and, in like manner, a definite speaker. Nothing that is anonymous will preach; nothing that is dead and gone; nothing even which is of yesterday, however religious in itself and useful." Hence Newman's insistence that "There is something more than composition in a sermon; there is something personal in preaching; people are drawn and moved, not simply by what is said, but by who says it. The same things said by one man are not the same as when said by another. The same things when read are not the same as when they are preached."[3] In short, the preacher persuades by what he is as well as by what he delivers. It helps, therefore, if he is a saint and an apostle.

In my early Jesuit days, it was not so much Newman's ideas that captivated me as his mastery of language. The words he chose always seemed so right; he could sustain, as few since, the periodic sentence; and the language was instinct with love. And so we young Jesuits imitated him, not to plagiarize but to get his feel for words, for style, for the ordering of a clause, a sentence, a paragraph. Of all this "The Second Spring" was a remarkable example: how to use language with reverence, with care, with discrimination, with feeling.

Good critics insist that Newman still speaks to us, still preaches effectively. Novelist Muriel Spark, who turned Roman Catholic "by way of Newman," gave first place in her 1961 reading to Newman's eight volumes of *Parochial and Plain Sermons*. His secret? Some call up his superb intelligence, his creative yet disciplined use of language, his abandonment of human ambition in pursuit of truth, his intense spirituality. Others appeal to Newman's rejection of "relevance," in the spirit of Dean Inge: "If you marry the Spirit of your generation, you will be a widow in the next."[4] It is an approach that may well turn many a modern off: to be timely by preaching the timeless. You would not know from Newman, writes a sympathetic critic, that the same century which produced Newman also produced a Marx and a Darwin. The ethical imperatives of the gospel are not brought directly to bear on the political, the economic, and the social. It was not that Newman was unconcerned about social issues, from slums to the exploitation of women and children. A fine historian has recently written:

> Few of the great ecclesiastical personages of the 19th century possessed Newman's pastoral instincts and, perhaps more significantly, his pastoral experience. None of them had had the care of a jail, an orphanage, and two poor schools, all within the confines of the Edgbaston parish and all with a disproportionately high Catholic clientele. None of them had sat, as Newman did, holding the hand of a parishioner growing black with cholera. . . .[5]

It was rather that Newman's apologetic stemmed from a conviction that the major problem underlying the specific issues was the modern movement to unbelief, the conclusion that this tidal wave could be met only by recovering the forgotten truths of revealed religion, not by accommodation to a middle-class "liberalism" he saw as a door to infidelity.

Who will dare to conclude that Newman should have preached otherwise? There were enough preachers who mimicked the radical social criticisms of the Hebrew prophets. Surely there was place for a preacher who saw *his own* prophetic vocation differently: to revitalize revealed religion in an unbelieving world, to move within a solid intellectual and doctrinal framework, to reflect a disappearing awe and reverence in the face of God and His creation, to transmit a profound personal spirituality, the cry of Augustine that we are made for God and our hearts will be restless until they rest in Him. I am not surprised that it is the timeless sermons of his age that have perdured to ours.

FATHERS OF THE CHURCH

In the same period of Jesuit juniorate, a young classics professor, Fr. Philip Walsh, put into my hands the seven letters of Ignatius of Antioch. In large measure these letters mapped out my intellectual journey, somewhat as the Exercises of Ignatius Loyola charted my spiritual pilgrimage. For the second-century martyr, with his prayer "God's wheat I am, and by the teeth of wild beasts I am to be ground, that I may prove Christ's pure bread," put me in touch with early Christianity and sparked a love for the Fathers of the Church that has been my life through five decades.

At that time, understandably, I did not connect the Fathers with the preaching I would take on as a priest less than eight years later. But as my immersion in patristics broadened and deepened, especially through doctoral studies under an unforgettable Johannes Quasten at the Catholic University of America, several facets of the Fathers took on pertinence for my preaching. In the first place, I was astonished at the large proportion of sermons in the patristic legacy.[6] The tradition to which the Fathers witnessed was transmitted not only in learned tomes, e.g. in Athanasius' *Discourses against the Arians* or Augustine's 15 books *On the Trinity,* but from the pulpit, in face-to-face contact with a believing, worshiping community. A second facet, which goes far to explain the first: The Fathers rarely divorced their search for God's truth from the living people for whom God spoke His truth. For them, theology was not an arcane discipline, done up ivory towers or behind ivied walls. Their theology was itself a spirituality, to be communicated in vibrant speech to pulsing people. Third, the Fathers saw themselves as men of the Bible; they were primarily interpreters of the word.[7]

From scores of patristic preachers and thousands of early Christian sermons, who in particular "grabbed" me and still have hold of me? Leo the Great (pope 440–61), for one. Why? Because he is lucidly clear and admirably succinct; his sentences are artfully constructed, neatly balanced; his antitheses and wordplays delight eye and ear; he makes theology come alive in Christ. Of Leo's 96 extant sermons, I still read for pleasure certain of the homilies for Christmas and Lent. The problem is, Latin rhetoricians like Leo are difficult to recapture in English; rarely can we reproduce the way words dance in his grasp, the nuances, the alliteration, the assonance.[8]

Influential, too, has been Origen (ca. 185–253), the "outstanding teacher and scholar of the early Church, a man of spotless character, encyclopaedic learning, and one of the most original thinkers the world has ever seen."[9] One early historian, Socrates, claims that Origen preached every Wednesday and Friday; his biographer,

Pamphilus, says he preached nearly every day. For Origen, "homily" has four characteristics.[10] (1) It has a liturgical dimension: Through the act of preaching, the Word is made flesh again in the community of faith and worship. (2) It has a prophetic quality: The preacher not only instructs minds but must convert hearts. (3) It is essentially and profoundly scriptural, often a running exposition of the biblical text. "Through him exegesis and preaching were so united that for long afterwards they remained one and the same."[11] (4) Origen's style is direct, familiar, conversational—not uninfluenced by contemporary rhetoric but not enslaved thereto.

Unfortunately, too few of Origen's homilies have been turned into English. Still, some delectable hors d'oeuvres are available in his homilies on Genesis and Exodus[12] and his two homilies on the Song of Songs.[13]

No need to repeat here the admiration I have expressed for Augustine and Chrysostom in the chapter "Thus Says the Lord." Each weds impressively two loves: the Book and the people. Worth noting, in addition, is Augustine's work *On Christian Learning,* surely his most important presentation of biblical scholarship.[14] The first two books deal with the secular and theological preparation required for successful study of Scripture; the third book, hermeneutics; the fourth, homiletics. The section on homiletics is not so much a "popular mechanics," a "how to" manual, as a small treatise on the basic relationships between rhetoric and preaching. Augustine assumes that his readers have been schooled in the rules of rhetoric. He is no enemy of eloquence; for eloquence, he believed with Cicero, is simply the speaker's effort to teach, please, and persuade—his appeal to intellect, feeling, and will. And yet, for Augustine, the soul of the preacher was not eloquence but wisdom.

> He helps his hearers more by his wisdom than his oratory, although he himself is less useful than he would be if he were an eloquent speaker also. But the one to guard against is the man whose eloquence is no more than an abundant flow of empty words. His listener is more easily charmed by him in matters that are unprofitable to hear about and, all too frequently, such eloquence is mistaken for truth. Moreover, this opinion did not escape the notice of those who believed that the art of rhetoric should be taught. They acknowledged that "wisdom without eloquence is of small benefit to states, but eloquence without wisdom is frequently very prejudicial, and never beneficial."[15]

How, concretely, was the preacher's wisdom to find expression? In sum, the sermon was indissolubly linked to Scripture and sacrament. It has been argued that "the most powerful influence on the content and shape of Augustinian preaching was that of the liturgy itself in which his sermons had their origin. . . . "[16] This is not to downplay the influence of Scripture; for Augustine the preacher read the word, interpreted the word, not in scholarly abstraction but as it revealed itself in the sacraments. Powerfully illustrative of this threefold unity (Scripture, sacrament, sermon) is the Easter Vigil. Augustine "has a profound conviction of the sheer power of this night"; the Church "is not only commemorating the death and resurrection of her Lord as she does his birth at Christmastide, but is actually engaging in a sacred action attesting all the happenings surrounding those momentous days and revealing their sacred meaning."[17]

As for Chrysostom, I add only one strong recommendation to preachers: Note, and imitate, his passionate attachment to St. Paul, so evident, for example, at the beginning and end of his commentary (32 homilies) on Romans. It grieved him sorely that some Christians were not only ignorant of the man, but did not even "know for certain the number of his epistles"! In our day, biblical criticism has made us intelligently uncertain of the exact number; but we can only blame ourselves for not knowing and loving Paul as Chrysostom did, for not preaching the Pauline Christ with some of his infectious enthusiasm.[18]

Also in the Age of the Fathers, I have profited from Gregory the Great (pope 590–604). Not so much from his 50 *Homilies on the Gospel* (pastoral talks that make good use of stories) or his 22 *Homilies on Ezekiel* (some remarkable passages on Christ, the Church, active and contemplative life, suffering). Rather his *Pastoral Care,* an impressively practical work that in the Middle Ages was for the secular clergy what the Rule of St. Benedict was for the religious orders. It is still highly useful for the four problems Gregory set himself to discuss: (1) the person and motives the pastoral office demands; (2) the virtues of a good pastor; (3) how to preach to different types of people; (4) the need for recollection, "return to oneself."[19]

It is Part 3 that interests me here. With psychological acumen Gregory details 36 contrasting sets of people that must be distinguished by the preacher and teacher. In his own summary:

men and women;
the young and the old;
the poor and the rich;
the joyful and the sad;
subjects and superiors;
slaves and masters;
the wise of this world and the dull;
the impudent and the timid;
the insolent and the fainthearted;
the impatient and the patient;
the kindly and the envious;
the sincere and the insincere;
the hale and the sick;
those who fear afflictions and, therefore, live innocently, and
those so hardened in evil as to be impervious to the correction of
affliction;
the taciturn and the loquacious;
the slothful and the hasty;
the meek and the choleric;
the humble and the haughty;
the obstinate and the fickle;
the gluttonous and the abstemious;
those who mercifully give of their own, and those addicted to
thieving;
those who do not steal yet do not give of their own, and those who
give of their own yet do not desist from despoiling others;
those living in discord and those living in peace;
sowers of discord and peacemakers;
those who do not understand correctly the words of the Holy Law
and those who do, but utter them without humility;
those who, though capable of preaching worthily, yet are afraid
to do so from excessive humility, and those whose unfitness or
age debars them from preaching, yet who are impelled thereto
by their hastiness;
those who prosper in their pursuit of temporal things, and those
who desire, indeed, the things of the world yet are wearied out
by suffering and adversity;
those who are bound in wedlock and those who are free from the
ties of wedlock;
those who have had carnal intercourse and those who have had
no such experience;
those who grieve for sins of deed and those who grieve for sins
of thought only;
those who grieve for their sins yet do not abandon them, and
those who abandon their sins yet do not grieve for them;

those who even approve of their misdeeds and those who confess
their sins yet do not shun them;

those who are overcome by sudden concupiscence, and those who
deliberately put on the fetters of sin;

those who commit only small sins but commit them frequently,
and those who guard themselves against small sins yet sometimes
sink into grave ones;

those who do not even begin to do good, and those who begin but
do not finish;

those who do evil secretly and good openly, and those who hide
the good they do, yet allow themselves to be thought ill of because
of some things they do in public.[20]

Whence came this knowledge? From uncommonly wide experience: in the world and the monastery, as papal nuncio and pope, dealing with soldiers and generals, with merchants and kings, with rich and poor, with the lofty and the lowly, with the manic and the depressive, with priests and bishops and patriarchs. Part 3 of the *Pastoral Care* stems from the mind and heart of a man who cared, who was frighteningly aware that office means responsibility, who wrote the work primarily to explain why the burden of a bishop made him sick at heart, why he tried desperately to decline the papal office to which popular acclaim elected him. Much of his career and personality, his ability and humility, reminds me of good Pope John XXIII.

This is not to canonize Gregory's own preaching. I can concur with Brilioth that his "preaching leaves a poor impression in contrast to that of Augustine or even of Leo the Great. It has little of the formal elegance which characterized his predecessors, and the sweep of thought which characterizes Augustine is entirely lacking."[21] I rarely sway to his allegorizing; I too sense the absence of a "spirit of prophecy."[22] I am simply asserting that Gregory's profound concern for the different types of people who have to listen to us calls for our admiration and imitation, however much we may have grown in psychological insight over the past 14 centuries.

CONTEMPORARY PROTESTANT PREACHERS

"Late have I loved you." The touching words Augustine addressed to God, the same words I speak penitently to my Protestant brothers and sisters. My undergraduate theology was shaped in pre-ecumenical days, when a Luther reached us through condemned propositions in Denzinger's *Enchiridion symbolorum;* he and his kind were consistently the "adversaries" to established theses. It was only in the early 60s that my mind and eyes were opened—initially and powerfully through involvement in the Lutheran-Roman Catholic dialogue. Close contact for more than a decade with theologians such as Joseph Sittler, Arthur Carl Piepkorn, Warren Quanbeck, and George Lindbeck shattered ingrained prejudices, humbled me. There were actually Protestants smarter than I! They were deeply devoted to the Lord, had a profound spirituality, loved the liturgy, and were engagingly human. The Reformers could no longer be cavalierly dismissed as hard-nosed, disgruntled rebels bent on destroying God's Church. And on a sheerly personal level, I shall never forget the Reverend Edwin Seymour, blind for most of his Presbyterian ministry, but incorrigibly convinced by experience that he sees more in his blindness than he ever saw before his accident. The last quarter century has enlarged and enriched my Christian sensibility immensely.

Not surprisingly, the Protestant theologian and the Protestant pastor were supplemented by the Protestant preacher—but a good bit later. Strange that it took so long. After all, the word, God's and the preacher's, has dominated Protestantism since, say, 1517. We Catholics used to excuse our pulpit inferiority by such observations as "You must remember, this is the way they have to make their living. If they're not good preachers, they lose their jobs. Our service of worship is not restricted to the pulpit." No longer a valid excuse, if ever it was. Not since Vatican II. Not when the liturgy of the word commands so prominent, so respected, so integral a place in the Roman Catholic Eucharistic service.

Concretely, what preachers in the non-Roman tradition have influenced me these recent years, and why? First and foremost, Frederick Buechner (1926–), convert from agnosticism and Presbyterian minister. A first-rate preacher and a seasoned novelist, he weds the two arts admirably. At least one reviewer was not surprised. He found Buechner's "religious sensibilities at work in his novels and the metaphor-making skill of the novelist enlivening and freshening his theological writing."[23]

I first heard of Buechner in an unusual way. Reviewing my book *Sir, We Would Like To See Jesus: Homilies from a Hilltop,* the Presbyterian pastor and preacher David H. C. Read wrote: "Only in the sermons of Frederick Buechner have I found such fresh language, such poetic vision, such unexpected twists and such a deeply personal witness to Christ."[24] It was obvious that Buechner would be "must" reading for me! I was not disappointed. Mulling over two collections of his sermons from the 60s, *The Magnificent Defeat*[25] and *The Hungering Dark*,[26] I was constantly arrested, delighted, amazed.

There is the "fresh language." Take his sermon on "The Road to Emmaus," at the point where the two disciples recognize Jesus when he breaks the bread:

> Much as they would have given to have had him stay there a minute or two more, they could not make him stay. They could not nail him down. And that is how it always is. We can never nail him down, not even if the nails we use are real ones and the thing we nail him to is a cross. He comes suddenly, out of nowhere, like the first clear light of the sun after a thunderstorm or maybe like the thunder itself; and maybe we recognize him, and maybe we do not, and our lives are never the same again either because we did not recognize him or because we did.[27]

There is the "poetic vision." In "The Annunciation" he has just spoken of the great medieval paintings of the event, where "the air is painted in gold leaf, and the figures of Mary and Gabriel stand there as still as death. There is no movement. None. Even the robe of the angel, still billowed out by the winds of Heaven, is frozen, and so is the wind itself. Time itself seems to have stopped. It is a moment beyond time."

> But that is only part of the truth, because when angels draw near, as they do, the earth begins to shake beneath our feet as it began to shake beneath Mary's feet, which was why she was greatly troubled. Instead of everything standing still and sure, suddenly nothing is standing still, and everything is unsure. Something new and shattering is breaking through into something old. Something is trying to be born. And if the new thing is going to be born, then the old thing is going to have to give way, and there is agony in the process as well as joy, just as there is agony in the womb as it labors and contracts to bring forth the new life.[28]

There are the "unexpected twists." The sermon "In the Beginning" moves so superbly through the darkness of our era that we expect the preacher to proclaim, in Christian hope, that the Creator will once again bring light out of darkness, that we shall see once more a staggering light such as followed the incomparable darkness that hung over our world when from the sixth hour to the ninth the sun was blotted out. But no, not a proclamation, only a question. "Are there in us, in you and me now, that recklessness of the loving heart, that wild courage, that crazy gladness in the face of darkness and death, that shuddering faithfulness even unto the end of the world, through which the new things can come to pass? . . . If not, God have mercy upon us, for we will soon be as yesterday when it is gone. If so, then we, even we, will have some part in the new heaven and the new earth that God is creating."[29] Or again, in "The Two Battles": "It is not until we love a person in all his ugliness that we can make him beautiful, or ourselves either."[30]

There is the "deeply personal witness to Christ." It pervades Buechner's preaching. Happily, I found the theory behind it excitingly expressed in his little book *Telling the Truth: The Gospel As Tragedy, Comedy, and Fairy Tale*.[31] He has just quoted from *King Lear*'s Edgar, stammering the curtain down on a stage littered with corpses:

> The weight of this sad time we must obey,
> Speak what we feel, not what we ought to say.
>   (Act 5, Scene 3)

Buechner goes on to comment:

> They are not the most powerful lines in the play, but they are among the most telling because in them it would seem that Shakespeare is telling us something about himself and about the way he wrote his play. What he has done in *Lear* is to look as deep as he can into the dark and ambiguous heart of things and then to body forth an impassioned statement about what he has found there. . . . He risks making a terrible fool of himself in *Lear*, and in scenes like the one where blind Gloucester thinks he is throwing himself off a cliff when there actually is no cliff, or where Lear starts tearing his clothes off and babbling nonsense, a single titter from the audience could destroy everything. But in the interests of truth-telling, there seems to be no risk that Shakespeare is not willing to run as if from the conviction that if the truth is worth telling, it is worth making a fool of yourself to tell. . . . What he said was what in the deepest sense he truly felt. He looked into the dark hearts of things, which is to say into his own heart and into our hearts, too, and told as close to the whole truth as he was able.

Buechner ends this section with a similar word for the preacher: "Drawing on nothing fancier than the poetry of his own life, let him use words and images that help make the surface of our lives transparent to the truth that lies deep within them, which is the wordless truth of who we are and who God is and the Gospel of our meeting."[32]

Novelist and preacher, Buechner is an artist with words, a sculptor. In a 1983 address celebrating the rededication of the library at New York City's Union Theological Seminary, he remarked: "Words are our godly sharing in the work of creation, and the speaking and writing of words is at once the most human and the most holy of all the businesses we engage in." He went on to say: "The ultimate purpose of language, I suspect, is so that humanity may speak to God."[33]

I have room only for inadequate references to other Protestant preachers who have influenced my preaching, often in subtle ways difficult to articulate. I think fondly of the Lutheran theologian Joseph Sittler, with whom I spent uncommonly profitable days within the Lutheran–Roman Catholic dialogue. I heard him preach no more than three times, at a convocation hosted by Bangor Theological Seminary in 1968; and I have already suggested my appreciation of his little book *The Anguish of Preaching*. Sittler's spoken word, even when unrehearsed, lent delight to the ear: measured syllables, rhetorical balance, lovely cadences, all with a view to gentle yet forceful Christian persuasion. And this simply the outer garment for Sittler's startling insights into God's word.

One of the Bangor sermons, "The Nimbus and the Rainbow," reflected on the story of Noah and the ark.[34] Sittler had been taught by Paul Tillich to "tread softly before the mystery of historical meaning and the profound complexity of the modes of historical transmission. Every effort to impose upon the reality of historical knowledge a single way of knowing is the mark of the humorless, and therefore the immature, mind. A university exists for the annihilation of such innocence."[35] After asking (1) where the story came from and (2) how the form of the older story was transformed by the community whose book Genesis is, Sittler sought (3) for "the proposal about God and man and the earth to which the episodic momentum of the story drives." This he did by "piercing the image of the rainbow, the sign of the covenant of God." Listen to his reflection.

There is, in the tradition, another ring of light—the nimbus, or halo—and in sameness and difference these two, the rainbow and the nimbus, invite the mind with the lure of the symbolic. For whereas the nimbus is the sign of the precision of grace, the rainbow is the sign of the theatre of grace. The nimbus encircles the head of a particular person—to say that here is one who trusted, accepted, dared in what he accepted, became by grace a personal incandescence of grace. Mary, for instance,

> "My soul magnifies the Lord
> And my spirit rejoices in God my Saviour;
> For he has regarded the low estate of his handmaiden."

But the rainbow is the sign of the scope of grace. The great story does not end with the man, Noah, encircled by a nimbus; it ends with a cosmic nimbus from God bent around the whole creation.

And God said: "This is the sign of the covenant which I make between me and you and every living creature that is with you, for all future generations. I set my bow in the cloud, and it shall be a sign of the covenant between me and the earth."

It is here being said to us that the life of history and the life of nature are not separate. The processes of both and the outcome of both are drawn into the crucial alembic of the decisions of man. The man, Noah, could listen or deafen himself; he could obey or not obey. Because he listened and obeyed, a little island of responsibility and care floated once upon the surface of chaos.

Sittler concluded by suggesting the sign-depth of the image for our day:

> The bow of God's promise and power and grace is over the city. Absolutely according to man's decision the city can become a theatre of grace in which humanity can be richly realized, or it can become a humanly intolerable hell, a stifling intersection of procedures for industrial convenience and, in Chicago's instance, conventioneers' frivolity.
>
> The bow of possibility is over Lake Michigan. How that magnificent given grace shall go is absolutely according to the elevation of evaluation. It can remain a kind of gracious counterpoint to the city—open, seeming-illimitable, an always clear out there to talk back to and strongly correct the fevers and the foolishness of our lives—or it can be turned over to sewage and the waiting algae.
>
> . . . A halo for Noah! Obedience to God and the year he put in deserves one! But the glow of the holy over and within the evil, the problem, the chaos and the sweat—is that perhaps the bow in life to which Hopkins made his salutation when he cried

> "The world is charged with the grandeur of God,
> It will flame out, like shining from shook foil"

or when he confessed

> "I say that we are wound
> With mercy round and round."

Sittler's rhetoric makes demands on the listener. Besides, "The Nimbus and the Rainbow" has to be replaced back in 1968, into the American furor over the "rape of nature." Moreover, to grasp his concern about the city and about nature, about "sewage and the waiting algae," you should be aware of Sittler's dissatisfaction with Vatican II's Constitution on the Church in the Modern World, where "the doctrine of grace remains trapped within the rubric of redemption, while at the same time the joys, hopes, griefs and anxieties that evoke the document are most sharply delineated under the rubric of creation. . . . What is required is nothing short of a doctrine of grace elaborated as fully under the article of God the Creator as a doctrine of grace has been historically developed under the article of God the Redeemer."[36] That much conceded, I pay him grateful tribute here because for years, though I did not advert to it, he was influencing my preaching with his wonderful wedding of God's word imaginatively recaptured and his sense of the sacredness and power of our own feeble syllables.

Most recently I have been stimulated by the published sermons of David H. C. Read, for three decades minister of the Madison Avenue Presbyterian Church in New York City. Author of 28 books, here is a preacher humble and daring enough to publish each Sunday's sermon. After devouring more of Read than of any other of my Protestant creditors, I believe William J. Carl III has caught his approach, his uncommon gift, with brevity and clarity:

> Read's sermons bear the mark of cultural sensitivity and theological depth. Holy Scripture, the *New York Times,* and the classics of Christian theology seem to inform every message. Read understands the questions of the culture. He has always kept his ear close to society's malaise and discomfort with religion. Read's pulpit ministry has concerned itself with answering culture's questions. . . .
>
> Read's congregation is not so much his own local parish as the broader public, particularly those resident aliens and tourists who find Christianity an oddity in a nuclear age, and those ex-

patriates and cynical citizens who have turned away from the nonsense of the gospel. They have turned away not as Greeks who sought wisdom and found the gospel to be foolish but because their own nagging and serious theological questions have not been answered. Like Cornelius, they want to know what it is all about. So they ask questions and make accusations. Read hears those questions and those waiting-room remarks. In fact, he "overhears" them, and he speaks to them directly. . . .[37]

Much of this, I suspect, stems from Dr. Read's rich experience of our bittersweet human condition. Page through *This Grace Given*,[38] the first half of his autobiography, what he characterizes as "one man's experience of God."[39] Share his touching remembrance of his Church of Scotland ancestors, "upholders of a strong morality of honesty, fidelity, and trust, and averse to anything that smacked of fanaticism."[40] Note the tremendous influence on his life and preaching from teachers who introduced him to the world of literature: English and French, Latin and Greek. Revel in his earlier experience of "theology at work" and "theology at war" as he moved from Edinburgh to Montpelier to Strasbourg to Paris to Marburg. See him face to face with Hitler in 1939 Germany. Listen to the chaplain in England, on the Belgian frontier, in France. Slog with this prisoner "across the long roads that led through Flanders, Belgium, and Holland to the Rhine."[41]

Being taken prisoner means being stripped down. Suddenly everything you have come to rely on is gone. Your possessions, your job, your plans, those dearest to you, your country—all these are, in a peculiar way, no longer there. There's just you—and God? People often ask if prisoners naturally turn to religion. I think many do, just as people would fill the churches today if they lived in a city that was under the threat of immediate nuclear attack. But it's also true that hunger and thirst can drive almost every other thought from the mind. I had a little Greek Testament with me when I was captured, and I read it on the road. But a friend marching beside me remarked one day that he didn't see me reading it when we were passing through a village where French women were thrusting bread into our hands as we passed. . . . All the texts on which one has preached . . . these suddenly seem either mere pulpit rhetoric or the most important words in the world. I knew then and ever after that they are real—even when the darkness falls and the foundations quiver.[42]

Five years a prisoner of war. "It was not quite the same person who returned to civilian ministry."[43]

Link such profound experience of living and dying (his own and others') to Read's love for Christ and the word and the Church, to his insatiable yearning to plunge deeper and deeper into the Mystery that is God and the mystery that is His every creation, to a rhetoric that can glow with the icy logic of the philosopher or the consuming fire of the prophet—and you have a preacher, if not for all seasons, surely for our post-Christian culture.[44]

I resonate especially to Read's ceaseless insistence on the centrality of Christ:

> In our world, with its relentless machinery of discovery, its confusion of tongues, its frantic search for techniques to cure our ills, its second-hand experience of life through the TV tube, its dependence on facts, figures and statistics, its obsession with the things we switch on and switch off, its search for the cyanide in a billion bottles of Tylenol, we all long for the human touch. And in our religious jungle our longing is the same. What the Christian Gospel offers is exactly that—the human touch of Christians who care. And why do we care? Because at the center of our religion is nothing other than the human touch of God. And his name is Jesus Christ.[45]

A Christ, however, who

> goes head-on toward the enemy, knowing well the malignity of the powers of evil that surround us all, and demonstrating that the path to victory goes rough and through the thorns of suffering. It is this real Jesus, who deliberately took the rough road to Jerusalem, who can brace us for our own encounter with our enemies and keep our eyes on the city of God. Toward the end of World War II, I preached on Palm Sunday, 1945, in a stalag in Germany to men who knew, as I did, that within a few days we should be either dead or liberated. And the text that came to my mind, the text I gave them, was just this, that "Jesus set his face to go to Jerusalem." That's the kind of Savior he is—the Son of God who has been there, who knows, and who can bring us through, whatever.[46]

How summarize what I owe to the Protestant pulpit? Not easy. It centers, I suspect, on biblical preaching. Not that my earlier, pre-Vatican II sermons were unscriptural; rather that the biblical heritage in my preaching was transmitted through, all but hidden in, the Church's doctrine. I rarely wrestled with the text myself; that had all been done for me. What was lost in such transmission was a personal experience of the word. It's the difference between seeing a movie, say the Mozart *Amadeus,* and reading a summary of the plot and its meaning; between an experience of the symbols and an explanation thereof.

Not that the Protestant pulpit did it all for me. The biblical resurgence within Catholicism in the wake of Pius XII's *Divino afflante Spiritu* (1943) and the scriptural focus exemplified by the documents of Vatican II have surely touched me more directly. Still, we Catholics owe a heartfelt "thank you" to non-Roman scholars and preachers. Much as we may object to a rigid *sola Scriptura* ("the Bible alone") divorced from the living experience of the Church, I find it a fine thing in retrospect that our Protestant brothers and sisters have kept thrusting the text in our faces and urging us to "take and read." Not the TV evangelists; rather the Achtemeiers and the Conzelmanns and the Käsemanns, the Buechners and the Sittlers and the Reads—scholars and preachers who have struggled with God in His word, have not found therein fast-acting placebos for the predestined, have linked what the word meant then to what it might be saying now, have tried to translate that word into syllables that speak to the heart of our cultures, to the root of our experience.

For all this, good friends, much thanks.

SELECT ANNOTATED BIBLIOGRAPHY

I end this chapter on "masters who just might help" with a very limited list of contemporary works on preaching that have attracted my attention. Since naked listing can frustrate the avid searcher, I have presumed to append brief explanatory comments.

ACHTEMEIER, Elizabeth. *Creative Preaching: Finding the Words.* Nashville: Abingdon, 1980. Her primary understanding of creativity in preaching seems to comprise faithful exegesis, sound theology, thoughtful sermon design, and careful use of language.

ACHTEMEIER, Elizabeth. *The Old Testament and the Proclamation of the Gospel.* Philadelphia: Westminster, 1973. Three main parts: the loss of the Bible in mainstream American Protestantism; the necessity of the OT for the Christian faith; preaching from the OT. The section on preaching is at once impressively learned and uncommonly practical: how to select OT texts (use of a lectionary; the church year); how to prepare the sermon (understanding the OT text; relating OT to NT; relating the text to the congregation); the miracle of preaching ("God's use of human language to reveal himself to his worshipers" [160]). A final chapter, on valid methods, includes as examples some of A.'s actual sermons.

BISHOPS, U.S. *Fulfilled in Your Hearing: The Homily in the Sunday Assembly.* Washington, D.C.: United States Catholic Conference, 1982. "The homily is preached in order that a community of believers who have gathered to celebrate the liturgy may do so more deeply and more fully—more faithfully—and thus be formed for Christian witness in the world" (18).

BURKE, John, O.P., ed. *A New Look at Preaching.* Wilmington, Del.: Michael Glazier, 1983. Five addresses (with five responses) delivered at the First National Ecumenical Scriptural-Theological Symposium on Preaching, convened at Emory University by the Word of God Institute: Walter J. Burghardt, "From Study to Proclamation"; Raymond E. Brown, "Preaching in the Acts of the Apostles"; Edward K. Braxton, "Preaching As Food for Thought and Action in the Church"; William J. Hill, "What Is Preaching? One Heuristic Model from Theology"; Leander E. Keck, "Preaching As Divine Wisdom." Elisabeth Schüssler Fiorenza's response to Burghardt is reprinted as an Epilogue in chapter 5 above.

CARL, William J., III. *Preaching Christian Doctrine.* Philadelphia: Fortress, ©1984. Written as a seminary text with an eye to the pastor's study. Carl argues that all preaching is doctrinal, "is always doctrine of some kind," and pleads for a more thoughtful theologizing from the pulpit. Not one right way to preach doctrine, but an array of possibilities. Carl calls up the purposes of classical rhetoric: didactic form, to teach the mind; poetic, to touch the heart; rhetorical, to move the will. Useful bibliography after each chapter. Three sermons in an appendix: Bruce Robertson on 1 Cor 13:12, Carl on Jonah, Luther on the Creed. Reviewer Patrick J. Willson confesses: "Try as I might, I cannot think of another book which so successfully combines serious learning *about* preaching with passion *for* preaching" (*Homiletic* 10 [1985] no. 1, 12).

CARROLL, Thomas K. *Preaching the Word.* Wilmington, Del.: Michael Glazier, 1984. Specifically on preaching in the patristic era: the Greek homily in Hellenistic culture, in the Alexandrian Church, in the fourth century (plus a separate chapter on Chrysostom); the Latin sermon in the African Church, in the fourth century (plus a

separate chapter on Augustine), in Roman tradition. Helpful information enlivened by about 250 quotations from patristic preaching.

COX, James W. *Preaching.* San Francisco: Harper & Row, ©1985.
Five chapters: importance of preaching, context (culture, worship,
sharing of meaning), content, the making of sermons, and delivery.
Good bibliographical appendix, with special recommendations
starred. David Read calls this "the most comprehensive treatment
of the homiletic art I have read in a long time," a "welcome 'high'
doctrine of preaching [that] has nothing to do with a prima donna
performance that is unrelated to the liturgy, the sacraments, or the
hunger in the pew" (*Reformed Journal*, May 1986, 30).

CRADDOCK, Fred B. *As One without Authority.* Enid: Phillips Univ.,
1971; Nashville: Abingdon, 1979. A theory of "inductive preaching." This "corresponds to the way people ordinarily experience
reality and to the way life's problem-solving activity goes on naturally and casually" (66). Takes seriously the power of the word to
create or destroy. The text shapes the sermon and at the same time
preaching is born in the congregation. A pivotal book in the field.

CRADDOCK, Fred B. *Preaching.* Nashville: Abingdon, 1985. Part
1: An overview: the sermon in context; a theology of preaching.
Part 2: Having something to say: study, the listener, the text, interpretation. Part 3: Shaping the message into a sermon. Part 2 is particularly useful: "He speaks clearly and simply, his method is quite
achievable by the average student, and yet he speaks out of a deep
awareness of recent developments in rhetorical and literary criticism" (Thomas G. Long, in *Homiletic* 10 [1985] no. 1, 10).

DODD, C. H. *The Apostolic Preaching and Its Developments.* New ed.
London: Hodder & Stoughton, 1951. Still useful on the primitive
preaching (kerygma) and two lines of development therefrom: the
eschatological valuation of facts of the past (life, death, and resurrection of Jesus) and the eschatological significance of facts of the
present.

FITZGERALD, George R., C.S.P. *A Practical Guide to Preaching.*
New York/Ramsey: Paulist, 1980. Useful, down-to-earth "helps and
hints for sermon preparation and delivery." The principal chapters
deal with (1) subject and theme, (2) critique of self as a communi-

cating person, (3) exegesis biblical and personal, (4) congregation analysis, (5) communicating the message, (6) images in preaching.

FULLER, Reginald H. *Preaching the Lectionary: The Word of God for the Church Today*. Collegeville: Liturgical, 1984. The revised edition (640 pp.) of Fuller's *Preaching the New Lectionary* (1974) "comprises articles originally published in *Worship* magazine (February 1971 through February 1974; October 1974; May 1981; January 1982). The material has been substantially reedited and rearranged, and commentary on Scripture readings not previously covered has been incorporated." New material includes commentaries on the readings for weddings and funerals. May well be the most useful single volume for preparation of sermons based on solid scriptural scholarship. More immediately pertinent to the Roman Catholic liturgy, but not exclusively. "Common use of the treasures of the Bible has long been cherished as a sign of fundamental unity across denominational boundaries. Formerly that commonality was ensured through the use of the so-called historic pericopes. The appearance of the *Ordo Lectionum Missae* broke that common bond, but a new consensus has almost spontaneously arisen on its foundations. The churches were ripe for such a change" (Eugene L. Brand, Foreword xi).

FULLER, Reginald H. *The Use of the Bible in Preaching*. Philadelphia: Fortress, 1981. How to move from a biblical text to a sermon on that passage. Mainly a step-by-step description of the route with illustrative examples. The meaning of a text is not exclusively lodged in historical concerns; it must also be explored in the context of a particular liturgical occasion and in relation to the other texts specified for that occasion by the lectionary.

FULLER, Reginald H. *What Is Liturgical Preaching?* London: SCM, 1960 [1957]). Still useful, and not only in its Anglican context. For Fuller, the purpose of a sermon is "to extract from the scripture readings the essential core and content of the gospel, to penetrate behind the day's pericope to the proclamation of the central act of God in Christ which it contains, in order that the central act of God can be made the material for recital in the prayer of thanksgiving" (22). Shows by examples how all this can be done effectively.

GONZÁLEZ, Justo L., and Catherine Gunsalus González. *Liberation Preaching: The Pulpit and the Oppressed*. Nashville: Abingdon, ©1980.

Summarizes liberation theology, expounds difficulties in hearing the text (e.g., lectionaries and the traditional commentaries; recommends "ideological suspicion"), recalls the forgotten interpreters (women, nonwhites, primitive Church), gives pointers toward a liberation hermeneutic of the Bible.

KECK, Leander E. *The Bible in the Pulpit: The Renewal of Biblical Preaching.* Nashville: Abingdon, 1978. Convinced that "it is far easier to preach the Bible unbiblically than to do so biblically" (11), Keck sets out what it is that makes preaching "biblical." He claims that "preaching is truly biblical when (a) the Bible governs the content of the sermon and when (b) the function of the sermon is analogous to that of the text. In other words, preaching is biblical when it imparts a Bible-shaped word in a Bible-like way" (106).

KILLINGER, John. *Fundamentals of Preaching.* Philadelphia: Fortress, 1985. Not so much a work of theoretical understanding as of practical assistance: Here, Killinger says from long experience, is what I have found to work. And so he treats of beginnings and endings, of illustrations, of style and delivery. Still, an ambitious program: Killinger is in search not of basic competence but of excellence. To that end, there is constant reference to the giants of the past: Fosdick, Buttrick, Brooks. . . .

LAUER, Eugene F. *Sunday Morning Insights.* Collegeville: Liturgical, 1984. Not sermons but ideas, insights, experiences for preachers, directors of liturgy, and regular worshipers. Includes all the Sundays of the three cycles, some propers of the saints, and some national holidays. A typical "insight" takes up a page or a bit more. Can be useful as a stimulus for a preacher's own mulling.

LEWIS, Ralph L., with Gregg Lewis. *Inductive Preaching: Helping People Listen.* Westchester, Ill.: Crossway, ©1983. Primary crisis in preaching today? Lack of congregational involvement. A promising solution? Not deductive (propositional) preaching, but inductive: "begins with the particulars of life experience and points toward principles, concepts, conclusions" (32). L.'s development of the inductive approach ends with four appendixes: two of his own sermons; a checklist of inductive characteristics; 96 inductive preachers from 20 centuries; a strategy for making traditional sermons inductive.

MARKQUART, Edward F. *Quest for Better Preaching: Resources for Renewal in the Pulpit.* Minneapolis: Augsburg, ©1985. A useful volume, practical without being banal. Markquart quotes the experiences and insights of experts constantly and effectively—e.g., Brooks, Buechner, Craddock, Keck, Steimle, Thielicke, Wilder. Fine chapters on the preacher as person, theologian, exegete, prophet, and storyteller. Helpful summaries at the end of each chapter, and a singular appendix outlining a 19-session course where a preacher works on preaching with "the wise men and women of his or her congregation" (213–18).

MURPHY-O'CONNOR, Jerome, O.P. *Paul on Preaching.* New York: Sheed and Ward, [1964]. Limits his investigation to "Paul's conception of that preaching whose object is the conversion of non-believers," i.e. missionary or kerygmatic preaching (xvii). Studies the place Paul assigns to preaching in God's plan of salvation; preaching as God's instrument and as a prolongation of Christ's ministry; the power of the word; the audience; and preaching as a liturgical act ("liturgical" with the connotation of worship alone).

OUTLER, Albert C., ed. *The Works of John Wesley* 1: *Sermons I: 1–33.* Nashville: Abingdon, 1984. A remarkable production of historical scholarship. I include it here (1) to recommend Outler's 100-page introduction to Wesley the preacher and (2) to point up a preacher whose message counted for more than his manner. "There are only occasional flights of eloquence in [the sermons]—all short. Wesley's message is Wesley's medium—it is a transaction with a reader responding to insights springing from shared traditions and a shared source in Holy Writ. . . . And always, it is the 'application' on which the whole effort is focused; this makes most of the sermons intensely personal and practical. Wesley was content that others might be more exciting if he could be more nourishing" (97).

RAHNER, Hugo, S.J. *A Theology of Proclamation.* New York: Herder and Herder, 1968. Insists that "Kerygma means . . . preaching the revealed divine truths according to the structure in which the divine Wisdom conceived and preached them, the very same structure in which the Church from the very beginning preached the divine revelation in her ordinary teaching . . . " (13). Insists on a renewed knowledge of Scripture and patristic theology. Considers in detail: the Trinity; original justice and original sin; hypostatic union; church, grace, and vision; life of Jesus; sacraments; priesthood.

RAHNER, Karl, S.J., ed. *The Renewal of Preaching: Theory and Practice.* Concilium 33. New York: Paulist, 1968. Short articles, soon after Vatican II, on various aspects of preaching, with informative surveys of preaching in Europe, South America, and the English-speaking world. I found most helpful (1) Karl Rahner's "Demythologization and the Sermon": the preacher as translator, turning the language of Scripture and tradition into a language that makes sense today; (2) Yves Congar's "Sacramental Worship and Preaching," which locates three links between word and worship: anamnesis, witness to faith, and spiritual sacrifice; (3) Franz Böckle's "Moral Sermons and Urgent Moral Issues," stressing the new situation in which the human person has to act, and certain basic issues in morality.

SITTLER, Joseph. *The Anguish of Preaching.* Philadelphia: Fortress, ©1966. Himself a creative Lutheran thinker and wordsmith, Sittler reflects on the current preaching situation by focusing on (1) the task of NT interpretation, (2) the anguish of Christology, and (3) the preacher's role as leader of a decision-making congregation (moral theology), "the possibility that preaching may work to dissolve the strange state of things in American Protestantism whereby the vision of the church's obedience is at odds with the popular piety in our congregations" (11).

SKUDLAREK, William. *The Word in Worship: Preaching in a Liturgical Context.* Nashville: Abingdon, 1981. Preaching "at its finest . . . is biblically centered, directed to the real questions of people and *taken up in worship*" (emphasis mine). Skudlarek stresses use of the lectionary, preaching in relation to sacraments, and preaching at weddings and funerals. A fine chapter on "Preaching at the Eucharist."

STOTT, John R. W. *Between Two Worlds: The Art of Preaching in the Twentieth Century.* Grand Rapids: Eerdmans, 1982. Convinced that "by far the most important secrets of preaching are not technical but theological and personal" (10), famed British preacher Stott stresses the theological foundations for preaching (convictions about God, Scripture, church, pastorate, and preaching), preaching as essentially bridge-building (between the biblical and the modern worlds), the call to study (Bible, theology, world), and personal characteristics (sincerity and earnestness, courage and humility).

THIELICKE, Helmut. *The Trouble with the Church: A Call for Renewal.* New York: Harper & Row, ©1965. A hard-hitting little book written out of "suffering love for the Church" (126) by a prominent Lutheran ethician who wrote his *Theological Ethics* "in order to do the theological background work for preaching" (78). Thielicke finds contemporary preaching ultimately unconvincing because our spiritual existence is unconvincing. He castigates the language of preaching: abstract and colorless, Christian categories not "in situation," preaching which, as Luther put it, would not entice a dog from behind a warm stove. He inveighs against *bondage* to principles, attacks the solution of "flight into busywork and liturgical artcraft" (81), in harmony with Bonhoeffer's "Only he who cries out for the Jews dare permit himself to sing in Gregorian." Emphasizes the need for dialogue with the laity, without "the dictatorship of the listeners" (31).

VOGELS, Walter. *Reading & Preaching the Bible: A New Semiotic Approach.* Wilmington, Del.: Michael Glazier, 1986. Asks if new methods of exegesis might yield better results for biblical preaching than the historical-critical method, which, for all its excellence, leaves the reader insecure about going to the text directly. One solution: semiotics, "the science of the signs," of hidden structures, a synchronic rather than diachronic method, a biblical text open to multiple meanings. Vogels offers the Bible reader "a 'do-it-yourself' method, that will enable him to go to the Scriptures feeling sure that his personal reading is faithful to the text" (12). The reader starts with the text as we have it. "The text . . . belongs to the reader, he gives meaning to it" (39).

WARDLAW, Don M., ed. *Preaching Biblically.* Philadelphia: Westminster, 1983. Wardlaw's introduction on the need for new preaching shapes is concretized by seven Protestant preachers shaping sermons by (1) the language of the text, (2) the context of the text, (3) plotting the text's claim upon us, (4) the interplay of text and metaphor, (5) the structure of the text, (6) the shape of text and preacher.

WAZNAK, Robert P., S.S. *Sunday after Sunday: Preaching the Homily As Story.* New York/Ramsey: Paulist, ©1983. Intended as a text for students, especially in the Roman Catholic liturgical tradition. Designed to assist reflection on three main goals of preaching: (1) cognitive: "to offer an interpretation of life based on the biblical view which calls for an awareness of who we are and who we are called to be"; (2) attitudinal: "to invite people to a change of heart"; (3) performance: "a caring ministry" (7). Fine chapters on the story of the preacher, the story of God, and the story of the listener. Should be supplemented by Waznak's article "The Preacher and the Poet," *Worship* 60, no. 1 (January 1986) 46–55.

WILLIMON, William H. *Integrative Preaching: The Pulpit at the Center.* Nashville: Abingdon, 1981. Preaching as the factor or instrument or activity that unifies a pastor's various functions: counselor, community builder, teacher, prophet, liturgist.

Homiletic. A Review of Publications in Religious Communication. Semiannual. A short article and an editorial are followed by reviews of books (some articles) about preaching, collections of sermons, works on history of preaching, biblical interpretation, theology, worship, communication theory, art and media, human sciences and culture, and dissertations. 3510 Woodley Road NW, Washington DC 20016.

Fortress Resources for Preaching (Philadelphia: Fortress). As of this writing, the series (booklets ranging from 61 pages to 109) contains seven titles: *Worshipful Preaching* by Gerard S. Sloyan (©1984); *Preaching Paul* by Daniel Patte (©1984); *Holy Week Preaching* by Krister Stendahl (©1985); *The Word of God in Words: Reading and Preaching the Gospels* by Bernard Brandon Scott (©1985); *A Trumpet in Darkness: Preaching to Mourners* by Robert G. Hughes (©1985); *The Passion As Story: The Plot of Mark* by John Blackwell (1986); *The Problem of Preaching* by Donald Macleod (1987).

POSTLUDE

Halfway through this book, I happened on a film that intrigued me. Its title: *Mass Appeal.* Two characters dominate the movie: a middle-aged pastor, Father Farley (played by Jack Lemmon), and a seminarian, Mark Dolson (played by Željko Ivanek). The pastor is comfortably busy, popular with his people, successful at the collection, quick with the wit, a bit frequent at the bottle. The seminarian is in bad odor with the seminary rector, who finds him immature, arrogant, suspiciously less than objective in objecting to the dismissal of an allegedly homosexual pair. The rector will (reluctantly) approve Mark for ordination to deacon, but only if Farley will then take him on for a month at St. Francis Church—a kind of final test.

Mark's first assignment from Farley is a sermon. Agonizing over the downtrodden, he wants to preach on social issues, take the parish to task for its apathy, attack mink hats and cashmere coats. But Farley is adamant; he doesn't want "song-and-dance theology." Mark begs: "Why can't I say what I want from the pulpit?" Farley tells him from experience what "works" and what doesn't, what will make Mark liked. But, Mark protests, are we preaching to be liked? He lashes out at Farley: "You'd be liked more if you were real and sober." Farley refuses to give in: "Don't 'kick ass' in your sermon." Give a "friendly" sermon. Don't be afraid to be "charming." Tell them about your youth and how the family would buy jelly doughnuts after Mass. If they cough, pick up the pace. "But," Mark objects, "if I have to listen for coughs, how can I hear the Spirit?"

Mark's first sermon is a disaster. In deference to Farley, he tries hard to do the jelly-doughnuts bit, but even that does not close off the coughing. So he goes on the attack, goes for the jugular: big hats, cashmere coats, blue hair. Says one irate parishioner on the way out: "I do not come to Mass to be preached to." 80% negative, Farley reports; 30% decrease in the collection, the Church's Nielsen rating. Mark: "What happened?" Farley: "You lost control." Mark: "I'm glad. . . . The Church needs lunatics." Farley: "The problem is, lunatics don't know how to survive."

Two generations, two backgrounds, two visions of priesthood, two approaches to God's people—two good men. The rest of the film is a poignant story of growth. Placid pastor and impassioned seminarian slowly see each other with new eyes; Farley even opens up about his early problems at home. But Mark is about to be dismissed from the seminary. Farley offers another slim chance: another sermon, this time on why Mark wants to be a priest, what he feels for the people. Get naked, Farley urges, naked like St. Francis of Assisi; then talk to the people as if to one person. Mark's sermon is searingly personal—even so, it bombs. Retelling his agonizing, profoundly symbolic experience of beautiful tropical fish turning into scavenging catfish (and this for one who felt called to be a "fisher of men"), he meets only blank stares, puzzlement, even "We have no choice but to be catfish, with all that garbage being thrown at us."

Two later scenes I found uncommonly moving. There is Farley's anguished sermon to a parish he has coddled for years, a parish that has coddled him. "I've baptized you, counseled you, married you, buried you; but I've never really cared enough for you to run the risk of losing you." His very need for their love has kept him silent, inactive. This is the first time he is saying what he wants to say. Only by being honest with them can he genuinely love them; only now is love possible. And there is Mark striding forth from seminary and parish to . . . where? Both, you sense, have fresh reason to hope. In different crucibles (or was it one crucible?) both have been refined, shaped anew. One of Farley's fresh insights is splendidly pertinent: "When Christ sent his apostles out into the world, he sent them in twos. I think I know now why he did that."

Why end this book with *Mass Appeal*? Not because it provides specific "homily hints." Rather because, imaginatively and torturously, it gets behind the preacher to the person. It lays bare so much that we hide even from ourselves. Sometimes it takes another—not necessarily younger or smarter or holier—to scratch our scabs, make the hidden trauma bleed a bit or badly, compel us to see ourselves as we really are—the first step on the road to healing.

The more honest I am with myself, about myself, the more "gracefully" a gracious God can work on and with me. And so, the more persuasive I am likely to be in preaching to God's people; the more likely to help them see Jesus; the more likely to love them as Jesus loved.

I may live to regret this, but I close this volume, this program for preaching, with a warm prayer that for the sake of my ministry there will always be a Mark Dolson in my life. Thank God, there have been many across these past five decades—younger and older, professors and students, priests and laity, women and men, Catholics and Protestants and Jews. Only a few as abrasive as Mark, but each and every one a grace in flesh, showing this priest and preacher "a still more excellent way" (1 Cor 12:31).[1]

NOTES

[1]Jerome Murphy-O'Connor, O.P., *Paul on Preaching* (New York: Sheed and Ward, [1964]) xiii.

CHAPTER 1

[1]Cf. *Oedipus the King,* lines 1528–30.
[2]Cf. *On the Crown* 169 ff.
[3]Cf. *Republic* 7, 1 ff.
[4]Plato, *Apology* 42.
[5]*Iliad* 1, 34.
[6]*Fourth Eclogue,* lines 5–6.
[7]*Odes* 1, 17.
[8]*Odes* 1, 11.
[9]*Odes* 1, 37.
[10]*The Life of Henry the Fifth,* Act 4, Scene 1.
[11]*The Tragedy of Romeo and Juliet,* Act 2, Scene 2.
[12]*The Tragedy of Hamlet, Prince of Denmark,* Act 3, Scene 1.
[13]*The Merchant of Venice,* Act 3, Scene 1.
[14]Gerard Manley Hopkins, "The Blessed Virgin Compared to the Air We Breathe," in W. H. Gardner and N. H. MacKenzie, eds., *The Poems of Gerard Manley Hopkins* (4th ed.; London: Oxford University, 1975) 93–97.

[15]Edmond Rostand, *Cyrano de Bergerac,* tr. Brian Hooker (New York: Random House, n.d.) 304–5.

[16]John L. McKenzie, "The Word of God in the Old Testament," *Theological Studies* 21 (1960) 205.

[17]Ibid. 206.

[18]For the different modes of Christ's presence in liturgical celebrations, see chapter 1-E in the instruction *Eucharisticum mysterium* of the Sacred Congregation of Rites, May 25, 1967 (translation in Austin Flannery, O.P., ed., *Vatican Council II: The Conciliar and Post Conciliar Documents* [Northport, N.Y.: Costello, 1975] 109). Note especially the final sentence: Christ's presence under the species of the Eucharist "is called 'real' not in an exclusive sense, as if the other kinds of presence were not real, but *par excellence.*" The words are taken from Paul VI's encyclical *Mysterium fidei* (*AAS* 57 [1965] 764).

[19]For simplicity's sake, I shall concentrate on the homily within the Mass; what I say can be applied *mutatis mutandis* to other liturgical events, e.g. a communal penance service.

[20]*Inter oecumenica* (= Sacra Congregatio Rituum, *Instructio ad executionem Constitutionis de sacra liturgia recte ordinandam,* Sept. 26, 1964) 3, no. 54 (*Normae exsequutivae Concilii oecumenici Vaticani II (1963–1969)*, ed. Florentius Romita [Naples: D'Auria, 1971] 58). This definition has been incorporated into the "General Instruction on the Roman Missal" in the Roman Missal of 1970, no. 41.

[21]Constitution on the Sacred Liturgy, no. 35.

[22]Ibid.

[23]Dogmatic Constitution on Divine Revelation, no. 10.

[24]For the homilist's consolation, the acts of Vatican II reveal a concern not to require of the homilist "a mere exegesis of the scriptural section of the liturgy but, connected freely with the text of one of the lessons or even of another detail in the word or rite of the liturgy itself, [the homily] should rather offer instruction for the religious and moral life of the faithful. . . . During the two festival circles of the Church's year it would be devoted more to the facts of salvation and their consequences, but outside these circles it would be all the more open for all the questions of the moral order of life. In all cases it should in some way, as mystagogical sermon, lead the faithful inwardly into the service, be in harmony with it and facilitate its inner celebration, rather than stand independently beside it" (Josef Andreas Jungmann, "Constitution on the Sacred Liturgy," in Herbert Vorgrimler, ed., *Commentary on the Documents of Vatican II* 1 [New York: Herder and Herder, 1967] 38).

[25]*Humani generis* (Denzinger-Schönmetzer [ed. 32] 3886 [2314]).

[26]John Gallen, "Liturgical Reform: Product or Prayer?" *Worship* 47 (1973) 606.

[27]Cf. Walter J. Burghardt, S.J., "A Theologian's Challenge to Liturgy," *Theological Studies* 35 (1974) 244.

[28]Jungmann, "Constitution" 38. See also *Inter oecumenici* 3, no. 55: If there is a set program of homilies for certain times, it should still preserve an intimate nexus with the more important times and feasts of the liturgical year or with the mystery of the redemption; "for the homily is part of the liturgy of the day."

[29]Yves Congar, O.P., "Sacramental Worship and Preaching," in *The Renewal of Preaching: Theory and Practice* (= Concilium 33; New York: Paulist, 1968) 51–63.

[30]Ibid. 54.

[31]Cf. ibid. 55–56.

[32]Ibid. 56.

[33]Constitution on the Sacred Liturgy, no. 59.

[34]Cf. Congar, "Sacramental Worship and Preaching" 58–59. See also Vatican II, Decree on the Ministry and Life of Priests, no. 4: "In the Christian community itself, especially among those who seem to understand or believe little of what they practice, the preaching of the word is required for the very administration of the sacraments; for these are sacraments of faith, and faith is born of the word and nourished by it."

[35]Congar, "Sacramental Worship and Preaching" 60.

[36]Ibid. 62.

[37]Joseph P. Fitzpatrick, S.J., "Justice As a Problem of Culture," in *Studies in the International Apostolate of Jesuits* 5, no. 2 (December 1976) 18–19.

[38]For a useful treatment of the problem of translation, see Karl Rahner, S.J., "Demythologization and the Sermon," in *The Renewal of Preaching* (n. 29 above) 20–38.

[39]Ibid. 21.

[40]Ibid. 25.

[41]*National Catholic Reporter*, Sept. 15, 1972, 2.

[42]Otto Semmelroth, S.J., *The Preaching Word: On the Theology of Proclamation* (New York: Herder and Herder, 1965) 200. See the whole section "Preaching As a Communication Which Summons" (179–202).

[43]Rod McKuen, *Listen to the Warm* (London: Michael Joseph, 1968) 112.

CHAPTER 2

[1]Antoine de Saint-Exupéry, *The Little Prince* (New York: Harcourt, Brace & World, ©1943) 7–9.

[2]See chapter 1 above; also my *Tell the Next Generation: Homilies and Near Homilies* (New York: Paulist, ©1980) 3–16, esp. 8–11.

[3]Some works which may prove helpful: William F. Lynch, S.J., *Christ and Apollo: The Dimensions of the Literary Imagination* (New York: Sheed and Ward, ©1960); Theodore W. Jennings, Jr., *Introduction to Theology: An Invitation to Reflection upon the Christian Mythos* (Philadelphia: Fortress, ©1976) esp. 9–84; Amos Niven Wilder, *Theopoetic: Theology and the Religious Imagi-*

nation (Philadelphia: Fortress, ©1976); Robert D. Young, *Religious Imagination: God's Gift to Prophets and Preachers* (Philadelphia: Westminister, ©1979); Urban T. Holmes, III, *Ministry and Imagination* (New York: Seabury, ©1976); Ray L. Hart, *Unfinished Man and the Imagination: Toward an Ontology and a Rhetoric of Revelation* (New York: Herder and Herder, 1968). Pertinent here, I suggest, is an understanding of symbol and of ritual; see, e.g., Mary Douglas, *Natural Symbols: Explorations in Cosmology* (New York: Penguin, 1978); George S. Worgul, *From Magic to Metaphor: A Validation of Christian Sacraments* (New York: Paulist, ©1980).

[4]I am aware that fantasy does not *have* to mean the bizarre; I am speaking of a common current usage. See *Webster's New International Dictionary of the English Language* (2nd ed. unabridged; Springfield, Mass.: Merriam, 1957) 918: "From the conception of *fantasy* as the faculty of mentally reproducing sensible objects, the meaning appears to have developed into: first, false or delusive mental creation; and second, any sense-like representation in the mind, equivalent to the less strict use of *imagination* and *fancy.* Later *fantasy* acquired, also, a somewhat distinctive usage, taking over the sense of whimsical, grotesque, or bizarre image making. This latter sense, however, did not attach itself to the variant *phantasy,* which is used for visionary or phantasmic imagination." See also Holmes, *Ministry and Imagination* 100–103.

[5]Holmes, *Ministry and Imagination* 97–98. Here Holmes is admittedly borrowing from Owen Barfield, *Saving the Appearances: A Study in Idolatry* (New York: Harcourt, Brace & World, n.d.).

[6]Cf. Holmes 88.

[7]Jennings, *Introduction to Theology* 49.

[8]Cf. ibid. 52.

[9]Sallie M. TeSelle, cited by Holmes, *Ministry and Imagination* 166, from the *Journal of the American Academy of Religion* 42 (1974) 635.

[10]Jennings, *Introduction to Theology* 51.

[11]Ibid. 51–52. See also Wilder, *Theopoetic* 80.

[12]Avery Dulles, S.J., "The Symbolic Structure of Revelation," *Theological Studies* 41 (1980) 55–56.

[13]Ibid. 56.

[14]A. N. Whitehead, *The Aims of Education and Other Essays* (New York: Macmillan, 1929) 139.

[15]Gerard Manley Hopkins, "As kingfishers catch fire . . . ," Poem 57 in W. H. Gardner and N. H. MacKenzie, eds., *The Poems of Gerard Manley Hopkins* (4th ed.; London: Oxford University, 1970) 90.

[16]Wilder, *Theopoetic* 57.

[17]Ibid. 67.

[18]Vatican II, Constitution on the Sacred Liturgy, no. 35.

[19]Frederick E. Flynn, in *Catholic Messenger* (Davenport, Iowa), Aug. 4, 1960, 13.

[20]Holmes, *Ministry and Imagination* 221.

[21]Here I am deeply indebted to Dulles, "The Symbolic Structure of Revelation" 55 ff. For objections raised against revelation as symbolic, and Dulles' reply, see ibid. 65–67.

[22]Ibid. 59. The quotation from Perrin is taken from his *Jesus and the Language of the Kingdom* (Philadelphia: Fortress, 1976) 33.

[23]See Dulles, ibid. 59–65.

[24]Walter J. Burghardt, S.J., "From Classroom to Pulpit: How Preach Dogma?" *Proceedings of the Catholic Homiletic Society*, Fourth Annual Convention, Dec. 1961 (published at Kenrick Seminary, St. Louis) 23–35.

[25]e. e. cummings, Poem 95 in *100 Poems*.

[26]Nathan Mitchell, "Symbols Are Actions, Not Objects," *Living Worship* 13, no. 2 (Feb. 1977) 1–2.

[27]A handful of further references that might prove useful for a preacher in the area of the imagination: Walter Brueggemann, *The Prophetic Imagination* (Philadelphia: Fortress, 1978); Andrew Greeley, "The Religious Imagination: A Sociological Approach," *Chicago Studies* 20 (1981) 267–80; Julian N. Hartt, *Theological Method and Imagination* (New York: Seabury, 1977). See also the March 1982 issue of *Thought* (Fordham University), totally devoted to "Faith and Imagination."

CHAPTER 3

[1]Here I am under obligation to Abraham J. Heschel's *The Prophets* (New York: Harper & Row, ©1962), especially the opening chapter, "What Manner of Man Is the Prophet?" (3–26).

[2]Ibid. 4.

[3]Ibid. 5.

[4]Cf. ibid. 13.

[5]Ibid. 14.

[6]Ibid. 14–15.

[7]Ibid. 19.

[8]Ibid. 21.

[9]Ibid. 24.

[10]On divine pathos, which is for Heschel a unique theological category, see ibid. passim, but esp. 24, 221–31, 489–92. For a strong critique of this category, see Eliezer Berkovitz, "Dr. A. J. Heschel's Theology of Pathos," *Tradition: A Journal of Orthodox Thought* 6 (spring–summer 1964) 67–104. He argues that Heschel's affirmation of divine pathos is based on a fallacious line of deductive reasoning and on a literalist interpretation of biblical texts.

[11]Ibid. 231.

[12]Ibid. 226.

[13]Ibid. 231.

¹⁴Ibid. 26.

¹⁵Joseph A. Wahl, C.O., *The Exclusion of Woman from Holy Orders* (Washington, D.C.: Catholic Univ. of America, 1959) 58.

¹⁶Second Vatican Council, Constitution on the Church in the Modern World, no. 1.

¹⁷Augustine, *First Catechetical Instruction* 1, 2, 3 (tr. Joseph P. Christopher, in Ancient Christian Writers 2 [Westminster, Md.: Newman, 1946] 15).

¹⁸Ibid. 1, 11, 16 (ACW 2, 40).

¹⁹Heschel, *The Prophets* 224.

²⁰See, in this volume, chapter 2, "Sir, We Would Like To See Jesus: Preaching As Imagining."

²¹*Theological Studies* 42 (1981) 3–19.

²²The reader may notice, and be surprised, that at this point I deal with the preacher as God's messenger only, not as God's counselor. It is simply that I do not see this characteristic of the Hebrew prophet as having particular pertinence for the Christian preacher.

CHAPTER 4

¹For a rich summary of the theology of Christian community, see Avery Dulles, S.J., *Models of the Church* (Garden City, N.Y.: Doubleday, 1974) 43–57. I am not denying that the Eucharistic liturgy creates invisible bonds among the faithful even when they do not recognize one another. I admit, with Jérôme Hamer, that what is distinctive in the Church is "the vertical dimension—the divine life disclosed in the incarnate Christ and communicated to men through his Spirit." But the communion given by the Holy Spirit is inadequate without the horizontal dimension, inadequate if it does not issue in "a network of mutual interpersonal relationships of concern and assistance" (Dulles 45–46; cf. Hamer, *The Church Is a Communion* [New York: Sheed & Ward, 1964] 159–64, 204).

²William J. O'Malley, "Ten Commandments for Homilists," *America* 149, no. 3 (July 23–30, 1983) 47–49.

³Constitution on the Sacred Liturgy, no. 2 (tr. *The Documents of Vatican II*, ed. Walter M. Abbott, S.J. [New York: America, ©1966] 137).

⁴References to a highly popular TV soap opera and two "deathless" night serials.

⁵Augustine, *First Catechetical Instruction* 1, 15, 23 (tr. Joseph P. Christopher, in Ancient Christian Writers 2 [Westminster, Md.: Newman, 1946] 50).

⁶From "I Have Given You an Example," in my *Still Proclaiming Your Wonders: Homilies for the Eighties* (New York/Ramsey: Paulist, ©1984) 67–73, at 72–73.

⁷Augustine, *Confessions* 9, 1 (tr. F. J. Sheed, *The Confessions of St. Augustine* [New York: Sheed & Ward, 1943] 183).

CHAPTER 5

[1]The reference is to a line in the Gilbert and Sullivan operetta *The Pirates of Penzance* (1879): "the very model of a modern major general."

[2]A reference to a popular TV show.

[3]A favorite early Christian expression for appropriating "pagan truth" in the interests of the faith: Whatever there is of truth among you really belongs to us.

[4]See Joseph Sittler, "A Protestant Point of View," in John H. Miller, C.S.C., ed., *Vatican II: An Interfaith Appraisal* (Notre Dame: University of Notre Dame, ©1966) 426; his "Ecological Commitment As Theological Responsibility," *Idoc*, Sept. 12, 1970, 75–85; and Vatican II, Constitution on the Church in the Modern World, no. 1.

[5]Constitution on Divine Revelation, no. 21.

[6]Raymond E. Brown, S.S., " 'And the Lord Said'? Biblical Reflections on Scripture As the Word of God," *Theological Studies* 42 (1981) 3–19, at 18. The whole article should be read for its careful effort to grasp the meaning of Scripture as *God's* word.

[7]Jerome, *Letter 22,* 17.

[8]So Josef Schmid, *The Gospel according to Mark* (Regensburg New Testament; Staten Island, N.Y.: Alba [1968]) 194.

[9]Sandra M. Schneiders, I.H.M., "Faith, Hermeneutics, and the Literal Sense of Scripture," *Theological Studies* 39 (1978) 719–36, at 731 and 732. See H.-G. Gadamer, *Truth and Method* (New York: Seabury, 1975) esp. 235–341.

[10]Schneiders, "Faith" 733.

[11]Ibid. 734–35.

[12]Joseph Mary Plunkett, "I See His Blood upon the Rose," in Thomas Walsh, ed., *The Catholic Anthology: The World's Great Catholic Poetry* (rev. ed.; New York: Macmillan, 1947) 428.

[13]Gerard Manley Hopkins, "As kingfishers catch fire . . . ," in W. H. Gardner and N. H. MacKenzie, eds., *The Poems of Gerard Manley Hopkins* (4th ed.; London: Oxford University, 1975) 90.

[14]Karl Rahner, S.J., and Paul Imhof, S.J., *Ignatius of Loyola* (New York: Collins, ©1978) 11, 12, 13, 17.

[15]The rest of this paragraph is indebted to Pierre Fransen, "Towards a Psychology of Divine Grace," *Cross Currents* 8 (1958) 229–30.

[16]Jean Mouroux, *The Christian Experience: An Introduction to a Theology* (New York: Sheed and Ward, 1954) 38.

[17]This summary of Gregory stems from Roger Leys, *L'Image de Dieu chez Grégoire de Nysse* (Brussels: L'Edition Universelle, 1951) 139–40.

[18]Henri J. M. Nouwen, *The Wounded Healer: Ministry in Contemporary Society* (Garden City, N.Y.: Doubleday, 1972) 25–26. This is apparently only one version of a very ancient story.

[19]Full text of this homily in my *Still Proclaiming Your Wonders: Homilies for the Eighties* (New York/Ramsey: Paulist, ©1984) 25–30.

[20]e. e. cummings, Poem 95 in *100 Poems.*

[21]Review of John Burke, O.P., ed., *A New Look at Preaching* (Wilmington, Del.: Michael Glazier, 1983), in *Worship* 59, no. 6 (November 1985) 555.

[22]Text taken from *A New Look at Preaching* (n. 21 above) 43–55, with the kind permission of Elisabeth Schüssler Fiorenza and Michael Glazier.

CHAPTER 6

[1]Constitution on the Sacred Liturgy, no. 35 (tr. *The Documents of Vatican II,* ed. Walter M. Abbott [New York: America, ©1966] 149–50).

[2]Dogmatic Constitution on Divine Revelation, no. 25 (*Documents* 127).

[3]Gerard Manley Hopkins, "God's Grandeur," in W. H. Gardner and N. H. MacKenzie, eds., *The Poems of Gerard Manley Hopkins* (4th ed.; London: Oxford University, 1975) 66.

[4]In this connection see Raymond E. Brown, S.S., " 'And the Lord Said'? Biblical Reflections on Scripture As the Word of God," *Theological Studies* 42 (1981) 3–19.

[5]See my article "Fathers of the Church," *New Catholic Encyclopedia* 5 (1967) 853–55.

[6]Hans von Campenhausen, *The Fathers of the Greek Church* (New York: Pantheon, ©1959) 10.

[7]*Acta apostolicae sedis* 35 (1943) 312.

[8]Pierre Benoit, in A. Robert and A. Tricot, *Initiation biblique* (3rd ed.; Paris: Desclée, 1954) 43 (translation mine).

[9]Here I am much indebted to F. van der Meer, *Augustine the Bishop* (New York: Sheed and Ward, ©1961) 412–52 ("The Servant of the Word").

[10]Ibid. 414.

[11]Ibid. 419–20.

[12]*Sermon 96,* no. 4.

[13]*Treatises on the Gospel of John* 7, 6.

[14]Van der Meer, *Augustine the Bishop* 440–41.

[15]Jaroslav Pelikan, ed., *The Preaching of Augustine: "Our Lord's Sermon on the Mount"* (Philadelphia: Fortress, ©1973) xxi.

[16]Van der Meer, *Augustine the Bishop* 443.

[17]See Johannes Quasten, *Patrology* 3: *The Golden Age of Greek Patristic Literature from the Council of Nicaea to the Council of Chalcedon* (Westminster, Md.: Newman, ©1960) 433–51.

[18]Philadelphia: Fortress, ©1966.

[19]Ibid. 12–13.

[20]Cf. Jared Wicks, S.J., *Man Yearning for Grace: Luther's Early Spiritual Teaching* (Washington, D.C.: Corpus, ©1968).

[21]I have used the translation in Gerhard Ebeling, *Luther: An Introduction to His Thought,* tr. R. A. Wilson (Philadelphia: Fortress, ©1970) 45–46.

[22]Jared Wicks, S.J., "Justification and Faith in Luther's Theology," *Theological Studies* 44 (1983) 15–16.

[23]For a development of some of these nourishments, see, e.g., Paul-Marie of the Cross, O.C.D., *Spirituality of the Old Testament* (3 vols.; St. Louis: Herder, ©1961–63).

[24]Cf. Carroll Stuhlmueller, C.P., *Thirsting for the Lord: Essays in Biblical Spirituality* (Garden City, N.Y.: Image Books, 1979) 62–70.

[25]Ibid. 69; For a critical study of Jeremiah (historical person not accessible to us), see Robert P. Carroll, *Jeremiah: A Commentary* (Philadelphia: Westminster, 1986).

CHAPTER 7

[1]In each instance I shall refer to a homily in one of my collections, specifically *All Lost in Wonder* (Westminster, Md.: Newman, 1960); *Tell the Next Generation* (New York/Ramsey: Paulist, ©1980); *Sir, We Would Like To See Jesus* (Paulist, ©1982); *Still Proclaiming Your Wonders* (Paulist, ©1984); *Grace on Crutches* (Paulist, ©1986).

[2]See *Tell the Next Generation* 30–33.

[3]See *All Lost in Wonder* 47–50.

[4]See *Tell the Next Generation* 44–48, 52–57.

[5]See *All Lost in Wonder* 87–91.

[6]See *Still Proclaiming Your Wonders* 90–96.

[7]See *Grace on Crutches* 111–17.

[8]See *Still Proclaiming Your Wonders* 134–38.

[9]See *Sir, We Would Like To See Jesus* 93–98.

[10]See *Grace on Crutches* 118–23.

[11]See *Still Proclaiming Your Wonders* 149–54, 155–59.

[12]Reginald H. Fuller, *Preaching the New Lectionary: The Word of God for the Church Today* (Collegeville, Minn.: Liturgical, 1976) 453.

[13]*Tell the Next Generation* 83–84.

[14]*Sir, We Would Like To See Jesus* 186–91.

[15]*Still Proclaiming Your Wonders* 201–10.

[16]*Grace on Crutches* 155–78.

[17]See *Still Proclaiming Your Wonders* 201–5.

[18]See *Grace on Crutches* 155–59.

[19]See *Sir, We Would Like To See Jesus* 192–95.

CHAPTER 8

[1]Second Vatican Council, Constitution on the Sacred Liturgy, no. 35. See also no. 52: "part of the liturgy itself."

[2]Reginald Fuller, *What Is Liturgical Preaching?* (London: SCM, 1957) 20.

29

[3]Ibid. 21. See also Campion Gavaler, O.S.B., "Theology of the Sermon As Part of the Mass," *Worship* 38 (1964) 201–7, at 203.

[4]Norman Pittenger, *Preaching the Gospel* (Wilton, Conn.: Morehouse-Barlow, 1984) 46. The whole chapter, "The Setting in Worship" (45–56), is worth pondering in our context. Pittenger observes that failure to follow these Reformers on this point "has been a tragedy," and notes that "it is only in our own time that the Reformed churches have begun to recover the centrality of the Eucharist in worship . . . " (46).

[5]Gerard S. Sloyan, *Worshipful Preaching* (Philadelphia: Fortress, 1984) 7.

[6]Ibid. 15.

[7]Second Vatican Council, Constitution on the Sacred Liturgy, no. 56.

[8]Gregory Dix, *The Shape of the Liturgy* (Westminster, Eng.: Dacre, 1945) 744.

[9]Yves Congar, O.P., "Sacramental Worship and Preaching," in *The Renewal of Preaching: Theory and Practice* (= Concilium 33; New York: Paulist, 1968) 51–63.

[10]Ibid. 55.

[11]Ibid. 56.

[12]Ibid. 57.

[13]Ibid. 60.

[14]John Burke, O.P., *Gospel Power* (Staten Island, N.Y.: Alba, 1978) 79.

[15]Gavaler, "Theology of the Sermon" (n. 3 above) 205.

[16]Sloyan, *Worshipful Preaching* 12.

[17]Robert Esbjornson, "Preaching As Worship," *Worship* 48 (1974) 164–70, at 166.

[18]Ibid. 170.

[19]Gilbert E. Doan Jr., "Preaching from a Liturgical Perspective," in Edmund A. Steimle et al., eds., *Preaching the Story* (Philadelphia: Fortress, 1980) 95–106, at 105.

[20]From a summary by James E. Kraus of Lechner's address at a meeting of the Ohio Regional Committee of the Liturgical Conference, in *Worship* 37 (1963) 425.

[21]Joseph A. Fitzmyer, S.J., *Pauline Theology: A Brief Sketch* (Englewood Cliffs, N.J.: Prentice-Hall, ©1967) 70.

[22]St. Thomas Aquinas, *Adoro te supplex*, tr. Gerard Manley Hopkins, in Robert Bridges and W. H. Gardner, eds., *The Poems of Gerard Manley Hopkins* (London: Oxford University, 1948) 186.

[23]Augustine, *First Catechetical Instruction* 1, 4, 7 (tr. Joseph P. Christopher, in Ancient Christian Writers 2 [Westminster, Md.: Newman, 1946; repr. New York, N.Y./Ramsey, N.J.: Newman, n.d.] 21).

CHAPTER 9

¹Cf. *Washington Star,* May 26, 1979, D-1 and D-2; quotation at D-2. Other quotations below are taken from the same article.

²T. Howland Sanks, S.J., and Brian H. Smith, S.J., "Liberation Ecclesiology: Praxis, Theory, Praxis," *Theological Studies* 38 (1977) 24.

³George G. Higgins, "The Church and Social Concerns," syndicated column, excerpted from *One Voice* (Diocese of Birmingham, Ala.), April 27, 1979, 4.

⁴As cited by Higgins, ibid.

⁵Pius XII, *Allocutio ad cultores historiae et artis,* May 9, 1956 (*AAS* 48 [1956] 212).

⁶Decree on the Apostolate of the Laity, no. 5; see also no. 7. In response to this quotation, one might dredge up the affirmation of *Gaudium et spes,* no. 42: "Christ, to be sure, gave his Church no proper mission in the political, economic, or social order. The purpose which he set before it is a religious one. . . . " Here the crucial terms are "missio propria" and "finis . . . ordinis religiosi." Discussion of these phrases is not possible here, but two observations seem to be in order. (1) *GS* 42 is not excluding the Christian community from playing a significant, transforming role in the social, economic, and political orders. Such an interpretation would make nonsense out of Part 1, chapter 4. The text reaffirms the legitimate autonomy that belongs to the temporal order. For the historical background of this chapter (nos. 40–45) and an insightful presentation of its meaning, see Yves Congar's chapter "The Role of the Church in the Modern World," in Herbert Vorgrimler, ed., *Commentary on the Documents of Vatican II* 5 (New York: Herder and Herder, 1969) 202–23. E.g., "The Church's function comprises everything human. . . . Consequently the Church must not be restricted to a 'religious' domain, identical in practice with public worship" (213). (2) There is a problem on what "Church" means in chapter 4. Charles Moeller argues, from the proposed amendments, that whereas in chapters 1–3 it means "the People of God," in chapter 4 it refers to the hierarchy (ibid. 61–62). Congar (ibid. 211 and 214 [see no. 28 for pertinent *relatio*]), without alluding to Moeller's position, says the Church in chapter 4 is "the People of God," "the social body." The difference in interpretation of "Church" is obviously not irrelevant to one's understanding of the Church's mission.

⁷1971 Synod of Bishops, *De iustitia in mundo* (Vatican Press, 1971) Introduction, p. 5. One may argue whether "constitutive" in the document means "integral" or "essential" (the 1976 document of the International Theological Commission, "Human Development & Christian Salvation," tr. Walter J. Burghardt, S.J., *Origins* 7, no. 20 [Nov. 3, 1977] 311, states that "it seems more accurate to interpret [*ratio constitutiva*] as meaning an integral part, not an essential part" [IV]—a discussable affirmation). What is beyond argument is that the Synod saw the search for justice as inseparable from the preaching of the gospel.

[8]1974 Synod of Bishops, "Human Rights and Reconciliation," *Origins* 4 (1974) 318.

[9]"Human Development & Christian Salvation" IV (tr. *Origins* 310–11).

[10]For a careful appraisal of "what the Old and New Testaments have to say about the relationship between salvation and human welfare, between salvation and human rights," see the document of the ITC (n. 7 above) III (tr. *Origins* 309–10). See also *The Social Message of the Gospels,* ed. Franz Böckle (=Concilium 35; New York: Paulist, ©1968).

[11]Address of Pope John Paul II opening the deliberations of the Third Assembly of Latin American Bishops, Puebla, January 28, 1979, III, 2. An English translation is available in *Origins* 8, no. 34 (Feb. 8, 1979) 530–38; but I have not used it for the passage quoted, because it translates *indispensable* as "essential" (536), apparently unaware of the problem to which I allude in n. 7 above. I take it that the Pope and/or his speechwriter consciously avoided a philosophical interpretation of the 1971 Synod's *ratio constitutiva;* it is enough that a facet of the Church's evangelizing mission be described as something which the Church may not refuse to do; it is not capable of being dispensed with; the Church cannot be released from this obligation. The Pope goes on to cite Paul VI's *Evangelii nuntiandi* 29: "evangelization would not be complete if it did not take into account the unceasing interplay of the Gospel and of man's concrete life, both personal and social" (tr. *Origins* 536).

[12]From the statement issued by the Catholic Bishops' Conference of the Philippines, after an emergency meeting in the week following the February 7 national elections; text in *Asian Focus,* Feb. 21, 1986, 8. My quotations from Cardinal Sin's talk are taken from a text delivered to Georgetown University by Sin and made available by the University in duplicated form.

[13]Brian Wicker, "Ritual and Culture: Some Dimensions of the Problem Today," in James D. Shaughnessy, ed., *The Roots of Ritual* (Grand Rapids: Eerdmans, 1973) 17. See also George G. Higgins, "The Mass and Political Order," *Proceedings of the Liturgical Conference,* Worcester, Mass., August 1955: "Shortly after World War II an extremely well-informed German priest told me, on what I am prepared to accept as reliable evidence, that the Nazis, far from being worried about the pre-war growth of the liturgical movement in Germany, secretly encouraged it. According to my informant, they felt that an intense preoccupation with the liturgy would serve to distract the attention of Catholics and make them less inclined to engage in political action. Whether this report is accurate or not, the record will show, I think, that some of those most actively engaged in the liturgical movement not only in Germany but in other countries as well did make the mistake of ignoring political and social problems or, even worse, of at least passively favoring political programs which they should have actively opposed" (130–31).

¹⁴Tissa Balasuriya, O.M.I., *The Eucharist and Human Liberation* (Maryknoll, N.Y.: Orbis, 1979).

¹⁵Joseph Gelineau, "Celebrating the Paschal Liberation," in *Politics and Liturgy,* ed. Herman Schmidt and David Power (=Concilium 92; New York: Herder and Herder, 1974) 107.

¹⁶"Editorial," ibid. 8.

¹⁷Gelineau, "Celebrating the Paschal Liberation" 107.

¹⁸Ibid. 111.

¹⁹Higgins, "The Mass and Political Order" 133.

²⁰The information and quotations in this paragraph are taken from a news article by William A. Orme Jr. in the *Washington Post,* July 21, 1986, A1 and A10.

²¹See D. Olmedo, "Mexico, Modern," *New Catholic Encyclopedia* 9 (1967) 775–83, at 780.

²²Yves Congar, O.P., "Sacramental Worship and Preaching," in *The Renewal of Preaching: Theory and Practice* (=Concilium 33; New York: Paulist, 1968) 60.

²³Cf. ibid. 54–56.

²⁴In Ambrose, *Letter 20,* 19.

²⁵See Socrates, *Church History* 6, 18; Sozomen, *Church History* 8, 20.

²⁶In *Origins* 8, no. 34 (Feb. 8, 1979) 543. I am aware that the Pope does go on to speak of a "more divine world" as well, "the vertical orientation of evangelization" (ibid.).

²⁷Karl Rahner, S.J., *The Shape of the Church To Come* (London: SPCK, 1974) 77.

²⁸Ibid. 76.

²⁹Cf. my *Seven Hungers of the Human Family* (Washington, D.C.: United States Catholic Conference, ©1976) 8–15, esp. 11–13.

³⁰See *Time* 113, no. 23 (June 4, 1979) 24.

³¹See ibid. 69.

³²George Higgins, "The Problems in Preaching: Politics/What Place in Church?" *Origins* 2, no. 13 (Sept. 21, 1972) 213. The whole article (207, 212–16) merits reading for its wedding of the theoretical and the practical, based on the respected author's long and varied experience.

³³Constitution on the Church in the Modern World, no. 43. In this connection I commend to preachers a splendid cautionary article by George G. Higgins, "The Social Mission of the Church after Vatican II," *America* 155, no. 2 (July 19–26, 1986) 25–29. Msgr. Higgins agrees with Karl Rahner that "clerical zeal for social reform . . . ought to be coupled with a realistic recognition of the fact that the clergy really do not have the answers to all of the complicated problems confronting the modern world," that "the limits of the church's possibilities and those of its official hierarchy are not to be regarded from the outset as identical" (27). He warns, with Charles Curran, against an uncritical baptism of every change that occurs. He suggests that "even the most radical kind of social reform . . . should be

compatible with a decent respect for technical expertise and the legitimate autonomy of the temporal order and also with a reasonable measure of what used to be known as liberal tolerance" (27). And though he fully agrees that "liberation is absolutely essential to evangelization," he notes that "the church cannot find a future simply in secular concerns, however pressing and urgent these may be, for *the church is meant to be a community of the transcendent*" (28; italics mine). He appears to agree with Thomas Gannon and George Traub that the main threat to Christian life today is not "angelism, docetism, self-obsession with ecclesiastical forms, musty incense and superstitious practices," but "a subtle but pervasive sense of hopelessness," that what is needed is a spirituality that "values precisely the poverty of its knowledge about the future. It does not attempt to outbid by its optimism all forms of human suffering and limitation, but strives to remain faithful to such experiences and, precisely through them, to realize all the painful breadth and depth of its hope—hope against hope" (28–29).

[34]Quoted by Higgins, "Problems in Preaching" 216.

[35]Quoted by Joel Porte, " 'I Am Not the Man You Take Me For,' " *Harvard Magazine* 81, no. 5 (May–June 1979) 50.

[36]Ibid. 50–51.

CHAPTER 10

[1]In point of fact, I *was* asked on one occasion to preach on Jews and Christians. It was a "first" on both sides, for me and for the Reform Synagogue in White Plains, N.Y., that welcomed me on February 21, 1964. See the sermon "Israel: A Light to the Gentiles?" in *Tell the Next Generation* 156–62.

[2]See Henri de Lubac, "Sur un vieux distique: La doctrine du 'quadruple sens,' " *Mélanges offerts au R. P. Ferdinand Cavallera* (Toulouse: Bibliothèque de l'Institut Catholique, 1948) 347–66.

[3]Dogmatic Constitution on Divine Revelation, no. 16. The Council makes explicit reference to Augustine, *Questions on the Heptateuch* 2, 73 (PL 34, 623).

[4]Constitution on Revelation, no. 16.

[5]Quoted by Salvador Muñoz Iglesias, "Old Testament Values Superseded by the New," in Pierre Benoit, O.P., Roland E. Murphy, O.Carm., and Bastiaan Van Iersel, S.M.M., eds., *How Does the Christian Confront the Old Testament?* (=Concilium 30; New York: Paulist, 1968) 99–100, from Adolf Harnack, *Das Evangelium vom fremden Gott* (2nd ed., 1924) 217.

[6]Pius XI, encyclical *Mit brennender Sorge*, March 14, 1937, in Claudia Carlen, I.H.M., ed., *The Papal Encyclicals 1903–1939* (Wilmington, N.C.: McGrath, 1981) 528.

[7]John L. McKenzie, S.J., "The Values of the Old Testament," in Con-

cilium 30 (n. 5 above) 5–32, to which these several paragraphs are deeply indebted.

[8]Ibid. 9.

[9]Ibid. 13.

[10]Ibid. 15.

[11]See M. J. Cantley, "Kingdom of God," *New Catholic Encyclopedia* 8 (1967) 191–95.

[12]Ibid. 194.

[13]McKenzie, "Values of the Old Testament" 18.

[14]Ibid. 26–27.

[15]See ibid. 28–29.

[16]See François Dreyfus, O.P., "The Existential Value of the Old Testament," in Concilium 30 (n. 5 above) 33–44, at 35.

[17]See Franco Festorazzi, " 'We Are Safe' (Jer. 7, 10): The Faith of Both Testaments As Salvific Experience," in Concilium 30 (n. 5 above) 45–59, at 47–55.

[18]See Elpidius Pax, O.F.M., "Fulfilling the Commandment (Deut. 6, 25)," in Concilium 30 (n. 5 above) 73–85, at 75–76, 79–80.

[19]See Hilaire Duesberg, O.S.B., "He Opened Their Minds To Understand the Scriptures," in Concilium 30 (n. 5 above) 111–21, at 112 and (quotation) 113.

[20]*Tell the Next Generation* 39–43.

[21]*Grace on Crutches* 100–105.

[22]*Tell the Next Generation* 100–103.

[23]*Sir, We Would Like To See Jesus* 93–98.

[24]Ibid. 126–31.

[25]Ibid. 173–77.

[26]*Still Proclaiming Your Wonders* 134–38.

[27]*Grace on Crutches* 118–23.

[28]Ibid. 140–45.

[29]Ibid. 146–51.

[30]Ibid. 19–23.

[31]*Still Proclaiming Your Wonders* 33–38.

[32]Ibid. 45–50.

[33]*Grace on Crutches* 49–53.

[34]Ibid. 160–64 and *Still Proclaiming Your Wonders* 201–5.

[35]*Still Proclaiming Your Wonders* 206–10.

[36]*Grace on Crutches* 170–74.

[37]New York/Oxford: Oxford University, 1983.

[38]Ibid. 11–34.

[39]Ibid. 16.

[40]Ibid. 17.

[41]Ibid. 18.

[42]Ibid.

[43]Ibid. 19.

[44]Ibid.

[45]Dominic M. Crossan, O.S.M., "Anti-Semitism and the Gospel," *Theological Studies* 26 (1965) 189–214, at 189. Note that Gerald G. O'Collins, S.J., "Anti-Semitism in the Gospel," ibid. 663–66, found Crossan's article "unsatisfactory on a number of points, some of which are quite important" (663). He was convinced that, though the study of NT words and events is of great import, "we must also explore the significance which Matthew, Luke, Paul, and other New Testament writers attach to these events and their theology of the obduracy of Israel. Only then can the Gospel be shown to supply no justification for anti-Semitism" (666). Also, Joseph A. Fitzmyer, S.J., has focused on a crucial text omitted by Crossan: "His blood be upon us and upon our children!" (Mt 27:25). In Fitzmyer's opinion, "Probably no other New Testament text has been so often quoted against the Jews since it was first written." See Fitzmyer's article "Anti-Semitism and the Cry of 'All the People' (Mt 27:25)," ibid. 667–71, quotation at 668. Cardinal Augustin Bea and others at Vatican II explained that the cry must be understood as the cry of a Jerusalem crowd with no right to speak for the whole Jewish people.

[46]Declaration on the Relationship of the Church to Non-Christian Religions, no. 4 (tr. *The Documents of Vatican II*, ed. Walter M. Abbott, S.J. [New York: America, ©1966] 665–66).

[47]Preachers should be aware of fresh approaches to, and more positive appreciations of, the Pharisees. See, e.g., Ellis Rivkin, *A Hidden Revolution* (Nashville: Abingdon, 1978); John T. Pawlikowski, *Christ in the Light of the Jewish-Christian Dialogue* (New York: Paulist, 1982); Leonard Swidler, "The Pharisees in Recent Catholic Writing," *Horizons* 10, no. 2 (fall 1983) 267–87.

[48]See the English translation and commentary by Joseph A. Fitzmyer, S.J., "The Biblical Commission's Instruction on the Historical Truth of the Gospels," *Theological Studies* 25 (1964) 386–408.

[49]*Instruction* VI.2 (tr. Fitzmyer 404). The three stages are developed in VII-IX (Fitzmyer 404–6).

[50]Ibid. IX (tr. Fitzmyer 405).

[51]Pontifical Biblical Commission, *Bible et christologie* (Paris: Cerf, 1984). The text is issued in Latin and French; the Latin is the official text, but the French was the working text. I am using the English translation by Joseph A. Fitzmyer, S.J., "The Biblical Commission and Christology," *Theological Studies* 46 (1985) 407–79.

[52]*The Bible and Christology* 1.2.5.2 (tr. Fitzmyer 422).

[53]See Eugene A. LaVerdiere, S.S.S., and William G. Thompson, S.J., "New Testament Communities in Transition: A Study of Matthew and Luke," *Theological Studies* 37 (1976) 567–97, esp. 571–78. Quotation at 576.

[54]Ibid. 578.

[55]*Instruction* X (tr. Fitzmyer 406).

[56]Lecture at Georgetown University, April 26, 1984; see also Tuch-

man's *The March of Folly: From Troy to Vietnam* (New York: Knopf, 1984) especially the very first chapter.

[57]*Discourse 1 against Judaizing Christians* 3, 1–3 (tr. Paul W. Harkins, *Saint John Chrysostom, Discourses against Judaizing Christians* [Fathers of the Church 68; Washington, D.C.: Catholic University of America, 1979] 10–11.

[58]Ibid. x.

[59]For a more detailed account of anti-Judaism and anti-Semitism in patristic theology and preaching, cf. Rosemary R. Ruether, *Faith and Fratricide: The Christian Theological Roots of Anti-Semitism* (New York: Seabury, 1974). This extensive study may be seen in summary in Ruether's essay "Anti-Semitism and Christian Theology," in Eva Fleischner, ed., *Auschwitz: Beginning of a New Era? Reflections on the Holocaust* (New York: KTAV, 1977) 79–92, 447–49. Note her thesis: "At its root anti-Semitism in Christian civilization springs directly from Christian theological anti-Judaism" (*Auschwitz* 79). Hence her demand for "a reexamination of Christology, for this is the original root of theological anti-Judaism" (ibid. 92).

[60]Marc H. Tanenbaum, "A Jewish Viewpoint [on Vatican II's Declaration on Non-Christian Religions]," in John H. Miller, C.S.C., ed., *Vatican II: An Interfaith Appraisal* (Notre Dame: University of Notre Dame, 1966) 349–67, at 355–56. In quoting Rabbi Tanenbaum, I am not conceding that genocide against the Jews was an inexorable consequence of Christian theology. On this see the remarkably nuanced essay by Yosef Hayim Yerushalmi, "Response to Rosemary Ruether," in *Auschwitz* (n. 59 above) 97–107.

[61]Tanenbaum, "A Jewish Viewpoint" 356.

[62]Roland H. Bainton, *Here I Stand: A Life of Martin Luther* (New York: Abingdon, 1950) 379.

[63]Joseph Elijah Heller and B. Mordechai Ansbacher, "Luther, Martin," *Encyclopedia Judaica* 11 (1971) 585.

[64]"Notes on the Correct Way To Present Jews and Judaism in Preaching and Catechesis in the Roman Catholic Church," June 24, 1985 (Vatican tr. from the French in *Origins* 15, no. 7 [July 4, 1985] 102–7). Behind this most recent document lie, of course, Vatican II's *Nostra aetate* (Declaration on the Relationship of the Church to Non-Christian Religions, no. 4; see n. 46 above), and the "Guidelines and Suggestions for Implementing the Conciliar Declaration *Nostra aetate*," issued Dec. 1, 1974, by the Vatican's Commission for Religious Relations with the Jews (see *Osservatore romano*, Jan. 4, 1975).

[65]"Notes" I.3 (*Origins* 103).

[66]Ibid. I.7 (*Origins* 103).

[67]Ibid. I.8 (*Origins* 103–4).

[68]Ibid. II.6 (*Origins* 104).

[69]Ibid. II.4 (*Origins* 104).

[70]Ibid. II.7 (*Origins* 104).

[71]Ibid. II.10 (*Origins* 104).

[72]Ibid. II.11 (*Origins* 104–5).

[73]Ibid. III.12–14 (*Origins* 105).

[74]Ibid. III.19 (*Origins* 105).

[75]Ibid. IV.21.A (*Origins* 106).

[76]Ibid. IV.21.E (*Origins* 106).

[77]Ibid. V.22 (*Origins* 106).

[78]Ibid. VI.25 (*Origins* 107).

[79]Ibid.

[80]Ibid.; emphasis in text.

[81]Ibid. VI.27 (*Origins* 107).

[82]My knowledge of and references to these reactions are drawn from the same issue of *Origins* that presented the Vatican Commission's document in English; cf. pp. 102–4, in the margins.

[83]See ibid. 105–6, in margins, for more favorable observations by Eugene Fisher, executive director of the (U.S.) National Conference of Catholic Bishops' Secretariat for Catholic-Jewish Relations, and by Msgr. Jorge Mejia, secretary of the Vatican Commission that issued the document.

[84]Thomas Stransky, C.S.P., "Focusing on Jewish-Catholic Relations," *Origins* 15, no. 5 (June 20, 1985) 66–70, at 70. The address was delivered at a conference in Rome, April 17–18, 1985, to mark the 20th anniversary of Vatican II's Declaration on the Relationship of the Church to Non-Christian Religions.

[85]Krister Stendahl, "Judaism and Christianity: A Plea for a New Relationship," *Cross Currents* 17 (1967) 453.

[86]For an elaboration of these four positions, see the carefully crafted article by J. Peter Schineller, S.J., "Christ and Church: A Spectrum of Views," *Theological Studies* 37 (1976) 545–66.

[87]On Romans 9–11 see Joseph A. Fitzmyer, S.J., in *Jerome Biblical Commentary* (Englewood Cliffs, N.J.: Prentice-Hall, 1968) 53:94–115; also Karl Hruby, "The Future of Jewish-Christian Dialogue 2: A Christian View," in Hans Küng and Walter Kasper, eds., *Christians and Jews* (= Concilium 98; New York: Seabury, ©1974–75) 87–92, esp. 91: "A consideration of the situation in the light of Paul's statements not only leads to a complete abandonment of the traditional theories of rejection and substitution, but also makes it possible and necessary to give *a positive interpretation* of the present existence of the Jewish people. To be able to fulfil their function for the Christian community, the Jewish people must preserve their identity and autonomy" (emphasis in text).

CHAPTER 11

[1]Basil the Great, *The Long Rules*, q. 17 (tr. M. Monica Wagner, C.S.C., in Fathers of the Church 9 [New York: Fathers of the Church, Inc., 1950] 271–72). For the first three paragraphs of this first stage of my development I have borrowed freely from my homily "For Your Penance,

Look Redeemed" in *Tell the Next Generation: Homilies and Near Homilies* (New York/Ramsey: Paulist, 1980) 45, but have inserted a few fresh ideas.

[2]San Francisco: Harper & Row, ©1964.

[3]Ibid. 9.

[4]Wilmington, Del.: Michael Glazier, 1986.

[5]Ibid. 12.

[6]Ibid. 9.

[7]See especially Buechner's *Telling the Truth: The Gospel As Tragedy, Comedy, and Fairy Tale* (San Francisco: Harper & Row, ©1977) chap. 3, "The Gospel As Comedy" (49–72).

[8]Ibid. 57–58. To capture the power and flavor of Buechner's argument, one must read the complete chapter.

[9]Ibid. 60.

[10]Ibid. 61.

[11]Ibid. 66.

[12]Ibid. 68.

[13]Ibid. 70–71.

[14]Ibid. 72.

[15]See Jean Leclercq, *Le défi de la vie contemplative* (Gembloux: Duculot, 1970) 360–61, 367–68.

[16]See the provocative essay by Thomas H. Clancy, S.J., "Feeling Bad about Feeling Good," in *Studies in the Spirituality of Jesuits* 9, no. 1 (January 1979).

[17]See Harvey Cox, *The Feast of Fools: A Theological Essay on Festivity and Fantasy* (New York: Harper & Row, 1969) esp. 139–57 on "Christ the Harlequin."

[18]Ignatius Loyola, "Rules of Modesty" (where "modesty" has to do with human and Christian decorum applied to the life of a Jesuit).

[19]Eugene O'Neill, *Lazarus Laughed,* Act 1, Scene 1; in *The Plays of Eugene O'Neill* (New York: Random House, 1955) 280.

[20]Philadelphia: Fortress, 1963.

[21]See ibid. v, the judgment of the translator, John W. Doberstein.

[22]Ibid. 24–26.

[23]Buechner, *Telling the Truth* 49–50.

[24]In *Grace on Crutches: Homilies for Fellow Travelers* (New York/Mahwah: Paulist, ©1986) 100–105, at 100–101.

[25]In *Sir, We Would Like To See Jesus: Homilies from a Hilltop* (New York/Ramsey: Paulist, ©1982) 88–92, at 90–91.

[26]Ibid. 65–69, at 68–69.

[27]Cf. Norman Cousins, *Anatomy of an Illness As Perceived by the Patient: Reflections on Healing and Regeneration* (New York: Bantam, 1979).

[28]Ibid. 39–40.

[29]Buechner, *Telling the Truth* 71.

CHAPTER 12

[1]Dietrich Bonhoeffer, *The Cost of Discipleship* (rev. ed.; New York: Macmillan, 1963) 45–48.

[2]New York: Kenedy, 1961. French original: Paris: Desclée de Brouwer, 1959.

[3]Raymond E. Brown, S.S., " 'And the Lord Said'? Biblical Reflections on Scripture As the Word of God," *Theological Studies* 42 (1981) 3–19, at 18.

[4]Ibid. 9.

[5]Ibid.

[6]Ibid. 10.

[7]"Instructio de historica evangeliorum veritate," *Osservatore romano*, May 14, 1964, 3 (with an Italian translation). I am using the English translation prepared, with added Roman numerals, by Joseph A. Fitzmyer, S.J., "The Biblical Commission's Instruction on the Historical Truth of the Gospels," *Theological Studies* 25 (1964) 386–408, at 402–8; this quotation at VI (404). See my chapter 10 above, on how to preach about the Jews.

[8]Ibid. VIII (404).

[9]Ibid. IX (405).

[10]Here I shall borrow, mostly verbatim, from my homily "Partying in Christ" in my *Sir, We Would Like To See Jesus: Homilies from a Hilltop* (New York: Paulist, ©1982) 121–25.

[11]See, e.g., Joachim Jeremias, *The Parables of Jesus* (rev. ed.; New York: Scribner's, ©1963) 65.

[12]See the informative article by Eugene A. LaVerdiere, S.S.S., and William G. Thompson, S.J., "New Testament Communities in Transition: A Study in Matthew and Luke," *Theological Studies* 37 (1976) 567–97.

[13]DS (32nd ed.) 3006 (1787). This is not the place to assess various theories of inspiration.

[14]Dogmatic Constitution on Divine Revelation, no. 8 (tr. *The Documents of Vatican II,* ed. Walter M. Abbott, S.J. [New York: America, ©1966] 115–16).

[15]Nikos Kazantzakis, *Report to Greco* (New York: Simon & Schuster, 1965) 15.

[16]Constitution on the Church in the Modern World, no. 43.

[17]See my homily "How Little Worthy. . . . " in *Sir, We Would Like To See Jesus* 110–14.

[18]Richard Bach, *Illusions: The Adventures of a Reluctant Messiah* (New York: Dell/Eleanor Friede, 1977) [4].

[19]Augustine, *First Catechetical Instruction* 1, 2, 3 (tr. Joseph P. Christopher, in Ancient Christian Writers 2 [Westminster, Md.: Newman, 1946] 15).

[20]Paul Claudel, "Saint Francis Xavier," in *Coronal* (New York: Pantheon, 1943) 190.

[21]Tim Reynolds, "Thomas, Dylan," *World Book Encyclopedia* 19 (ed. 1975) 200.

CHAPTER 13

[1]For a text see Daniel M. O'Connell, ed., *Favorite Newman Sermons* (Milwaukee: Bruce, ©1932) 13–29.

[2]The text of this essay can be found in Newman's *Lectures and Essays on University Subjects* (London: Longmans, Brown, Green, Longmans, and Roberts, 1859) 187–220. My direct source for the quotations that follow is W. D. White, ed., *The Preaching of John Henry Newman* (Philadelphia: Fortress, ©1969), specifically from his Introduction (1–63). The volume contains 13 fine selections from Newman's *Parochial and Plain Sermons.*

[3]In White, *The Preaching of John Henry Newman* 24–46.

[4]Quoted by White, ibid. 51; cf. W. R. Inge, *The Diary of a Dean* (London: Hutchinson, 1949) 12.

[5]Marvin R. O'Connell, "Newman: The Victorian Intellectual As Pastor," *Theological Studies* 46 (1985) 329–44, at 335.

[6]Besides the usual manuals (Altaner, Quasten), see the informative recent work by Thomas K. Carroll, *Preaching the Word* (Message of the Fathers of the Church 11; Wilmington, Del.: Michael Glazier, 1984).

[7]See the second section of my chapter "Thus Says the Lord: The Word Forms the Preacher" in this volume.

[8]Leo's Latin style, with French translation, can be gathered from the four volumes of his sermons in the series Sources chrétiennes: 22, 49, 74, 200 (Paris: Cerf, 1947, 1957, 1961, 1973).

[9]Johannes Quasten, *Patrology* 2: *The Ante-Nicene Literature after Irenaeus* (Westminster, Md.: Newman, 1953) 37.

[10]See Carroll, *Preaching the Word* 43–62.

[11]Ibid. 61.

[12]In the series The Fathers of the Church 71 (Washington, D.C.: Catholic Univ. of America, 1982).

[13]In the series Ancient Christian Writers 26 (Westminster, Md.: Newman, 1957; repr. New York, N.Y./Ramsey, N.J.: Newman, n.d.).

[14]The Latin word *doctrina* in the title (*De doctrina christiana*) is sometimes rendered "instruction," sometimes "doctrine." English translation in FC 4 (New York: Fathers of the Church, 1947; 2nd ed. 1950) 19–235.

[15]*On Christian Learning* 4, 5 (tr. FC 4, 173).

[16]Carroll, *Preaching the Word* 180.

[17]Ibid. 183.

[18]The translations of Chrysostom's sermons can be located in Johannes Quasten, *Patrology* 3: *The Golden Age of Greek Patristic Literature: From the Council of Nicaea to the Council of Chalcedon* (Westminster, Md.: Newman, 1960) 433–59; updated in the Spanish translation by Ignacio Oñatibia, *Pa-*

trología 2: *La edad de oro de la literatura patrística griega* (3rd ed.; Madrid: Biblioteca de Autores Cristianos, 1977) 481–510. Since Chrysostom's style is very much part of his homiletic fame, Quasten's caution (*Patrology* 3, 433) on his sermons is worth noting: "The written form in which we possess them today does not go back to a copy prepared for publication by the author but in most cases to notes of his stenographers. The manuscripts present not infrequently two editions of the homilies, the one in a comparatively smooth style, the other in a rather rough state. The former is a deliberate later revision of the latter. Thus the superiority and greater antiquity of the rough text is too evident to be called in question. The smooth text is without authority."

[19]The work is neatly introduced, translated, and annotated by Henry Davis, S.J., *St. Gregory the Great: Pastoral Care* (Ancient Christian Writers 11; New York, N.Y./Ramsey, N.J.: Newman, 1978 [1950]).

[20]*Pastoral Care*, Part 3, chap. 1 (tr. ACW 11, 90–92).

[21]Y. Brilioth, *A Brief History of Preaching* (Philadelphia: Fortress, 1965) 66.

[22]Ibid.

[23]Thomas G. Long, in *Theology Today* 32 (1975–76) 450.

[24]*America*, Dec. 25, 1982, 417.

[25]New York: Seabury, ©1966.

[26]New York: Seabury, ©1969.

[27]*The Magnificent Defeat* 86.

[28]Ibid. 61–62.

[29]Ibid. 26.

[30]Ibid. 42.

[31]New York: Harper & Row, ©1977, at 5–6.

[32]Ibid. 24.

[33]For more detailed information on Buechner, his religious background and convictions, his theological works, and the significance of his novels, see Marie-Hélène Davies, *Laughter in a Genevan Gown: The Works of Frederick Buechner 1970–1980* (Grand Rapids: Eerdmans, ©1983).

[34]I am quoting from the text as it appeared in the *Alumni Bulletin of Bangor Theological Seminary* 43, no. 2 (April 1968) 12–14.

[35]Ibid. 12.

[36]See Joseph Sittler, "A Protestant Point of View," in John H. Miller, C.S.C., ed., *Vatican II: An Interfaith Appraisal* (Notre Dame: Univ. of Notre Dame, ©1966) 422–27, at 426.

[37]William J. Carl III, *Preaching Christian Doctrine* (Philadelphia: Fortress, ©1984) 109.

[38]David H. C. Read, *This Grace Given* (Grand Rapids: Eerdmans, ©1984).

[39]Ibid. ix.

[40]Ibid. 7.

[41]Ibid. 102.

[42]Ibid. 105–6.

[43]Ibid. 129.

[44]Commercially published collections of Dr. Read's sermons still available for purchase are: *God's Mobile Family* (New York: Madison Avenue Church Press, 1966); *Giants Cut Down to Size* (Cincinnati: Forward Movement Publications, 1970); *Overheard* (Nashville: Abingdon, 1971); *Curious Christians* (Nashville: Abingdon, 1973); *Unfinished Easter: Sermons on the Ministry* (San Francisco: Harper & Row, ©1978). The ongoing Sunday sermons can be procured from the Madison Avenue Presbyterian Church, 921 Madison Ave., New York, N.Y. 10021 (subscription: $15 per year; $.50 per copy).

[45]From the sermon "Faith's Foundations: (2) The Centrality of Christ," Feb. 23, 1986, duplicated copy from Madison Avenue Presbyterian Church, p. 6.

[46]From the sermon "On the Road with Jesus," in *Unfinished Easter* (n. 44 above) 82.

POSTLUDE

[1]For a very negative reaction to the film, see the review by Tom O'Brien in *Commonweal* 112, no. 2 (Jan. 25, 1985) 51; he found it superficial. Perhaps it is; my competence as a film critic is open to serious question. I can only confess that *Mass Appeal* spoke profoundly to me as priest, as preacher, as a fallible human person in whom the yearning to love and the need to be loved are often in tension.

INDEX OF SUBJECTS

theology: 58–59; feminist, 68–77; ignorance of, 9
translation: homily as, 12–16, 187

Vatican II: on content of homily, 221; on expertise of pastors, 185; on homily as liturgy, 108; on Jews and the crucifixion, 148; on proper mission of Church, 230; on sacraments and faith, 11; scriptural focus of, 208; on sources of preaching, 79; on tradition, 181
vision: and imagination, 20

weakness, human: 39–40
weddings: different approaches to, 104–6

witness: preaching as act of, 84–89
woes: beatitudes and, 99–101
women: need for proclamation by, 68–77
word: homiletic, 6–16; made flesh today, 11–16; preacher as the, 15–16; and sacrament, 111–14; and sacrifice, 6–7; and worship, 11–12
word of the Lord: 175–81; see New Testament, Old Testament, Scripture
words: 1–16, 188, 200–205
worship: as anamnesis, 11, 111–12; homily as, 110–11; as spiritual sacrifice, 11–12, 112; as witness to faith, 11; word and, 111–14

INDEX OF PERSONS